A Double Duty

Jim Wallace

Jim Wallace

A Double Duty

The Decisive First Decade Of The North West Mounted Police

Bunker to Bunker Books
Winnipeg
1997

Copyright © Jim Wallace, 1997.

All rights reserved. No part of this publication may be reproduced, stored in a retrieval system, or transmitted in any form or by any means, electronic, mechanical, photocopying, recording or otherwise, except brief passages for purposes of reviews, without the prior permission of the publisher.

Care has been taken to trace the ownership of copyright material used in the text, including the illustrations. The author and publisher welcome any information enabling them to rectify any reference or credit in subsequent editions.

Canadian Cataloguing in Publication Data

Wallace, James B., 1932 -

"A Double Duty": the decisive first decade of the North West Mounted Police.

Includes bibliographical reference and index.
ISBN 0-9699039-8-7

1. North West Mounted Police (Canada) - History.
2. Northwest, Canadian - History - 1870-1905.*
3. Police - Prairie Provinces - History.
4. Frontier and pioneer life - Prairie Provinces. I. Title.

FC3216.2.W34 1997   363.2'09712   C97-920082-2
HV8157.W34 1997

Bunker to Bunker Books,
34 Blue Spruce Cres.,
Winnipeg, MB,
R2M 4C2.

- Dedicated to-

Jessica Bryce Wallace

in the hope that she may inherit her Grandfather's love
of Canada and its history.

"But that little force had a double duty to perform: to fight, if necessary, but in any case to establish posts in the far west."

Commissioner George A. French

CONTENTS

Preface — viii
1 Canada Expands Westward — 1
2 The Force Is Forged — 19
3 Planning and Preparation — 33
4 Fort Dufferin to Roche Percée — 57
5 Roche Percée to Fort Macleod — 71
6 Sweet Grass Hills to Fort Dufferin — 91
7 Roche Percée to Fort Edmonton — 96
8 Flawed Planning, Intelligence and Logistics — 103
9 Establishing Law and Order in the West — 111
10 Problems of Command — 125
11 Swan River Barracks — 139
12 Changes on the Plains — 160
13 Sitting Bull And The Sioux — 174
14 Problems on the Plains — 196
15 Tension Rising — 216
16 Trouble in the Force — 237
17 A Decisive Decade — 245
Appendix A - What Happened to Them? — 249
Notes — 252
Bibliography — 267
Index — 272
Photo Credits — 278

PREFACE

This book covers the first decade in the history of the North West Mounted Police, 1873-1883, a decisive period in the history of Western Canada. Many early authors were so laudatory in describing the Great Trek of 1874 that the early years of the Mounted Police became enshrined in the mists of mythology. A more objective and balanced point of view has since been presented by writers such as R.C. Macleod, S.W. Horrall and Philip Goldring, whose analyses of the shortcomings, political influence and internal problems have given us a much clearer and more realistic view of events.

This work examines the beginnings of the force and the difficulties encountered by the first Commissioner, George French, who organized and trained the force then led it West, only to come in conflict with his political masters. It also tells how the small force initially won the respect of the aboriginal peoples then saw this relationship deteriorate over the decade as the force was required to enforce unpopular government policies. The men of the force had to cope with the influx of the Sioux following the Battle of the Little Big Horn and widespread starvation among the tribes on the plains as the buffalo disappeared. By the end of the decade regressive government policies had alienated the aboriginal people and set the stage for the North West Rebellion.

One of the '74 Originals, Frederick Bagley, wrote of his resentment of those who, in writing of the early days of the force, intentionally distorted facts in order to create drama. I hope this book would have met with his approval. There is no need to distort the facts, the story has its own drama, and I have attempted to remain unbiased, objective and analytical in presenting the facts. Along with many other Canadians, I have had a lifelong admiration and respect for the place of the Royal Canadian Mounted Police in Western Canadian history. As my research progressed I found that some of my idols had feet of clay; however, ultimately, my admiration and respect both for the organization and individual members remains intact and undiminished.

- Preface -

This book draws on personal accounts, such as diaries and letters, newspaper accounts, archival material and a detailed search of relevant government files. The policy files provided a framework which the personal reminiscences brought to life. Faced with numerous variations in spelling I have chosen to use one form which has remained throughout, except where a different form appears in quotations. Place names, as far as possible, are those in use when the events took place.

I am indebted to members of the force who left diaries, letters and other material describing life in the early years of the force, as well as those who carefully filed official documents I was able to read over a century later. I received considerable assistance from the Provincial Archives of Manitoba, the Hudson's Bay Company Archives, the Glenbow-Alberta Institute Archives and last, but not least, the National Archives of Canada. I would also like to acknowledge the considerable assistance of the Historical Section of the Royal Canadian Mounted Police, particularly Glenn Wright.

I wish to give special thanks to the many people who assisted me in some way: Dr. Ruth Cook for reading the first draft and making many useful suggestions as well as encouraging me to continue; Susan Fonseca for proofreading and editing; Nina Jakubowicz for research assistance and support; Renata Jakubowicz for driving me endless miles in Alberta looking for lost fragments of history; and last, but not least, three old Armed Forces comrades, Jerry Holtzhauer for research at the National Archives and Mike Dorosz and Don Macnamara for tracking down elusive reference material. While the assistance of these many individuals was appreciated, the responsibility for any errors or omissions remains mine.

Jim Wallace

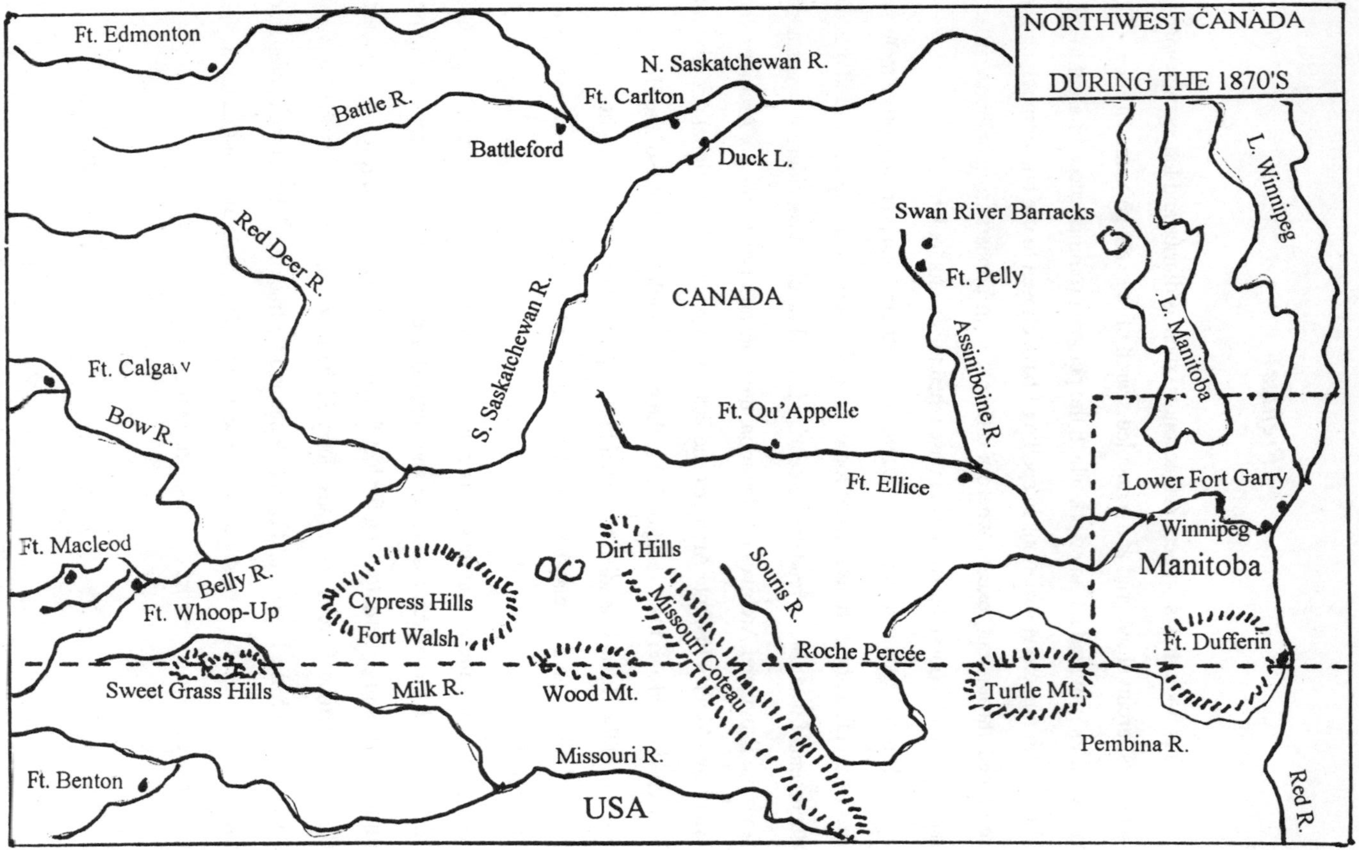
NORTHWEST CANADA
DURING THE 1870'S
Ft. Edmonton
N. Saskatchewan R.
Battle R.
Ft. Carlton
Battleford
Duck L.
Swan River Barracks
Ft. Pelly
L. Winnipeg
L. Manitoba
CANADA
Red Deer R.
S. Saskatchewan R.
Assiniboine R.
Ft. Calgary
Bow R.
Ft. Qu'Appelle
Ft. Ellice
Lower Fort Garry
Winnipeg
Manitoba
Ft. Macleod
Dirt Hills
Souris R.
Belly R.
Cypress Hills
Fort Walsh
Ft. Whoop-Up
Missouri Coteau
Roche Percée
Ft. Dufferin
Sweet Grass Hills
Milk R.
Wood Mt.
Turtle Mt.
Pembina R.
Missouri R.
Ft. Benton
USA
Red R.

- 1 -

Canada Expands Westward

A hot July sun beat down on a long column of scarlet clad horsemen, winding its way across the hills and plains of southern Manitoba. Each of the six divisions rode matched horses. Two nine-pounder field guns pulled by four-horse teams accompanied the force. Behind this column was a long trail of wagons, Red River carts, agricultural machinery and cattle on the hoof. This sight, unlike anything seen before or since, was the great march of the North West Mounted Police, moving westward in 1874 to bring law and order to the newly acquired Northwest Territories. To understand the motivation behind this tremendous undertaking, which contained a drama so rarely found in Canadian history, we must go back in time to the period immediately after Confederation in 1867.

Canada was then a new country occupying only a small part of the territory that now makes up the nation. It consisted of Prince Edward Island, Nova Scotia, New Brunswick, and parts of present day Quebec and Ontario. British Columbia was a well established separate crown colony, while the area between Ontario and British Columbia was in the possession of The Governor and Company of Adventurers of England trading into Hudson's Bay. The Hudson's Bay Company was formed in 1670 when King Charles granted his cousin Rupert and sixteen other investors a charter to trade in a vast area of North America. In this region, which became known as Rupert's Land, the Company was primarily interested in trading with the aboriginal peoples. The Company had no interest in settlement, which they actively discouraged, but had an obvious commercial incentive to maintain the trust and friendship of the Indians, who provided the furs on which their business depended.

In this huge territory controlled by the Hudson's Bay Company there were several Indian tribes. The traders established good working relations with most of the aboriginal peoples but were not warmly welcomed by the Blackfoot Nation. This

- *A Double Duty* -

alliance of Blackfoot, Peigans and Bloods occupied what is now Southern Alberta from the foothills of the Rockies to the Cypress Hills and from the Red Deer River south into present day Montana. The fierce and warlike Blackfoot allowed the Sarcee to settle in their territory in an often uneasy association, but kept other intruders out of their hunting grounds.

At one time the fur trade was dominated by two rivals, the Hudson's Bay Company and the newer North West Company which was formed in the 1870's when traders from Montreal banded together to compete effectively with the British traders. When the rivals amalgamated in1821, the Hudson's Bay Company took over the two North West Company posts in Blackfoot territory, Chesterfield House on the South Saskatchewan River, close to the present Alberta-Saskatchewan border and Old Bow Fort, near the present site of Calgary. Due to the hostility and aggression of the Blackfoot Nation, these posts were soon closed. The Blackfoot then had to either travel to Fort Edmonton to trade, deal with the Cree who acted as intermediaries, or trade with American traders from Montana. Because their hunting grounds were more suitable for buffalo hunting than for fur trapping, the Blackfoot were not as extensively involved in trading as other tribes but did depend on traders for rifles, ammunition and metal utensils.

Because the Blackfoot were not as deeply involved in the fur trade and actively discouraged outsiders from entering their hunting grounds, they remained relatively isolated for many years, but this isolation did not completely protect them from disasters. White men, although few in this area, introduced tuberculosis, measles, syphilis and, worst of all, smallpox. In 1830 the Blackfoot Nation lost two-thirds of its people to smallpox and after a second epidemic decimated the tribes in 1869-70, their weakened condition made them ripe for exploitation as American whisky traders moved in from Montana.

The Blackfoot were nomadic and dependent on the buffalo for food, shelter, clothing and fuel. Along with other plains Indians, they originally killed buffalo by techniques such as herding them over a cliff at a buffalo jump but, as they obtained horses from the south and rifles from the traders, their ability to kill buffalo increased. The successful use of buffalo leather belts for industrial purposes in the eastern United States dramatically increased the demand for buffalo hides. There was also an increase in the demand for pemmican, a concentrated, portable concoction made of dried buffalo meat and grease, with berries sometimes added for flavour.

This demand for buffalo hides and meat changed the traditional way of life of the aboriginal peoples, especially the Blackfoot. After successive smallpox epidemics decimated and demoralized the Blackfoot Nation, American traders moved into their territory and the Indians began to exchange buffalo robes and wolf hides for whisky. Up until this time the Indians had killed buffalo in numbers necessary to provide food and shelter. Hunters now killed buffalo by the thousands, both for meat and for robes, but there were also some who slaughtered "for portions only of the meat, the remainder being left to rot on the prairie."[1] The Hudson's Bay Company was not interested in trading in buffalo robes, which were heavy and not easily transported to the east by the company's canoe routes. American traders, on the other hand, could move loads of robes south to Fort Benton by wagons or carts then ship them down the Missouri by steamboat. It is not surprising that traders based in Montana took the initiative in this trade.

These American traders had a free hand. By the late 1860's the United States, nearing the end of its first century as a nation, saw the conclusion of a bloody civil war. Attention turned westward where land, gold and the hope of quick fortunes lured many of the footloose veterans of two armies. Although much of the land in the west was still in the possession of aboriginal tribes who had no desire to give it up to the newcomers, the United States Government sided with the whites and the army took the land in a series of protracted "Indian Wars." Settlers, miners and railway companies all regarded the native population as a threat so there was some popular support for the government policy of either putting them on reservations or destroying them. The Territory of Montana was largely lawless and throughout the west there was some apprehension

- A Double Duty -

about the Indians since the Sioux had killed a large number of settlers in Minnesota in 1862.

The discovery of gold in the Black Hills of South Dakota resulted in considerable pressure for additional westward expansion in the United States. Many Americans had a vision of "Manifest Destiny," that the destiny of the United States was to expand to fill the North American continent. Under pressure from prospective settlers, miners and railroaders, the United States government ignored treaties and forced the Indians off their lands, so the United States Army was continuously involved in contentious conflicts with various tribes.

The new Canadian government in Ottawa also had a vision, perhaps not as grandiose as "Manifest Destiny", but still astonishingly ambitious for a nation with such a small population and modest national income. In contrast to the situation in the United States, Canada's vision of the west called for strong government institutions based on law and order, with little or no local control. Canadians believed that the lawlessness and anarchy in the American west was the product of local autonomy and they were not anxious to import American problems. Sir John A. Macdonald, the Prime Minister, wanted to bring British Columbia into Confederation to create a nation from sea to sea and the price of British Columbia's entry was to be a Canadian transcontinental railway, similar to those moving steadily across the plains of the United States. The politicians believed that such a transcontinental railway would bring settlers and ensure the economic future of Canada, but before they could have the railway built the Government of Canada needed to gain effective control of Rupert's Land.

In 1868 the British Parliament passed legislation authorizing Canada to acquire Rupert's Land from the Hudson's Bay Company. Britain prepared a Deed of Surrender to the Crown, with the company receiving £300,000 and over 6 million acres of land in various parcels throughout the Territories. Britain then transferred Rupert's Land to Canada. In 1869 the sovereign powers of the Hudson's Bay Company passed to

- Canada Expands Westward -

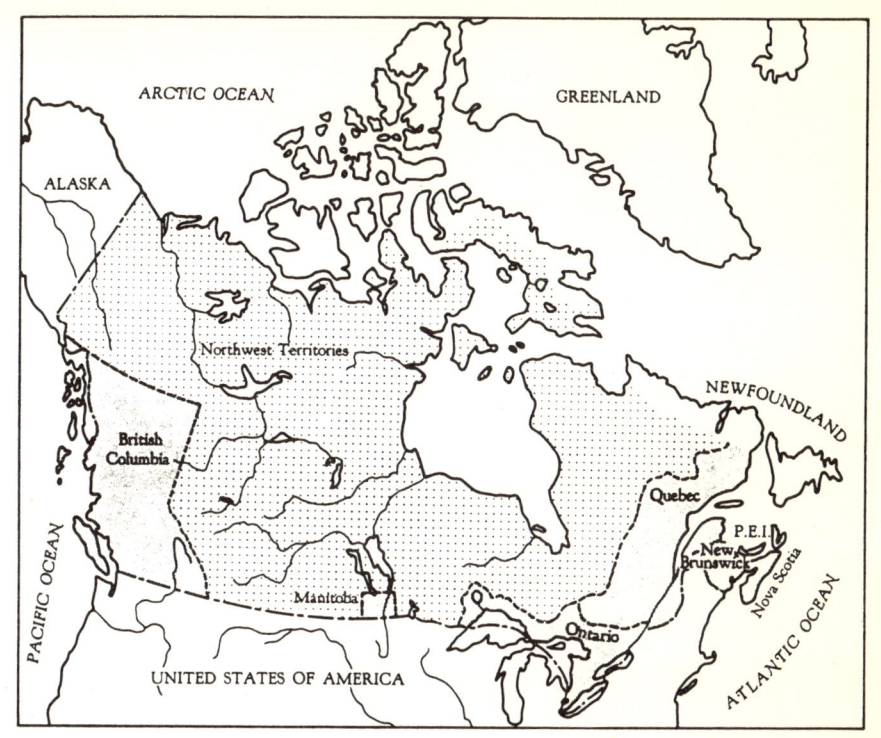

Canada's Frontier, 1870 to 1873

Canada but there was no machinery for local government, no legal system and no means of controlling the territory.

Ottawa, being out of touch with reality, decided to govern the whole of their new possession as a single territory. In a display of arrogance that many westerners still believe prevails, there was no consultation on the matter with the people living in the territory. Sir John A. Macdonald's chief concern was to bring about completion of the railway and settlement of the west without becoming involved in a costly Indian war that could bankrupt the nation. The annual revenue of Canada at this time was about $20 million, roughly the same amount as the United States expended annually fighting

- A Double Duty -

Indians on the western plains. In 1869 the only significant settlements in the Northwest Territories acquired by Canada were in what is now Manitoba, so the failure to undertake adequate consultations was felt most strongly in the Red River Settlement.

The fur trade employed a large number of men, mostly French Canadians in the North West Company and Scots in the Hudson's Bay Company. Many of these men had Indian wives and, over time, half-breed or Métis settlements grew up around the fur trade, especially at Red River. The Métis were employed in large numbers as hunters to provide pemmican or as boatmen, moving furs and trade goods. An agricultural community of Scottish settlers was established at Red River in 1811 when Lord Selkirk obtained a land grant. Before the union of the two companies, the rivalry between the French Canadian North West Company and the British Hudson's Bay Company created a rift between the two groups which was only partly healed by the merger. The combination of the two fur trading companies reduced the need for workers in the trade and some of these displaced workers took up subsistence farming at the Red River Settlement.

When Canada purchased Rupert's Land the Métis, the first nonindigenous settlers in the area, found that they were outnumbered by increasing numbers of white settlers. Their growing concern about language rights, schools and title to the lands they occupied, caused them to rally around Louis Riel, a Métis they believed could represent their aspirations. At this point "some credible reassurances from the British government, the Hudson's Bay Company, or the Canadian government that the rights and property of the inhabitants would be respected and some minimal consultation with community leaders, would have prevented trouble; but there was no consultation and the promises to respect local rights came too late to be believed."[2]

Canada passed an Act under which Rupert's Land would be governed by a governor, with an appointed council of seven to fifteen members. William McDougall, former Minister of Public Works for Canada, was appointed the first governor. Before Rupert's Land became part of Canada, McDougall, displaying a complete lack of sensitivity, ordered surveys at Red River using the system of sections and townships employed in Ontario. This created great apprehension among Métis settlers whose farms at Red River were laid out in lots running back from the river, as done in Quebec. When the Métis and surveyors confronted each other, trouble started.

Meanwhile, William McDougall, a pompous man with delusions of grandeur, started on his way to Red River well in advance of his official appointment as the governor. In his entourage was Captain Donald Roderick Cameron, an officer of the Royal Artillery and son-in-law of Sir Charles Tupper the former Premier of Nova Scotia and one of the Fathers of Confederation. Captain Cameron, who was appointed to the Council to look after military and police matters, is described in contemporary accounts in an unflattering way. Sir John A. Macdonald, a friend and colleague of Tupper's, wrote to Cameron, giving an idea of how he saw the area being policed, "I have no doubt that, come what will, there must be a military body, or, at all events, a body with military discipline at Fort Garry. It seems to me that the best Force would be *Mounted Riflemen* trained first as Cavalry, but also instructed in the Rifle exercises." He added that "they should be instructed . . . in the use of artillery and should be styled *Police* and have the military bearing of the Irish Constabulary." Macdonald went on to warn Captain Cameron that he had observed that Cameron and McDougall did not get along well and to impress upon him the "importance of cordial action together."[3]

William McDougall's moment of glory was shortlived. By the time his entourage reached the border at Pembina, the Red River Settlement was in a state of rebellion under the leadership of Louis Riel. Riel's followers stopped McDougall and Cameron when they arrived at the border at Pembina. The new Governor, barred from entering the Red River Settlement, withdrew to the United States. Captain Cameron was turned back at a barricade on the way to Fort Garry after peering at it through his monacle, to the amusement of the Métis.

There was a clear need for surveys to be completed before an orderly system of land ownership could be introduced, but it was unwise to act in haste. At Red River Settlement, the settlers' genuine concerns about the lack of political and property rights

- A Double Duty -

for those who lived there turned to apprehension as surveyors crossed what the settlers regarded as their land, laying out sections and townships. On November 24, 1869 Riel and his followers seized the Hudson's Bay Company post at Fort Garry and elected a council and provisional government. They then drew up a Bill of Rights demanding the right to have a Legislature, a just land policy and representation in Parliament. The Government of Canada sent a three-man commission to negotiate with them but, unfortunately, at this point tragedy intervened when Riel captured and executed an Ontario Orangeman, Thomas Scott, a leader in opposition to Riel's provisional government.

Thomas Scott's death caused a storm of protest in Ontario so the government in Ottawa sent a military expedition, under Colonel Garnet Wolseley, to quell the Red River uprising. The troops came by the long and time consuming Dawson Route via the Great Lakes and a series of rivers and portages to Fort Garry only to find that Louis Riel had fled to the United States. After a brief stay, during which they allegedly consumed all the liquor in Winnipeg, the main body of the force returned east, leaving a small Militia garrison in Fort Garry under Major A.G. Irvine, who was later to become the Commissioner of the North West Mounted Police. In the Red River Expeditionary Force there were several other future members of the Mounted Police, including James Macleod, Sam Steele, Arthur Griesbach and William Herchmer. Following the departure of Riel, negotiations with Ottawa continued and resulted in an agreement for the creation of the Province of Manitoba by the Manitoba Act of 1870.

When Riel fled from the advance of Colonel Wolseley's forces he spent the three years from 1870 to 1873 in the United States, mostly in Minnesota, hoping to hear that he had been pardoned for the killing of Thomas Scott. In 1873 he went to Ontario to press his case and eventually received a pardon, contingent on his leaving Canada for five years. He also had to give up his seat in Parliament. In 1875 in Washington, D.C. he experienced a religious revelation which caused his friends to have him committed under an assumed name to asylums in Quebec for two years. Following his release in

- *Canada Expands Westward* -

1878 he returned to the United States and eventually drifted west to Montana where nomadic groups of Métis were still hunting the rapidly diminishing buffalo.

While national attention was focused on the troubles at Fort Garry, all was not well further west. The Indians watched, with increasing concern, what was happening below the border and they were becoming worried about their future and the security of their lands and way of life. Lawlessness was spreading, life was cheap and many white traders, who held Indians in contempt, were moving across the border to trade with them. In the United States the army was increasingly used to force Indians from the lands that were theirs by tradition or treaty. In Montana, authorities started to enforce a United States law of 1832, banning sales of liquor to Indians. When the Hudson's Bay Company relinquished its control over Rupert's Land in 1869 and no system of law enforcement filled the vacuum, the American whisky traders moved across the boundary to establish themselves in what is now southern Alberta and Saskatchewan.

Most of the trading posts, euphemistically termed "forts," were hastily-built log cabins occupied in the winter months, when prime furs were available, by traders from Fort Benton, Montana. Their activities were seasonal and they usually burned their posts when they left in the spring. If they did not burn the "forts" the Indians did it for them. The traders dealt in a normal range of trade goods such as flour, salt, tea, tobacco, blankets, guns and ammunition but many of them also dealt in locally concocted "whisky." While the recipe varied from "fort" to "fort" the concoction was usually some kind of alcohol, diluted with swamp water and mixed with an astonishing variety of other ingredients, often heated in a large kettle and served hot in tin mugs. "The trader stood at the wicket, a tubful of whisky beside him, and when an Indian pushed in a buffalo robe to him through the hole in the wall he handed out a tin cupful of the poisonous decoction. A quart of the stuff bought a fine pony."[4]

Recipes that have survived include ingredients such as bitters, black chewing tobacco, black molasses, Jamaica ginger, red peppers, red ink, castile soap and water. One ingredient not mentioned in the recipes is lye, which was added to give the mixture "bite." It appears that the lye tended to settle to the bottom of the containers and there were reports of deaths from drinking the last of the batch! While the "whisky" itself killed some customers, many more died of freezing when they passed out or became involved in drunken brawls.

The results of this trade were devastating. Paul F. Sharp wrote that "whiskey traders callously stripped the proud Blackfoot of every possession. Robes, pelts, horses, weapons, even squaws, were bought and sold for a few cups of Whoop-Up bug juice, with the traders enjoying a quick profit and the Indians speedily reduced to miserable poverty."[5] The most notorious of the whisky trading posts was Fort Whoop-Up, situated not far from where the City of Lethbridge, Alberta now stands. Two traders from Fort Benton, John J. Healy and Alfred B. Hamilton, established Fort Whoop-Up in 1869, near the forks of the St. Mary's and Old Man's Rivers. Originally called Fort Hamilton, it was not a substantial structure the first year and the Indians burned it when the traders abandoned it in the spring. The traders returned the next year and built a stronger "fort" of heavy timbers chinked with mud and buffalo dung.

While there are many variations on the origin of the name Fort Whoop-Up, most came from someone saying they were "whooping it up" when asked about their activities. Stories of trading in guns and whisky with the Blackfoot gave the government in Ottawa cause for concern. To add insult to injury, the American traders were allegedly flying the Stars and Stripes over Fort Whoop-Up, although the flag may actually have been a combination of the owner's crest and a striped flag. The reports of a United States flag flying over a fort on Canadian territory caused great indignation in Canada. When word spread through the western United States that Healy and Hamilton had netted $50,000 in their first season at Fort Whoop-Up, many other traders moved into the territory.

As things settled down in the west following the passage of the Manitoba Act in 1870, there was more discussion of a police force for the Northwest Territories, although there was no real effort made to provide security for life or property. In 1870 there was a proposal for a mixed force of whites, and English and French speaking

- Canada Expands Westward -

Métis, with headquarters at Fort Garry. It was to be under the command of Captain D.R. Cameron, who had apparently recovered from the ignominy of his expulsion from Red River by Riel's men. There were to be 200 men, fifty of them to be recruited in Eastern Canada and the remainder in the west. It was intended that a number of the men recruited in the east would be bilingual. The proposed enlistment was for three years with pay of fifty cents a day and the force was to be ready by May 1, 1870. Cameron chose Spencer repeating rifles and revolvers as weapons.

In the House of Commons, the Opposition questioned Sir John A. Macdonald about whether Captain Cameron was raising a force and, if so, how and where. Sir John responded that the government had appointed Mr. McMicken and Mr. Coursol in Winnipeg as Police Commissioners and they were engaging men in Lower Canada. Alexander Mackenzie, Leader of the Opposition, acknowledged that Captain Cameron might be "a most efficient officer in his own place but not in the position proposed."[6] Cameron, however, assisted by Sergeant A.H. Griesbach, continued to plan the requirements for the force and purchased and warehoused a considerable amount of equipment and stores in Ottawa before the government decided to postpone any further action on the police force and filed the plan away.

In 1871 the government continued to procrastinate and, being in a precarious financial position, the politicians were quite happy to postpone any military or police venture that would cost money. Events in Manitoba and the Northwest Territories would not stand still, however, and the government was soon forced into action. On July 20, 1871 British Columbia joined Confederation, with the stipulation that work must begin within two years on a railway to connect the west coast with eastern Canada. The building of the railway was to be the dominant force in Canadian politics for the next decade or more.

Meanwhile, nothing was being done to establish law and order in the new territory acquired two years previously. The Indians, uncertain about their future, continued to be apprehensive about what was happening below the border, while there was pressure in the United States to annex the vast area held tenuously by Canada. As

- *A Double Duty* -

Philip Goldring describes it, "the Dominion's possessions west of Manitoba were a house of cards. A stiff breeze of American annexationism or an energetic flurry of Indian hostility could have brought the whole thing tumbling down."[7]

While reports of the American traders' activities did not stir those in Ottawa to action they did cause considerable concern to Lieutenant Governor Archibald in Fort Garry. He sent Lieutenant William Butler, who had been Colonel Wolseley's Intelligence Officer on the Red River Expedition, to investigate the situation in the west and report back to him. Butler, later to be Commander in Chief of the British Army, travelled 2,700 miles on horseback, and by wagon and dog sled. There is a description of the journey in his book *The Great Lone Land*.[8] Butler was back in Fort Garry in February 1871 and reported to Archibald that there was an urgent need to establish law and order, to avoid conflicts like those in the contiguous American states between the Indians, particularly the Sioux, and the United States Army. He also reported that the traders were systematically debauching the Indians with liquor. Butler recommended a police force of 100 to 150 men, one third of them mounted.

Shortly after receiving Butler's report, Lieutenant Governor Archibald received a letter from W.J. Christie, Chief Factor of the Hudson's Bay Company at Edmonton House, describing a visit from chiefs representing the Plains Cree. The chiefs wanted to know the government's intentions regarding their land. Christie ended the letter saying "I take this opportunity of most earnestly soliciting, on behalf of the Company's servants, and settlers in the district, that protection be afforded to life and property here as soon as possible, and that Commissioners be sent to speak with the Indians on behalf of the Canadian Government." Sweet Grass, a Cree chief, attached a message to Archibald saying, "we heard our lands were sold and did not like it; We don't want to sell our lands; it is our property, and no one has a right to sell them."[9]

There was still a lack of concerted action in Ottawa regarding the formation of a police force, although the matter got some support from politicians anxious to find employment for Captain Cameron, who now seemed fated to serve in India if he could not find a position in Canada. In correspondence between Sir John A. Macdonald and

- Canada Expands Westward -

Sir George Cartier it was noted that "Cameron's wife is so delicate that if she were to accompany her husband to India there is but little chance of their being able to see her again. This may be prevented by an early organization of a mounted police."[10] The "their" refers to Sir Charles Tupper and his wife, Captain Cameron's in-laws.

The Prime Minister also faced a political problem in Manitoba. The influx of new immigrants from Ontario in 1872 had changed the political balance from Conservative to Liberal and caused fears of unrest. There were calls for both a military force and police but the parsimonious Sir John A. Macdonald believed the requirement could be met with a combination of the two. He expressed the opinion "that two companies will be quite sufficient for all purposes for which they are required." To combine the characteristics of a military force and a police role he noted that "we must have a mounted police under a Stipendiary Magistrate, . . . to keep things quiet on the border."[11]

Still pondering how to establish law and order in the Northwest Territories, Sir John A. Macdonald sent Colonel P. Robertson-Ross, Adjutant General of the Canadian Militia, on a fact finding trip through the west. Robertson-Ross left Fort Garry on August 10, 1872 with his sixteen year old son, a guide, a Saulteaux boy, ten horses and two carts. He reported that his party met with no major difficulty or problems. On his return he recommended to the Prime Minister a regiment of 550 mounted riflemen. He also stressed the importance of red coats, stating that the Indians believed they could trust men wearing red coats. In his diary Colonel Robertson-Ross was fairly accurate in locating Fort Whoop-Up at the forks of the Old Man's and Belly Rivers, about ten miles from the actual location at the forks of the Old Man's and St. Mary's Rivers. His published report erroneously placed the location at the junction of the Bow and Belly, some sixty miles northeast

As 1872 progressed, Sir John A. Macdonald continued his search for a Commissioner for his new police force. He wanted someone with colonial experience, preferably in India, where policing was modelled on the Irish Constabulary. He had earmarked the job for Captain Cameron, who seemed to have been perpetually in need

- A Double Duty -

of employment, and also promised a commission in the North West Mounted Police to Lawrence Herchmer, son of an old friend from Kingston. Each of them had the desired experience in India, but by the time plans for the police were becoming firm, both men had been given positions on the Boundary Commission.

The North American Boundary Commission was formed jointly by Britain and the United States in 1872 to survey and mark the boundary between Lake of the Woods and the Rocky Mountains. Sir John A. Macdonald, in his seemingly endless search for a position for Captain Cameron, had nominated him to be the Commissioner. The British reluctantly agreed, preferring a Sapper or Royal Engineer officer. Macdonald had Captain Herchmer appointed Commissary Officer. The marking of the boundary was a major undertaking and in the years 1873-1874, the combined Boundary Commission parties of Britain and the United States deployed considerably more men and animals in the west than the Mounted Police. The United States party had a large military escort, both infantry and cavalry, for their protection. This escort was commanded by Major Marcus Reno, who later became infamous at the Little Big Horn.

Fort Dufferin, near Emerson, Manitoba, became the headquarters and main supply depot of the Boundary Commission. For the next year or so the activities of the Boundary Commission and those of the Mounted Police were to coincide in many ways. Forty-four non-commissioned officers and men of the Royal Engineers, specifically brought out from Britain for the task, made up the main body of the British side of the Boundary Commission. They started by erecting the barracks, offices, a cookhouse and stables, later used by the Mounted Police.

With Captains Cameron and Herchmer no longer available, Sir John A. Macdonald continued his search for a commander for his new police force. In October 1872 he offered the position to Colonel J.C. McNeill, aide to Governor General Lord Lisgar. He told McNeill that "it involves the watching of the Frontier from Manitoba to the foot of the Rocky Mountains; and it will have its civil side as well as military side, as the person in command will have to hold the position of Stipendiary or Police

- *Canada Expands Westward* -

Magistrate."[12] McNeill ceased to be a candidate when he left for the Ashanti Campaign in West Africa.

As 1872 ended, Alexander Morris replaced Archibald as Lieutenant Governor while, to the west, the activities of the whisky traders increased, hunting decimated the buffalo at an alarming rate, and the exploitation and debauchery of the Indians continued unabated. Morris viewed the situation with some alarm and did not agree with the idea that there was a choice between providing police in the Northwest Territories or troops at Fort Garry. Early in 1873 he wrote to Sir John A. Macdonald pointing out that, "the most important matter of the future is the preservation of order in the North West and little as Canada may like it she has to stable her elephant. In short the Dominion will have to maintain both a military and police force for years to come." Morris cautioned Macdonald not to "diminish the military force below its present strength and the police should also be under military discipline and if possible be *red coated* as fifty men in red coats are better than 100 in other colours." He warned that "the presence of a force will prevent the possibility of such a frightful disaster as befell Minnesota and without it might be provoked at any moment."[13]

Above all else, Sir John A. Macdonald feared the outbreak of an Indian war when settlers started to arrive in the west. This would be disruptive to construction of the transcontinental railway and thus had the potential to derail his vision of a nation from sea to sea, if promises to British Columbia were not fulfilled. It was essential there be no protracted and costly Indian wars like those in the United States. Therefore, it was necessary to bring order to the territory and extinguish Indian title to the land, thus making it available for settlement. The North West Mounted Police were to be an instrument of this Indian Policy.

Canada believed that Rupert's Land belonged to them on the basis of exploration but, under pressure from the Colonial Office, they reluctantly accepted the Hudson's Bay Company's ownership rights. They saw Indian title only as an "encumberance upon the underlying title to the lands held by the sovereign." Title was vested in the Crown but aboriginal right to use the land was seen as "an encumberance on that title

- A Double Duty -

which had to be extinguished before the Crown could alienate the land to private owners. Extinguishment required compensation, which might take the form of land reserves, money payments, educational or medical services, etc."[14] To gain control of the lands the government decided to negotiate treaties that would extinguish aboriginal title in return for immediate cash payments, annual "treaty money" and gifts of food and ammunition. They agreed to provided reserves in locations chosen by the bands and to give them animals, equipment and seeds as an inducement to abandon their nomadic way of life and take up farming. There was hope that, in time, this would lead to their becoming self-sufficient farmers. All these concerns and more occupied the mind of Sir John A. Macdonald as he prepared to put forward legislation to create his police force and continued his search for an Imperial Officer, preferably with colonial experience, to lead it. Unknown to him events were taking place in the Cypress Hills to the west which, while not responsible for the formation of the North West Mounted Police, would certainly accelerate its recruitment and training.

The Cypress Hills, in what is now southern Alberta and Saskatchewan, were a haven which provided food, fuel and water to nomadic Indians of the many tribes who frequented the area from time to time. It was also a favourite spot of the Métis buffalo hunters who often spent the winter in the hills as "hivernauts." By 1873 less desirable elements, wolfers and traders, also visited the region. Wolfers travelled through the area seeking wolf and coyote pelts which they obtained by killing the animals with buffalo meat laced with strychnine. This indiscriminate poisoning, which also killed Indian dogs and, occasionally, people created bad relations between the wolfers and the Indians. Fearing the Indians, the wolfers attempted to put pressure on the traders to stop supplying the Indians with rifles and ammunition. The traders would not be coerced so the attempt was unsuccessful, leaving the Indians and wolfers coexisting in an aura of mutual distrust.

By 1873 there were thirteen or more trading posts in the Cypress Hills, dealing in conventional trade goods such as tobacco, blankets, flour and tea as well as whisky. The trader's business success, and often his life, depended on maintaining good relations with the Indians who provided him with furs, so they were not happy with the animosity created by the wolfers. This animosity culminated, in May 1873, in what has become known as The Cypress Hills Massacre. Two of the many traders, Moses Solomon and Abe Farwell, had established trading posts on opposite sides of Battle Creek and there, in May 1873, about 300 Assiniboines under their leader, Little Soldier, made their camp. The Assiniboines believed that Moses Solomon cheated them in their trading and intermittently fired at his post to express their irritation.

A group of wolfers, led by John Evans and Thomas Hardwick, arrived at Abe Farwell's post on the evening of May 31 in a foul mood. They had travelled for two weeks unsuccessfully tracking 40 horses stolen from them by Indians just outside Fort Benton. Abe Farwell, and his interpreter, Alexis Lebombard, who were preparing to leave for Fort Benton with the winter's furs, received them politely and invited them to return to the post in the morning. After breakfast the following day, the wolfers returned and settled down to do some serious drinking. The Assiniboines, who had earlier received some whisky from Abe Farwell as a reward for recovering a horse belonging to a trader named George Hammond, were also drinking.

While Farwell and his companions packed robes into carts, the wolfers and Indians drank. When George Hammond found that his horse was missing once more, he immediately assumed that the Indians had taken it and appealed to the wolfers for assistance. They were more than willing to get involved and the men immediately picked up their weapons and moved out. Goldring writes that "just as the party gained the east bank of the creek, Lebombard saw Hammond's horse being led back into the fort. He called out to Hammond in French, but the latter just looked back quickly and then ignored his call and pressed on toward the camp."[15]

The Assiniboines were drunk and when some Métis warned them of the danger from Hammond and his companions, chaos erupted. Women and children fled, while many of the men were in an alcoholic stupor and incapable of effective action. As the wolfers took up positions in a small coulee overlooking the Indian camp, Abe Farwell

- A Double Duty -

shuttled back and forth between the Indians and the wolfers in a vain attempt to avert a disaster.

A shot rang out. Nobody is sure which side fired first but it started a slaughter. The wolfers poured rapid fire into the Assiniboine encampment from their concealed positions in the coulee, with supporting fire from others on the roof of Solomon's post. The Assiniboines, caught in this fire, had no real chance since their muzzle loaders were no match for the wolfer's repeating rifles. Those in the Indian camp able to do so scattered. Hardwick led a few men on horseback across the creek to outflank the Indians hidden in the bushes, but other Assiniboines on the hill drove them back. A few men ran to assist but the Indians fired on them as they tried to cross the creek and one of the white men, Ed Legrace, was killed. The wolfers wrecked the Assiniboine camp and shot the survivors, except several women whom they raped. They wrapped Legrace in a blanket, built a rough coffin and buried him in a shallow grave under Solomon's post. Solomon and Farwell then packed their goods and left, and as the last cart disappeared, the two posts burned to the ground.

- 2 -

The Force Is Forged

Sir John A. Macdonald wanted a police force on the model of the Royal Irish Constabulary. Unlike the system in Britain, this force would be armed and under central control. The British had used this type of force successfully in colonies, such as India, with large native populations. Macdonald was enamoured with the Royal Irish Constabulary which appears to have been exactly what he wanted for the Northwest Territories. The noted Canadian historian, George F. Stanley believes this was because "the Royal Irish Constabulary had developed against a background of religious and civil strife and social unrest, such as Macdonald feared might develop in the Canadian prairies between the whites and the native peoples, Métis and Indian."[1]

On May 3, 1873 Sir John A. Macdonald introduced a Bill in the House of Commons authorizing the formation of a police force for the Northwest Territories. The Bill, which passed on May 23, 1873, allowed a strength of 300 men, although only 150 were recruited initially. The specific duties of the force included suppression of the whisky trade, collection of customs duties and calming unrest among the aboriginal peoples. Applicants had to be of sound constitution, able to ride, active and able bodied, of good character and between the ages of eighteen and forty. They also had to be able to read and write, either in English or French. While commonly called the North West Mounted Police, this was not the official title of the force until the Act of 1873 was amended in 1879.

Enlistment was initially for three years and Sub-Constables or Constables who completed their term with good behaviour could qualify for a land grant of 160 acres in the Province of Manitoba or the Northwest Territories. The pay was parsimonious, especially when the hardships were considered. This was characteristic of the often shabby treatment meted out to the policemen in the early years by a series of seriously cash-strapped governments. Those in Ottawa neither understood nor appreciated the sacrifices made by many of the men. Sam Steele, a prominent figure in the history of the North West Mounted Police, later wrote that "the government probably relied on the spirit of adventure regardless of compensation which is innate in every Anglo-Saxon in his early manhood."[2] Sub-Constables were paid seventy-five cents a day and Constables one dollar. The Commissioner received from $2,000 to $2,600 a year and Superintendents from $1,000 to $1,400 a year. In comparison, in the United States Army on the western plains, a Colonel received $3,500 a year and a Second Lieutenant $1,400. A private received $13 a month and sergeants $22 a month.

The original draft of the Bill had used the term *Mounted Rifles* and this apparently caused some consternation in the United States when it became known that there was to be a military force to patrol the international boundary. Sir John A. Macdonald swiftly remedied this problem by picking up his pen, crossing out *Mounted Rifles* and substituting *Mounted Police*. Word of the Cypress Hills Massacre reached Ottawa after the actual decision to form the Mounted Police was made. While it was not, in itself, responsible for the creation of the force, the Cypress Hills Massacre resulted, to some extent, in the hasty recruiting and training of the first contingent.

A new force of this type required experienced leaders. Luckily, James Macleod, recently made a Companion of the Order of St. Michael and St. George (CMG) by Queen Victoria for his exemplary service on the Red River Expedition, was in need of a new appointment. While visiting in Scotland, he learned that through the good offices of Sir Alexander Campbell, a Cabinet Minister in Sir John A. Macdonald's government, he would be given a commission in the soon to be formed Mounted Police. Campbell felt that Macleod would make a good second-in-command who could get the force organized while the search for a Commissioner continued.[3] Macleod does not appear to have been considered for the top appointment at this time, possibly because he lacked colonial or Royal Irish Constabulary experience.

Having laid the legal framework for the foundation of the Mounted Police, Sir John A. Macdonald turned his mind to other things, such as the "Pacific Scandal," which arose when rumours circulated that a group which received contracts to build the transcontinental railway to the west had donated large amounts to the Conservative

- The Force Is Forged -

Party's election fund. Despite his denials this scandal threatened the life of Macdonald's government and preoccupied the Prime Minister. Throughout the summer of 1873, the actual formation of the force had a very low priority. Lieutenant Governor Morris kept pressing Ottawa to do something about the situation in the west, especially the whisky traders at Fort Whoop-Up, but Ottawa denied his requests and told him "circumstances at Fort Whoop-Up are not grave enough to send a force there."[4] In response Morris warned that "the government may find itself in Indian difficulties of the gravest nature."[5]

Even with the appointment of recruiters, the formation of the force moved along very slowly. Macdonald wrote to Morris telling him that "our present idea is to drill them all winter here, and send them up, with their horses as soon as the Dawson route is open in the Spring. Do not you think, on consideration, that this is by far the best plan?"[6] Morris obviously did not think so! In response to vague reports of a Métis conspiracy to prevent further treaties between Canada and the Indians, he sent a further telegram to Sir John A. Macdonald asking, "what have you done as to Police force, their absence may lead to grave disaster."[7]

Sensing a potential political disaster if there was any further delay, Sir John A. Macdonald capitulated, telling the Governor General that Morris "is so pressing about the necessity of having the mounted police there that although we intended to concentrate them at Toronto and Kingston for the winter and give them a thorough drilling before going west, we found it necessary that the Force should be sent up before the close of navigation. It would not be well for us to take the responsibility of slighting Morris' repeated and urgent entreaties. If anything went wrong the blame would be laid at our door. I shall hurry the men off at once. No time is to be lost. The Dawson route is not open after the middle of October."[8]

Recruiting for the force had started in a desultory fashion with recruiters assigned to different geographical areas of eastern Canada. Now, with the commitment to have the force recruited and moved to Fort Garry before the Dawson Route closed, the tempo increased and the new officers needed assistance. Sir John A. Macdonald

- *A Double Duty* -

advised Colonel Powell, acting Adjutant General of the Canadian Militia, that a great deal of help would be required from military sources. The deputy adjutant generals of the military districts provided the recruiting officers with support which made it possible for them to recruit the men and get them to Collingwood.

The recruiters, who became the first commissioned officers of the new force, received instructions to round up whatever men they could get and rush them to Collingwood where the Militia would arrange for their movement to Fort Garry. This was a routine movement for the Militia since they had been sending troops west via the Dawson Route since 1870. Colonel Powell made the necessary arrangements with the Northern Railway, which operated both the trains from Toronto to Collingwood and the steamships from Collingwood to Thunder Bay and arranged with the Department of Public Works for the movement from Thunder Bay to Fort Garry. Major D.A. McDonald was sent to Collingwood to act as Movement Control Officer, responsible for the reception, equipment and onward dispatch of the contingents as they arrived.

While recruiting was under way, Sir John A. Macdonald continued his seemingly endless search for a Commissioner. To make the position more attractive, he asked the Governor General to have the War Office regard the appointment of Commissioner as pensionable military service for a British officer. On September 25, 1873 an Order-in-Council appointed nine commissioned officers - Jarvis, Young, Macleod, Winder, Carvell, Walsh, Brisebois and Clark, with Lieutenant Colonel W. Osborne Smith, Deputy Adjutant General in Military District 10 at Fort Garry, appointed Commissioner on a temporary basis. The officers were selected partly for military experience and background but largely by political considerations, while the men were drawn, in large part, through the militia. Jarvis and Young had served in the British Army, Macleod and Walsh in the Canadian Militia, Brisebois in the Papal Zouaves and Carvell was a cavalry officer in the Confederate Army during the Civil War.

The new recruits moved in three contingents. The first group of 31 men, under Inspector James Morrow Walsh, sailed from Collingwood, Ontario on October 4, 1873 on the *Cumberland*. The second contingent, consisting of Winder, Carvell, Brisebois

- The Force Is Forged -

and 62 men sailed on October 8 on the *Chicora*. The third contingent of three officers, Young, Macleod and Breden, and 53 men sailed on the *Frances Smith* on October 10.

Inspector Walsh left a detailed account of the trip of the first contingent that gives some idea of the problems they encountered.[9] He was from Prescott and had recruited in eastern Ontario around Ottawa and along the St. Lawrence to Kingston. His group of thirty-two men was ready by October 1, and they left Ottawa by train that evening at 9:30 p.m. The party had their first casualty at Prescott Junction in the early hours of the following morning. T. O'Neill, a trumpeter, had an abbreviated career with the new force when he received his discharge for "being drunk and riotous" and insisting on making a disturbance.[10] Inspector Walsh returned him to Ottawa.

At Prescott William Walsh, the nephew of Inspector Walsh, joined the group and a short time later, at Belleville, an additional seven recruits boarded, including Sam Steele and two of his brothers, Richard and Godfrey, along with Percy Neale. Sam Steele was destined to become one of the best known officers in the force as well as having a distinguished military career. When the draft reached Toronto there was a three-hour wait for the Collingwood train and by departure time they were short one man, Sub-Constable J. Nelson, so left without him. Obviously needing help in controlling his eager recruits, Inspector Walsh appointed Lawrence Fortescue, a former officer in the Royal Marine Light Infantry and Samuel B. Steele, recently a sergeant in "A" Battery Dominion Artillery to act as noncommissioned officers. Percy Neale, also a former sergeant of "A" Battery, was appointed to act as Quartermaster Sergeant. The party arrived at Collingwood late that evening where Major McDonald met them and billeted them in the Railway Hotel.

The next morning, Sub-Constable John Todd of Ottawa, who was later to gain some notoriety in the force, went to the beach to practice with his revolver. Presumably it was a personally owned weapon since the force had not issued revolvers at that point. Some boys allegedly jostled him while they played on the beach and Todd accidentally shot himself in the fleshy part of the forearm and went to the local hospital for treatment. Inspector Walsh informed Ottawa that Todd would not be fit to sail for a

- A Double Duty -

week and left him in the charge of Major McDonald.[11] That day the detachment paraded at 9:00 a.m. and Major McDonald issued the men essential items such as a greatcoat, towel, soap, tin plate, cup, knife, fork and spoon from Militia stores. Later in the day they were issued blankets. Sub-Constable Nelson, having caught the night train, rejoined his mates. The steamer sailing was delayed for 24-hours so the men remained at Collingwood. Inspector Walsh issued a memo requesting that they "abstain from too free use of intoxicating liquors" and said that by their conduct they would show themselves worthy of the trust placed in them.

After doing squad drill the next morning the party embarked on the steamer *Cumberland* in the afternoon. Inspector Walsh appointed J.H. McIllree, later an Assistant Commissioner, R.E. Steele and R. Killaly to act as corporals and had a guard mounted and sentries posted so that the men could not leave the ship at ports. To their surprise, Sub-Constable Todd rejoined them before they sailed. The doctors suddenly decided he had improved more rapidly than expected and declared him fit to continue the trip.[12]

The detachment reached Prince Arthur's Landing early on the morning of October 8 and immediately started to unload. Inspector Walsh informed Ottawa of their safe arrival and reported that Todd was well.[13] They left by wagon at 7:30 a.m. via the Dawson Route, a series of water crossings by tugs and barges or steamboats, linked by portages of corduroy road. Travel for the first fifty miles was by wagon, followed by another 385 miles of rivers and lakes with forty-seven portages and, finally, 110 miles overland from the Northwest Angle to St. Boniface - a total distance of 545 miles. The Wolseley Expedition of 1870 took three months of hard going to reach Fort Garry but by 1872, new roads and improved portages had reduced transit time to three weeks.

On October 9, Inspector Walsh had his party on the move at 2 a.m., arriving at Lake Shebandowan at 6:00 a.m. only to find no steamer there. The steamer eventually arrived and sailed the next day at 6:30 a.m. The whole of October 10 was spent alternately crossing lakes and portages. On October 11, the detachment crossed Lake Windegooshean, a three-hour trip in open boats. More than fifteen hours and a few

- *The Force Is Forged* -

portages later they pitched their tents for the first time and stayed at Sturgeon Portage for the night. There was a slight delay the following morning when the Indians initially refused to row the boats because it was Sunday, but they eventually got underway and progressed well until halted at Island Portage because, once again, there was no connecting steamer. The steamer arrived next morning and they resumed their journey via vessels and portages to Rainy River, Fort Frances and the North West Angle, where they arrived about 5:30 p.m. on October 17, 1873.

At the Northwest Angle, low boats or scows towed by a tug carried the men from the ship to the shore, a distance of about two miles. The detachment and their baggage left the ship at 6:30 p.m. in snow, rain and bitter cold and as they neared the shore, the tug cast off the tow ropes and left them to drift. There are differing versions of what happened. Inspector Walsh complained that Engineer George Dixon, in charge of the tug, had put the vessel ashore, extinguished the boiler fires and left his men to drift until the barges grounded. He said that the action exposed the wounded man, Todd, and another man suffering from rheumatism, to snow, cold and wind. The detachment was left adrift for a time and then brought ashore. Walsh went on the attack, reprimanding Dixon for delaying their journey. Dixon complained that Walsh "commenced abusing me in the most ungentlemany manner, telling me he should think nothing of shooting a thing such as me, calling me a murderer, a God damn black hearted villain." He reported Walsh "continued abusing me for full half an hour, in a very vile manner, and would not allow me to say anything in defence." Inspector Walsh filed an official complaint but an investigation ended with contradictory versions of events.[14]

This is an early indicator of the personal characteristics of James Morrow Walsh that were to mark his career. He was quick to act, stood up for his men and had a vocabulary that was to become legendary in the west. Walsh followed the sound military practice of looking after his troops and when he believed that Dixon had unnecessarily exposed them to snow and cold he found it unacceptable. When Walsh perceived Dixon as responsible for his men's discomfort he ensured Dixon knew of his annoyance. After a miserable trip, the sight of the person who cast them adrift getting

- A Double Duty -

a tongue lashing from the Inspector, fairly or not, probably worked wonders for the group morale and spirit of the detachment.

On October 18 the detachment started to march to 30 Mile Shanty, with their baggage following in three wagons and four bullock carts. They arrived at Birch River that evening and stayed there the next day, unable to march due to the condition of their boots and the need to wait for the baggage carts. Other than Militia greatcoats, the force had not been issued uniforms at this time so the men would have been marching in the footwear and clothing in which they left home, much of it highly unsuitable for the conditions they now encountered. The men rode in wagons for the next few days, arriving at Fort Garry on October 21. Here, they left Sub-Constable Todd for medical treatment at the military hospital and went on by steamer to Lower Fort Garry, also known as the Stone Fort.

The second contingent, consisting of Winder, Carvell, Brisebois and thirty-two men, sailed on the *Chicora* on October 8. The Grand Trunk railway lost part of Brisebois' baggage, just the start of his troubles in the Mounted Police. Sub-Constable Fullerton recalled that the food was poor but the officers had several boxes of beef for their own use and somehow one dark night a box was broken open on a portage and the smell of cooking meat was later wafting through the camp. Similarly, a 20-gallon keg of whisky, loaded into a scow in the rain, somehow turned into water.[15]

The third and last contingent, composed of three officers, Young, Macleod and Breden, with fifty-three men, had a much more difficult time. They boarded the *Frances Smith*, which sailed from Collingwood on October 10, 1873. They encountered a severe storm enroute and all aboard were ill, with the exception of James Macleod. On arrival at Prince Arthur's Landing, they made the fifty mile trip to Shebandowan without difficulty but the weather then turned cold and it snowed heavily. At Shebandowan, the party found the stopping house closed and locked. They decided to push on. They could not go back since the last boat of the season had already sailed eastward from Prince Arthur's Landing. Sergeant Major Bray reported that they broke into all the stopping houses and "every morsel the cook left behind was well taken care

- *The Force Is Forged* -

of." At Rainy River they got a very welcome meal of boiled corn and whitefish from some Chippewa Indians.[16]

The contingent got as far as Fort Frances, the Hudson's Bay post on Rainy Lake, with great difficulty then had to wait there for a steamer to cross Lake of the Woods. After waiting three days for a storm to subside, they made the crossing, only to have to break ice for fifty yards to get ashore at the North West Angle. Due to the severe weather they had to abandon a large part of their equipment in a blizzard and this was to cause considerable difficulty for them during the ensuing winter. There were carts waiting at the North West Angle with tents in them, but the tents were frozen hard and could not be pitched. The men walked to Fort Garry under adverse circumstances and, on the last night on the trail, slept in a blizzard then walked ten miles without breakfast the next morning in a temperature of $-10°F$. As they approached Saint Boniface, Archbishop Taché met them and invited them to his palace where they were given hot baths, good food and comfortable beds. The next morning they crossed the river, one by one, on the treacherous newly formed ice.[17] The third contingent reached Lower Fort Garry by sleigh and the force was finally assembled and ready to start training but, with their stores frozen in on the Dawson route, they were a scruffy crew - the complete opposite of most people's vision of the ultra-smart Mounted Police.

Pending the appointment of a Commissioner, the Deputy Adjutant General commanding Military District 10 (Manitoba), Lieutenant Colonel W. Osborne Smith, was in charge of the force. He arranged contracts for the purchase of horses and supplies. He negotiated with the Hudson's Bay Company to provide food under contract and arranged accommodation for the whole force in Lower Fort Garry. The officers' mess was in the "Big House," the former residence of Governor George Simpson. Osborne Smith arranged for the erection of two large stables later described by him as "very flimsy."[18] He also arranged for the provision of bedding and whatever items of uniform were available and, since the force had yet to procure weapons, the Militia provided 50 Snider-Enfield carbines and 46 Snider-Enfield Short Rifles for training purposes.

- A Double Duty -

In October 1873, Sir John A. Macdonald finally found a Commissioner for the Mounted Police, George French, a Royal Artillery captain seconded to Canada with the acting rank of lieutenant colonel while commanding the School of Artillery at Kingston. Although he lacked the colonial experience in India that the Prime Minister considered an asset, he had, apparently, served for a short time in the Irish Constabulary as a young man. The Secretary of State for War in London wrote that there was "no objection to Captain G.A. French holding the appointment of the Commissioner of Police in command of the Mounted Police in the North West Territories of Canada and retaining his position on the Seconded List of the Royal Artillery."[19] Writers often describe Commissioner French as an "experienced officer." This is misleading. George Arthur French was a junior captain in the Royal Artillery, promoted to that rank in December 1872, a year before his appointment as Commissioner of the North West Mounted Police.[20] As a junior officer he served largely with garrison artillery and there is no indication that he had any operational experience that would be especially beneficial in Western Canada.

On November 3, 1873 Lieutenant Colonel Smith came to Lower Fort Garry for a ceremony where each man received a warrant of enlistment on signing the articles of engagement. The first man to enlist was A.H. Griesbach, the first Regimental Sergeant Major, who had previously served in the 15th Hussars and the Cape Mounted Rifles as well as on the Red River Expedition in 1870. A misunderstanding became apparent when the men were signing the articles of engagement. Several of those recruited by Inspector Carvell in Quebec and New Brunswick refused to be attested because they would have to serve for three years, after which they would be allowed to resign on giving six months notice. Due to a miscommunication between Captain Young and Carvell, the men had been assured that they could resign at any time on six months notice. When the ceremony was completed, Lieutenant Colonel Osborne Smith returned to Winnipeg, leaving Superintendent Jarvis in command with Inspector Walsh as adjutant, veterinary surgeon and riding-master. Since Winnipeg, twenty miles away, was the centre for communication, Staff Constable Arthur Stewart, acting as Orderly

- The Force Is Forged -

Room Sergeant, was attached to the Provisional Battalion of Infantry there and the Army also provided offices for the Commissioner.[21]

Shortly after this, on November 6, 1873, Sir John A. Macdonald was forced to resign as a result of the Pacific Railway Scandal. His government was replaced by that of the Honourable Alexander Mackenzie, with the Honourable A.A. Dorion as Minister of Justice responsible for the Mounted Police. Hewitt Bernard, the Deputy Minister of Justice at the time of the formation of the Mounted Police, survived the change of government, despite the fact that he was Sir John A. Macdonald's brother-in-law.

The new Prime Minister, in marked contrast to Macdonald, was a temperance supporter and he took the control or limitation of the liquor trade seriously. The need for action was reinforced by the entreaties of Lieutenant Governor Morris. Mackenzie was not completely in favour of a semi-military police force so, while planning and training for the expedition continued, he explored other alternatives. He apparently even considered a joint expedition with the United States but was dissuaded by the Governor General, Dufferin, who argued that if Canadians went alone they would look like allies of the Indians. Dorion, the Minister of Justice and Bernard, the Deputy Minister, supported the use of the Mounted Police.[22]

Training was now underway in earnest under very harsh conditions with "much inconvenience and discomfort being caused by the fact of a great portion of their uniform and winter clothing being frozen in on the Dawson route."[23] The experienced Sergeant Major Griesbach and Sergeant McIllree were in charge of discipline and foot drill while Staff Sergeant Sam Steele, an expert horseman, was in charge of equitation. While most of the recruits had previous military service of some kind, few of them apparently knew how to ride. Since few of the available horses had ever been saddled, the combination of novice riders and unbroken horses made for exciting equestrian drills.

Sam Steele recalls that "our work was unceasing from 6 a.m. until after dark. I drilled five rides per day the whole of the winter in an open *menage*, and the orders were that if the temperature was not lower than 36 below zero the riding and breaking should go on." He noted that, with very few exceptions, the horses were untrained broncos so none but the most powerful and skilled riders tried to deal with them. Steele recalls that even when he had them "gentled" enough to let recruits mount, the men were repeatedly thrown violently to the frozen ground.[24]

Training continued through November and into December, turning the recruits into Mounted Riflemen but giving them no training in the law. The work was demanding and hard but offered some opportunity for recreation. Sam Steele found that "although we had much work at Stone Fort there were some amusements, such as balls, parties and rifle matches; but with the thermometer in the thirties below zero there was little pleasure in shooting." With an eye to what lay ahead he also "took notes of all the information I received, and was pretty well acquainted with the customs of the Indians, hunters and traders before I left Fort Garry."[25]

Commissioner French arrived at Fort Garry in December 1873. He had not served in the west before. Two months later he returned to Ontario where he remained until he came to Fort Dufferin with the second contingent in June 1874. He thus had a total of about three months experience in Western Canada when he led the force westward from Fort Dufferin This lack of experience was of concern to Lieutenant Governor Morris who wrote to A.A. Dorion, the Minister of Justice, noting that "Colonel French is an entire stranger to the North West, I hope I can consult with French and Cameron as to dealing with the Indians."[26]

James Walker, who had known Lieutenant Colonel French at the Artillery School, served with him in the North West Mounted Police and remained one of his staunchest supporters over the years, described him as holding "ingrained views about the organization and administration of a police force and equally seasoned resentment against any attempt at outside interference." He also described him as "a strict, but not humourless, disciplinarian who was intolerant of incompetence, particularly in politicians."[27] These views were to contribute to his ultimate downfall.

Commissioner French travelled to Fort Garry and advised the Minister of Justice that he had been "duly sworn in . . . on 16 December." He reported that Lieutenant

- *The Force Is Forged* -

Colonel Osborne Smith had purchased thirty-three horses for $175 each, nearly all halfbred Red River ponies, adding that "a very large number of horses will be required for the Force and it appears quite hopeless to expect to obtain them in this Province." He pointed out that "the horses used by the Boundary Commission are imported from Ontario for less than $175 each and if horses from Ontario were imported via Duluth or the Dawson Route I believe they would cost less than this amount."[28]

Comm. French   GAI NA-23-1

Commissioner French, known as a keen disciplinarian, arrived in his appointment to find that thirty members of the Mounted Police had signed a petition asking for the promotion of Sub-Inspector Brisebois. Ottawa had already dealt with the matter and French wrote to Colonel Bernard, Deputy Minister of Justice, expressing surprise "that a matter of discipline should be dealt with without reference being previously made to the Officer Commanding the Corps, and I think it is to be regretted that I have thereby been prevented from discovering the ringleaders in what I consider a most flagrant violation of the Rules of Discipline."[29] This was an early skirmish in what was to be an ongoing struggle over who was in charge of the force. French suspected that Brisebois had personally initiated the petition and this early notoriety probably did nothing to enhance Brisebois' career prospects. French indicated that he did not consider Brisebois qualified for promotion and the promotion was denied.

Despite Sir John A. Macdonald's desire for the plain and simple, a decision was made to have a scarlet tunic. This had the advantage of being clearly different from the blue of the United States Army, which was in constant conflict with the Indian tribes south of the border. Colonel Robertson-Ross reported that the Indians did not like the dark uniforms of the Rifles and recalled the 6th Regiment at Fort Garry who wore red.

- *A Double Duty* -

Commissioner French welcomed the decision and wrote to the Minister of Justice that "a scarlet tunic has I believe been decided upon and from what I can learn here there are very good reasons for the decision."[30] The Governor General informed the British Ambassador in Washington that "the expedition will be commanded by Colonel French, an artillery officer, and though nominally policemen the men will be dressed in scarlet uniforms and possess all the characteristics of a military force."[31]

By its training, organization and discipline, the force took on a military aura that survives to this day. Commissioner French, while frequently reminding his men that they were not soldiers, created a force "which in every respect had more the characteristics of a first-class cavalry regiment than those of an ordinary rural police."[32] There was no legal or police related training. There were a considerable number of unsuitable recruits as a result of hasty recruiting and those who were below standard had to be removed. A medical board discharged nineteen men who were unable to meet medical standards and several others were released on disciplinary grounds. The hard work, harsh conditions and demanding discipline also incited several others to desert.

As 1874 came in, the men in Lower Fort Garry continued their training under great hardship and miserable conditions. Their newly appointed Commissioner acquainted himself, to the extent possible, with the conditions they would face on their trek to the west and the necessary equipment and logistic arrangements. An immediate weakness showed in the latter. While many experienced and capable commissary officers had applied for the appointment, the post of Quartermaster had gone to an inexperienced officer. The lack of an experienced and capable logistics officer was to have serious consequences on the march west.

- 3 -

Planning And Preparation

The challenge of leading a newly formed police force into a sparsely settled region to wipe out the liquor trade and establish law and order was a daunting undertaking. If the force was to move west in 1874, the planners had to pay immediate attention to logistics, especially supplies and transportation. Before deciding what he was to take and how to get it there, Commissioner French had to know what he faced in terms of potential enemies, topography, and climate. In military terms he needed up-to-date intelligence. There was no record of an officer being assigned as "Intelligence Officer" to collect, collate and confirm any available information. The Boundary Commission, on the other hand, also faced travelling from Fort Dufferin to the Rocky Mountains, and Captain Cameron divided his organization into seven departments, each with its own head reporting directly to him. One of these departments was "Intelligence" and Cameron instructed all members of the Boundary Commission to report on any items of interest.

In December 1873, Lieutenant Governor Morris, considered by some to have been alarmist, wrote to the Minister of the Interior that he had "positive information that there are no less than six forts of United States traders (any one of which is as large as the H.B. Co.'s post at Carlton or Pitt) fully armed and equipped, in our territory, and the question we now have to solve is, how to deal with the matter and avoid an Indian war, which may, at any moment, burst out, and involve the Dominion in enormous expense, and expose the people of the Territories and this Province, to the fearful atrocities which overwhelmed Minnesota a few years ago."[1]

Morris had some legitimate cause for concern. He received a report that Fort Whoop-Up was armed with cannon and the Indians would laugh at a small force but "offer no opposition to a good force."[2] Colonel J.B. Mitchell, then the Sergeant Major of "E" Troop, recalled that reports came in that the whisky traders who were causing all the trouble were preparing to defend Fort Whoop-Up and Fort Standoff. Hunters

- A Double Duty -

who had been in the area reported that the forts were stocked with guns, provisions and fighting men. Colonel Mitchell's assessment was that carbines would be useless against a fort of ten-inch logs.

Having apparently accepted the intelligence that Fort Whoop-Up housed a large number of lawless desperadoes, well protected by fortifications and prepared to fight anyone attempting to dislodge them, Commissioner French set out to plan his march westward.[3] His initial planning assumed that there would be little chance of obtaining supplies in the west so it would be necessary for the force to carry food and forage as well as the tools and material to build stables and living quarters. He estimated a minimum requirement of 300 men, which meant 150 more would have to be recruited, and he saw a need for 250 additional horses which could not be found in Manitoba. At this point he was fully aware that some of the horses would be required to pull carts, wagons or guns.

Most of the 300 men would move west to subdue the whisky traders at Fort Whoop-Up. About 80 of them would be left on the Bow River where they would have to build their own accommodation. Another 80 would be distributed along the North Saskatchewan, with rations and quarters obtained from the Hudson's Bay Company, while 100 more would return to Manitoba. Because of the reports of large numbers of outlaws in heavily timbered forts with underground galleries, Commissioner French decided it would be necessary to have field guns with the force. Given this proposed disposition, French decided that the force would carry rations based on a 12-month supply for the 80 personnel going to Bow River, a 150-day supply for those going to Fort Ellice or Fort Carlton, and a 90-day supply for those going to the North Saskatchewan, where the Hudson's Bay Company would provide rations and quarters. He realized that there would be some supplies of pemmican and game available but he was reluctant to depend on it.

At the request of the Honourable Alexander Mackenzie, the Hudson's Bay Company had agreed to provide free to the Mounted Police any spare quarters that were available at Edmonton. It was specified that any repairs or additions would be at the

- Planning And Preparation -

expense of the Canadian government.[4] This meant that the portion of the force going to the Saskatchewan would not need to carry material for the construction of a post.

Based on Commissioner French's plan, the force would carry 209,050 pounds, or over 100 tons, which presented enormous problems in transportation. There had to be a reduction in the weight of pork packed in barrels with brine, which was 65 percent deadweight. They could carry bacon as a substitute but it was more expensive. Since a good ox would make 600 pounds of ration meat and needed no transportation if driven on the hoof, they substituted beef in the form of 125 oxen for some of the pork. This reduced the ration load to about 125,000 pounds. If some of the oxen pulled Red River carts they could also transport 70 to 80 thousand pounds of other rations, and 25-two horse wagons could carry the remaining 50,000 pounds.

Regarding forage, Commissioner French wrote that "there will be little difficulty as to the supply of grass." One can only wonder how often he looked back on those words. He had obviously not yet read reports of the Palliser Expedition that had travelled part of the same route some fifteen years before in conditions remarkably similar to those encountered by the Mounted Police. Commissioner French also appears to have been unaware, at the time, that horses imported from Ontario would not eat prairie grass until acclimatized. He did, however, realize that carrying oats in quantity would be a problem "and yet horses at hard work must, if at all possible, have grain of some sort." Using a half ration of five pounds as the minimum possible, 350 horses would require 175,000 pounds of oats for 30 days, requiring 27 Red River carts for transportation and a 90-day supply would require 81 carts or 27 wagons.

Thus, for food and forage alone, the force would require 100 Red River carts drawn by oxen, which would be available afterward for beef, and 50 wagons drawn by 100 of the available horses. In addition there would be large quantities of camping equipment, tools, building materials, agricultural implements, medical and veterinary supplies, small arms, gun and mortar ammunition and personal baggage. Having made his initial estimate, Commissioner French then asked Superintendents Jarvis, Macleod,

- A Double Duty -

Winder and Carvell for their estimates and they must have come as a shock to him, with Macleod's estimate for one Troop coming to over 100 tons.

There were also many useful suggestions, some of which he appears to have adopted. James Macleod, having had experience manhandling 200 pound barrels of pork in brine over portages on the Dawson Route during the Red River Expedition, noted that bacon was "more handy to carry" and that pork barrels leaked from rough usage and the pork had to be rebrined from time to time or it would go rancid. He recommended eliminating coffee from the ration and doubling the amount of tea. Regarding cattle on the hoof he prophetically wrote that "with the knowledge of the fact that considerable stretches of the road we must travel are bear [sic] of any supplies of grass under certain circumstances, I think it would be hazardous to trust such a supply."[5]

Jacob Carvell, whose experience as a Confederate cavalry officer probably gave him some experience with existing on short rations, recommended that they take three-quarters of a standard ration for 180 days and Jarvis, who had been in the west surveying the previous summer, recommended only taking grain for one month "by which time prairie grass would be sufficiently grown to nourish the horses." He also recommended light carts rather than wagons due to the difficulty of crossing rivers and negotiating narrow trails.[6]

For reasons which are not clear, Commissioner French was adamant that the force should not be dependent on the Militia for supplies even though the Department of Militia & Defence had provided the Mounted Police with transportation, weapons, clothing, bedding and other assistance, at Fort Garry and Toronto. He informed the Minister of Justice that he wished "it to be particularly understood that from previous as well as present experience I object to the Force under my command being dependent on the officials or contractors of the Militia Department for their supply." He concluded that the stores and provisions should be taken west by the force's own horses and that cattle for slaughter should be driven on foot by the force, instead of carrying large quantities of pork or pemmican.[7]

- *Planning And Preparation* -

Commissioner French decided that it would be essential to have some field guns with the force due to the absolute necessity of reducing the outlaws' forts. The inclusion of field guns was reasonable if one accepted the reports about Fort Whoop-Up which Commissioner French appears to have believed without hesitation. Had he obtained more accurate intelligence he may well have considered using the much lighter and more easily transported 7-pounder mountain gun. This would have eased the burden of the horses that had to haul the guns and the ammunition for them. He considered the possibility of taking a subunit of the Militia artillery but ultimately decided to have the artillery as an integral part of the Mounted Police, on the model of the Cape of Good Hope Frontier Police. He requisitioned two 9-pounder muzzle loading rifles, asking for the newer 6-cwt model that was lighter and had an increased range, but the equipment eventually provided was the 8-cwt model in use in the Canadian Militia at the time.

On February 5, 1874 Commissioner French left via Fargo for Ottawa to seek permission to recruit up to the full strength of 300 authorized by the Act. This proposal met with no opposition and, in addition to the increase in manpower, the government authorized the purchase of additional horses, arms, ammunition and stores. French had also asked that James Macleod be appointed Assistant Commissioner and the Minister of Justice gave his approval.

Commissioner French was very busy in the spring of 1874 interviewing prospective recruits for the additional 150 vacancies in the force. He was also personally involved in the purchase of horses for the force and supervising the training in Toronto. French realized he would need all the help he could get training the new recruits, so he had Inspector Walsh come from Lower Fort Garry to Toronto in March 1874.[8] There are indications that French was either unwilling or unable to delegate responsibility and he kept an overwhelming number of matters in his own hands. He could reasonably have delegated supervision of the purchase of horses to an officer like Sub-Inspector Walker who had considerable expertise on the subject. Training at Toronto could have been largely delegated to Inspector Walsh and Intelligence to

- A Double Duty -

Inspector Jarvis, leaving French to devote the necessary time to planning and preparation for the march.

By April the second contingent of 150 men was undergoing training at the New Fort in Toronto with uniforms, saddles and weapons provided from the military sources that Commissioner French wanted nothing to do with. As in the first contingent, there were many "old soldiers." The sergeant major was Tom Miles, a former captain in the 13th Hussars, ably assisted by Sergeant Francis, a Crimean War veteran, said to have taken part in the Charge of the Light Brigade. There was also room for young men of outstanding ability such as J.B. Mitchell, who had trained at the Artillery School under Commissioner French.

At first all was confusion as things got sorted out, but one young recruit recorded that "outstanding from the muddle was that thorough soldier and disciplinarian Colonel French, who seemed to be here, there and everywhere, giving special attention often accompanied by devastating remarks, to some of the incompetents wished upon him by the Ottawa gang." The same recruit wrote that "conspicuous among the trained officers was Major James M. Walsh, whose erect bearing and quick, energetic movements gave early evidence that he possessed that virile character which was in after years to earn him the name 'Sitting Bull's Boss'."[9]

William Parker, a new recruit, wrote home that when he arrived he had to go and fill his bed with straw.[10] This was his introduction to the palliasse, a mattress shaped bag, used by the military for decades, which was filled with straw to make a bed. Later on, the standard "bed" for the North West Mounted Police in the west was three planks, supported by two trestles, covered by a buffalo robe and a palliasse filled with straw.

The youngest member of the Mounted Police, did not get in easily. When Fred Bagley, then fifteen years old, tried to enlist, Commissioner French who had served in the British Army with his father, immediately informed Mr. Bagley of what his son was trying to do. After a heated confrontation, his father finally agreed that young Fred could go as a trumpeter, but for no more than six months. His parents saw him again fourteen years later.[11] The newly recruited Fred Bagley was issued a scarlet Norfolk

- Planning And Preparation -

jacket and blue trousers with the double white stripe of the Military Train down the outside seams. He had his picture taken in his new uniform and years later remarked "that a present day glance at the photograph, which I still have, shows a rather goofy looking youth, the fit of whose uniform reminds one forcibly of those well known French towns, Toulon and Toulouse."[12]

The greatest weakness among the recruits in Toronto, as it had been in Fort Garry, was riding. The riding school obviously afforded amusement to spectators and numerous bruises to the participants. As Fred Bagley described it "a visit to the riding school revealed dashing horsemen galore. Many of them dashing from their saddles and over their horses heads, causing such sarcastic remarks as 'Who the H__l told you to dismount Sir'?" He also described how one recruit, a former professor in a famous French college was seen leaning forward from his saddle and embracing his horse's neck, drawing a roar from the Sergeant Major, "That's right young fellow me lad, kiss 'im and 'e'll be good to you."[13]

The French professor, Jean D'Artigue, confessed, "I must say here, that most of us had overrated our proficiency in horsemanship; for when we came to ride without stirrups, many laughable falls ensued; men having lost their balance would cling to their horses in every imaginable position, till the drill instructor coming up, would give the horse a smart lash with the whip, which would make him rear and plunge, till freeing himself from his rider, he would gallop away to the stable."[14] Commissioner French, noting the lamentable lack of riding skills, commented that "it was too much to expect that much advance could be made in riding in such a limited time and with untrained horses; however, I consoled myself with the reflection that, whereas little drill and no target practice could be carried out on our long march to the West, there would be ample opportunity for the practice of equitation."[15]

Sergeant Major Mitchell was more optimistic, observing that the English saddles in use were slick and the recruits were not allowed to use stirrups. They had to leap onto their horses but after early awkwardness they could soon get astride gracefully. With an eye to the future he also placed the most promising men, well-built recruits

- A Double Duty -

from the farm or other outdoor work, in "E" Troop which he was to lead.[16] Not so optimistic was Fred Bagley, whose duty as trumpeter was to "tag along after some officer whose knowledge of military maneuvers was of very recent acquisition and who, although on his way, was in a dense mental fog as to where he was headed for."[17] The drills of the force's own Horse Artillery Troop, under Inspector Jackson, were spectacular "and the drivers and gunners of that troop made the most of the sensation they caused as with gun carriages and limbers rumbling thunderously they rushed furiously from point to point."[18]

With the passage of time and hard work the troops in Toronto started to resemble a disciplined military unit and their thoughts frequently turned to the time when they would join the others in Manitoba. Twice during their training Commissioner French addressed them on parade, describing the dangers and the hardships ahead and informing them that anyone who now believed it had been a mistake to enlist was free to leave.

While Commissioner French was in Ontario recruiting, buying horses and supervising training, activity continued at Fort Garry. During this time the authorities called upon the force at least twice to act as policemen. The first of these came at the end of 1873 when Lieutenant Colonel Osborne Smith at Fort Garry received a letter from W.T. Urquhart, Secretary of the North-West Council, stating that it was believed men from Manitoba, alleged to be in the lumbering business, were selling liquor to Indians at Big Black Island and suggesting that the police investigate. He then said that he hoped to obtain further evidence so immediate action was not required. Finally, on December 24, 1873, he wrote to Commissioner French that he had no more information but suggested some policemen be sent to determine if something illegal was occuring.[19] In the Lower Fort Garry Post Journal for December 29, 1873 an entry records that Major Macleod left the post on that date with a party of police officers, to arrest liquor sellers on Lake Winnipeg. The Post Journal entry for January 7, 1874 notes that the Mounted Police party who went to search for liquor and liquor sellers returned without finding the one or the other.[20] There are many versions of what

- *Planning And Preparation* -

happened on this expedition, including a report that the men "found that the birds had flown, but had thoughtfully left a couple of 'kegs' of whisky in their deserted shack." The patrol supposedly poured the whisky on the ground and destroyed the shack by fire.[21] It is likely that both the whisky and the burning shack warmed up the members of the patrol.

In April 1874 information was received that an American trader enroute to Fort Edmonton had said he would be taking liquor with him, contrary to the law. A search warrant was given to Inspector Crozier who had to move quickly to capture the trader. He called on the Lieutenant Governor and told him that he could not proceed unless he could purchase a wagon, harness and provisions for his men. The Lieutenant Governor bought a wagon for $75.00, harness for $20.00 and advanced Inspector Crozier an additional $200.00.

Off went Crozier and his men. After six or seven months, when nothing more had been heard, the Secretary to the Lieutenant Governor wrote to Commissioner French saying that the Lieutenant Governor had never been officially informed of the result and requesting a report on this case, an accounting for the $200.00 and information on the whereabouts of the wagon and harness.[22] French responded by pointing out that since Crozier had gone to Portage La Prairie in Manitoba, which fell within provincial jurisdiction, the expenses appeared to be chargeable to Manitoba and he advised the Lieutenant Governor to refer the matter to the Minister of Justice. To further confuse the issue it appears that Crozier had traded the wagon for two Red River carts somewhere along the way.[23] Nothing could be found in the files to suggest the outcome of the case, possibly the first federal-provincial squabble over policing costs in western Canada.

An incident occurred at Fort Garry at this time that had both immediate and long term implications for relations between the Mounted Police and the Canadian Militia. Two members of the force, John McIllree and Percy Neale, were in Fort Garry when a fire broke out in the Militia barracks and they immediately went to help fight the blaze. When the fire was extinguished, Lieutenant Colonel Smith appeared through the smoke and ordered McIllree to "rejoin his company," obviously believing him to be a soldier. He apparently did not appreciate McIllree's response that he had no company and placed him under close arrest. When Percy Neale told Smith he was mistaken, the colonel told him to "go to hell." After McIllree was freed the two men reported the incident to Commissioner French who ordered an inquiry. Lieutenant Colonel Smith refused to appear or cooperate. James Macleod, who conducted the official inquiry, concluded that Smith's conduct was unwarranted and that he had lied in his allegations.[24]

Philip Goldring considered that French's support for his men contributed to the development of an *esprit de corps* which might help sustain the force through years of difficulties. It may also have been responsible for a deterioration in relations between the Militia and the Mounted Police. This incident had no negative influence on the subsequent careers of the two members involved, since John McIllree received a commission shortly thereafter and retired, many years later, as an Assistant Commissioner while Percy Neale later became a Superintendent. In 1880, when James Macleod was to be replaced as Commissioner, Lieutenant Colonel Osborne Smith wrote to Sir John A. Macdonald asking that he be considered for the appointment.[25] One can only imagine how McIllree and Neale would have reacted had Smith become their new commanding officer.

While training continued at Fort Garry so did the preparations for the march west. The Paymaster, Dalrymple Clark, writing to his uncle, Sir John A. Macdonald, who was now in the Opposition, complained that "we are purchasing ox carts for the march to the West and by the regulations I am so tied down that I must also see every ox cart and set of harness before paying for them." He added that "the authorities that be appear to know very little about the difficulties that exist here during the spring weather and consequently I have been kept on the road between here and the Lower Fort for the last month."[26] James Macleod was also involved in purchasing Red River carts and other requirements in Fort Garry. To help him in his negotiations, Commissioner French agreed that Macleod could hire his future brother-in-law, Willie

- Planning And Preparation -

North West Mounted Police March At Lower Fort Garry   HBCA N9206

Drever, who had experience with cart trains. In June, just before leaving Lower Fort Garry, Macleod informed Commissioner French, who was still in Toronto, that transport was progressing satisfactorily.[27]

The statute authorizing the formation of the Mounted Police provided that the Governor-in-Council could locate the headquarters of the force at any place in the Northwest Territories or the Province of Manitoba. In May 1874 the government selected Fort Ellice, on the grounds that all known trails in the area converged there. A report from A.A. Dorion, the Minister of Justice, brushed off any perceived problem in obtaining the required building materials in this relatively remote location, noting that "it is believed that with some trifling encouragement an enterprising man could readily be found who would establish the mill and provide the requisite supply of boards."[28]

On May 5, 1874 Sub-Inspector Shurtliff took ten men to Fort Ellice to establish the first detachment of the Mounted Police. Their main duty was to check cart traffic on the Fort Garry-Fort Edmonton trail for illicit liquor. They also took some agricultural implements with them to plant oats and other crops to supply the bulk of the force, which would be returning to Fort Ellice in November. Commissioner French told Ottawa that "the idea of wintering any large portion of the Force at Fort Ellice this winter is entirely out of the question. The Governor entirely agrees with me as to the unsuitability of Fort Ellice as a headquarters for the Force. If the Department chooses to set his opinion and mine aside they can do so, but they must take the responsibility thereof. I am making such arrangements as I can, without expenses, to provide for the wintering of the Force at the Stone Fort, Winnipeg and Dufferin."[29]

Lieutenant Governor Morris arranged to send messengers with presents for the Indians to pave the way for the arrival of the Mounted Police. The messengers were to "state that the Queen is sending the Mounted Police for the preservation of law and order and prevention of aggression by lawless American traders and the introduction of liquors;" they were to "ask for their good will" and were told the "cooperation of the Indians is not sought in actions the police take." They were also to "state that the Boundary Commission is marking the line between British and American territory;" and that it was "intended to make a treaty this season."[30]

The Lieutenant Governer asked J.A. Grahame of the Hudson's Bay Company to provide assistance since some of that company's officers were "familiar with the language of the Blackfeet and other tribes between Fort Edmonton and the International boundary line and have influence."[31] This request was made shortly before the force was due to depart from Fort Dufferin and one is left wondering why it was not done much earlier, given the importance of the mission. As a result, the Hudson's Bay Company had W. McKay at Fort Pitt take the message to the Plains Crees. He took "four horses and two carts; and a supply of tea, sugar, tobacco, ammunition and a few other articles to the amount of six hundred dollars." He delivered the message and distributed the presents, encountering no major difficulties, other than "two families belonging to Big Bear's band, who objected to receive present, stating it was given them as a bribe to facilitate a future treaty."[32]

- Planning And Preparation -

The Hudson's Bay Company had no officers immediately available to visit the Blackfoot and, in any case, Grahame considered it would be a mistake for the Company to become involved as middlemen.[33] Morris then asked the Reverend John McDougall, a Methodist missionary living with the Stoneys at Morley, to deliver the message. He was out hunting when the courier arrived but his wife sent a man to give him the letter from Lieutenant Governor Morris and he immediately set out for Blackfoot Crossing. The Reverend McDougall relished being the messenger, seeing himself as the 'John the Baptist' of the coming system of law and order on the plains.

When he arrived at Blackfoot Crossing the traders were in full operation there and "it being evening we were forced to camp near the trading shop and knowing that if the Indians in camp were drinking we would be subject to any amount of annoyance and danger I sent a note to the traders stating our position and errand and requesting them as a favour to stop the flow of liquor for at least two days until we got through with the camp."[34] His request was ignored. McDougall met with Crowfoot and Old Sun, and explained that policemen in scarlet tunics were coming across the plains and would build posts in the Blackfoot hunting grounds. He said they were coming to stop the traders selling whisky to the Indians and to stop the Indians from killing each other. He explained the system of British justice and how all would be treated equally. Crowfoot and the other chiefs offered cooperation and assistance.

When he left Blackfoot Crossing the Reverend McDougall proceeded to Fort Whoop-Up where he found Joseph Healey and one other man, the rest being away visiting the Boundary Commission. He wrote that the whisky traders enjoyed these rough and tumble visits to the Survey Camp. Now both the Indians and the whisky traders were aware that the police would be coming but he also said that "more than once we were taunted" by the American traders "about the tardiness and inefficiency of our country's soldiers."[35]

As their rudimentary training drew to an end, the time eventually came for the two parts of the force, those at Lower Fort Garry and those at New Fort in Toronto, to assemble at Fort Dufferin, the Boundary Commission post just north of the present

- A Double Duty -

Emerson, Manitoba. In May, Superintendent Carvell took a dozen men from Lower Fort Garry to Fort Dufferin to prepare the camp. On June 7, 1874 the three troops at the Stone Fort left, "with considerable regret, but with high hopes," via Winnipeg, to meet their comrades.[36] Sub-Constable Finlayson reported that they "had considerable difficulty in starting - ox carts breaking down and oxen running away."[37] This situation was to repeat itself often in the coming weeks. The men travelled slowly along beside the Red River in hot weather until they arrived at Fort Dufferin on June 18.

On June 6, 1874 the other part of the force, consisting of 16 officers, 201 men and 244 horses left Toronto in two special trains via Chicago and St. Paul to Fargo, North Dakota, then the western terminus of the Northern Pacific Railroad. At Sarnia they picked up nine additional carloads of unassembled wagons and agricultural implements, with two more cars, containing 34 horses, being added at Detroit. This time the men did not have to endure the hardships suffered by the earlier contingent on the Dawson Route because the American government allowed them to move through the United States, provided they travelled unarmed and in civilian clothes with their arms, ammunition and equipment packed in boxes and sealed in the freight cars.

Sub-Inspector Walker, highly regarded by Commissioner French, was placed in charge of the horses for the trip. He reported moments of pandemonium as men who had no practical experience loaded frightened horses that had never previously been near a train. Following a stirring farewell with bands playing and people waving, the two trains pulled out of the Grand Trunk Depot at 2:00 p.m. but "before the first train was out of sight, though, it was forced to stop abruptly to eject a stowaway seeking a free ride to adventure."[38] Quarters were cramped on the trains and the need to unload horses three times a day for feed and water created a lot of work for the men at stops along the way. The government allowed a dollar per man per day for "boarding expenses" on the trip. Sub-Constable D'Artigue says that through Ontario this was adequate because the Commissioner had arranged in advance for meals at railway stations for 25 cents a man. But, he reported, "in Chicago, no arrangement

- Planning And Preparation -

Loading Horses At Toronto   NLC C61344

of that sort had been made; there we had to pay 50 cents for every meal we took, hence a good deal of grumbling on our part against Yankees!"[39] Sergeant Major Mitchell was given $200 to $300 in Canadian funds to feed the men and he exchanged this at a 10 percent premium which bought them more delicacies. Nobody called on him to account for the exchange.[40]

It rained steadily during the stop in Chicago where the train was left at stockyards afloat in muck and filth. The air was filled with the smell of pigs. The two officers and 30 men detailed to look after the horses found themselves in a pitched battle with hordes of hungry rats which "emerged from every nook and cranny, driving the horses from their feed boxes until the recruits on duty stepped in with clubs."[41] In Chicago Fred Bagley got his first taste of "western" adventure when he saw Frank James, brother of the notorious Jesse James, sitting on the verandah of the small frame hotel near the stockyards, with his feet up on the railing.

The journey continued to St. Paul where the men unloaded the horses in steady rain and walked them into town to the stables. At this stop, Sub-Inspector Walker purchased agricultural implements such as mowing machines and hay rakes as well as provisions, including a one year supply of oats, flour and bacon, which added another freight car to the train. In addition, the Commissioner took on a dozen new men in Chicago and St. Paul, including E.H. Maunsell, later well known in Alberta ranching circles.

The train reached the end of the rails on the morning of June 12 and work began in earnest on the edge of the plains. The wagons had been stowed in freight cars unassembled and not packed as complete units so it was eventually found necessary to unload all the cars, lay the various parts out on the prairie and somehow sort things out. Sub-Constable E.H. Maunsell, a typical green recruit, observed, that while an assembled wagon may not appear to be complicated, it is a different matter when one has to be put together by men who know nothing about wagons. Somehow they got the job done then tackled the more difficult task of assembling the harness. Their helplessness was alieviated, to some extent, by their officers being equally inept.

At dawn on June 13, "D" Troop pulled out with 29 wagons, "E" Troop was two hours behind and "F" Troop cleared things up at the detraining point. By June 14, everything was loaded and the column camped six miles from Fargo, ready to head north to Fort Dufferin. Supper, in at least one case, consisted of boiled pork, hardtack and strong black tea. Fred Bagley noted that his dinner that day was "one soda biscuit, a chunk of fat bacon and the seventeenth part of a small loaf of bread."[42]

When the column tried to get moving, they immediately ran into trouble. Although Commissioner French's initial planning had recognized the need for at least 100 horses to pull wagons there appears to have been little or no attempt to differentiate between saddle horses and draft animals when they were purchased. The horses acquired were riding horses, not accustomed to working in harness and they refused to pull wagons. James Walker said that "some started kicking and some fiery teams, with inexperienced drivers, started across the prairie with loaded wagons, out of control, and had to be rounded up by men on horseback. The men and horses repeated this circus every morning during the 160-mile march to Fort Dufferin."[43]

- *Planning And Preparation* -

The problems with horses continued to plague the force on the march west as well. The force's veterinary surgeon recognized this failure to match horses and tasks, noting that "they were good horses no doubt, but selected by standards more suited to the English cavalry and the parade square than to the task before them. They were riding horses but many of them were forced into harness to drag wagons, carts and the two nine-pounder field guns or 'killers of horses' as one trooper called them. They were sleek and slender animals previously fed a highly concentrated diet and therefore simply unable to eat enough dry prairie grass to fulfil their energy requirements."[44]

Commissioner French, anxious to get back on Canadian soil, set a fast pace with long daily marches. He later reported that on the trip from Fargo to Fort Dufferin the wagons were lightly loaded, 11 cwt. being the maximum load. The Veterinary Surgeon, John L. Poett, says that "although the waggons were lightly laden, the length of journey they accomplished each day, viz., 30 miles or thereabouts, began to tell severely on the still enfeebled constitutions of some of them."[45] Not everyone agrees that the wagons were lightly laden. Inspector Denny considered that the long daily marches from Fargo to Fort Dufferin "were a mistake, and with our heavily loaded wagons had much to do with animals giving out and dying subsequently on the longer and more arduous journey across the plains."[46]

The matter was also of concern to the men. Sub-Constable D'Artigue recalled, "that day we travelled thirty miles. Rather a long march for horses that had just ended a long journey by railway, and after leaving Fargo, living on grass too tender yet to be substantial. Furthermore, most of them were not broken to harness. The same speed was kept up the two following days, the result being that the horses failed rapidly in flesh and in strength. On the morning of the June 18 we found many of them disabled, and two of them went down to rise no more."[47] Since Commissioner French had personally supervised the purchase of many of the horses and also set the rate of march when on the move, he would appear to have been, in large part, directly responsible for the problems encountered with the horses.

- *A Double Duty* -

Not surprisingly, the food on the march was the source of many complaints. Sub-Constable D'Artigue described one meal as "a large cup of tea and a tin plate holding a slice of bacon and two or three biscuits."[48] This would have been luxury to Fred Bagley who said he got "23", i.e. tea only, or "wet and dry" which was tea or water and hardtack. The men were relieved on June 19 when they reached Fort Dufferin. Named in honour of the Governor General, Fort Dufferin consisted of a few log cabins, a Hudson's Bay Company store, and some whisky saloons. Commissioner French described Dufferin as having " . . . many disadvantages. There are several low public houses there, it is close to the Boundary Line, and although it might appear invidious to call this the worst place on the Red River for mosquitoes, yet its claims in that direction are generally admitted."[49] Except for the public houses the description remains valid. At Fort Dufferin the three troops from Toronto met the men of "A", "B" and "C" Troops who had arrived from Lower Fort Garry the previous day. They camped in separate troop lines and fortuitously made different arrangements for their horses.

"D", "E" and "F" Troops tethered their beautiful eastern horses inside a ring of loaded wagons at night. On June 20, the night after their arrival at Fort Dufferin, there was an intense prairie thunderstorm which gave the impression of being constant thunder and lightning the whole night. About midnight this caused 250 frightened horses to break loose, trample the sentries, overturn the wagons forming their corral and stampede across the Pembina bridge. The men who went out eventually recovered all of the horses except one, believed to have drowned in the Pembina River. There were six personnel injured in the stampede but only one seriously; Sub-Constable Latimer, who was on picket duty, received a scalp wound from ear to ear.

Sub-Constable D'Artigue wrote that the storm "formed an imposing sight, capable of frightening men less resolute than ourselves."[50] Canvas wagon covers were torn off by the wind and when they hit the horses, the terrified animals charged straight through the tent lines. There was total confusion and the "continuous rolls of thunder

- Planning And Preparation -

The Stampede at Fort Dufferin   NLC C61346

made conversation impossible, and the stentorian voices of Sergeants Major unheeded, as they shouted orders, which nobody paid attention to . . . ."[51]

Sub-Inspector Walker pursued the horses to Grand Forks, North Dakota, sixty miles from camp, where he got them turned and started to drive them back. He arrived at camp 24 hours after leaving, having "caught and rode five different horses, was wet through and dried three times and had ridden 120 miles by trail."[52] The effort exhausted everyone and the glamour of their western adventure was a bit tarnished. Fred Bagley summed up the feeling when he said "not much Fennimore Cooper romance about this."[53] This stampede did a considerable amount of damage to the horses, much of which only became evident when the hardships of the subsequent trek began to take their toll.

After the horses had been rounded up, preparations for the march continued, with a great deal of work remaining to be done. A large quantity of bulk supplies, such as oats, bran, and charcoal had to be moved from the river to the camp. In addition, those farriers who had not deserted, had to shoe all the horses. Supplies of flour and

- A Double Duty -

oats, shipped as deck cargo on the river steamer from Fargo, were damaged by rain and an attempt had to be made to have them replaced. The force also lost a large quantity of oats when a barge sank after an accident on the Red River, creating a critical shortage of oats. As a result the "the force had therefore to leave with a very trifling supply of oats or the expedition could not have been made in this year."[54]

On July 3, Commissioner French paraded the entire force, as he had done on previous occasions, to ensure that all were aware of the potential hardships they faced: starvation, thirst and possible death. He told them that any members who "were not prepared to take their chances of these privations to fall out, and they could have their discharges, as there were plenty of good men to take their places."[55] The combination of hard work, poor food and potential hardships acted as an incentive so that 31 men had deserted by the time the march started.

Unlike the Boundary Commission, the Mounted Police had no photographer on the march. Although it would have been technically possible, it would have required bulky and fragile equipment and, perhaps more important, additional expense. There is a pictorial record of another kind, however, as Henri Julien, an artist and correspondent for the *Canadian Illustrated News* accompanied the force and left several sketches as well as a diary.

Many problems delayed the departure, including the late arrival of pistols from Britain. A critical item in any policeman's equipment is his personal weapon. In the original planning for a police force in 1870, Captain Cameron realized the need for a repeating rifle and had wisely arranged for the purchase of Spencer rifles. Parsimony now replaced prudence and the weapons issued were single shot Snider-Enfield carbines and Adams revolvers. Neither was the ideal weapon but the carbines at least were a bargain at a time when even the Indians were acquiring Winchester repeating rifles. Another factor in the choice might well have been a reluctance to arm the force with weapons largely dependent on foreign ammunition.

The Snider-Enfield carbine was a muzzle loader design converted to a breech loader and only accurate up to about 200 yards. In 1871, when the British Army took

- Planning And Preparation -

Fort Dufferin

NLC C-061462

the Martini-Henry into use, over 2,000 obsolete Snider carbines were shipped to Canada for a nominal price. Three hundred of these went to the Mounted Police. "Winchester and Spencer-armed Indians came to look upon Snider-equipped Mounties with amusement and, much more to the point, with disdain."[56]

The Adams revolvers were a real problem. Their late arrival caused delays and their condition on arrival was terrible. Major General Griesbach, son of a distinguished member of the North West Mounted Police, observed that "the Adams revolver was a typical British side-arm. The English people are not pistol or revolver conscious and when they bring out a new weapon of that type it begins its career obsolescent and shortly becomes obsolete."[57] The force received some 330 Adams Side Rod Ejector or "First Model" revolvers at Fort Dufferin a week before their departure. They were in terrible condition with bent ramrods, twisted frames, loose trigger guards and, in many cases, cylinders that would not revolve. Revolvers that do not revolve are not very useful!

A report from the Department of Justice expressed the opinion that these revolvers "never belonged to the Imperial Stores. It is true that they have the Imperial sale mark ⇒⇐ upon them, but if they were furnished by a contractor it appears probable that this sale mark must have been put upon them on account of their sale to the Dominion Government." They were described as having been "packed in the most

53

careless manner, thrown loosely into boxes, with no protection but a piece of thin paper, the ram rods being in many cases bent and the sticks injured and many screws (particularly those attaching the trigger guard) were loose." The armourer managed to come up with several serviceable weapons. After much correspondence the government agreed to retain the revolvers and the War Office granted a price reduction of £1-6-4 on each pistol.[58]

The artillery troop was equipped with two 9 pounder muzzle loading rifles. Each gun, with its carriage and limber, weighed approximately 3800 pounds and was pulled by a four-horse team. The guns were capable of firing common shell against buildings or stockades such as those likely to be found at a trader's fort and could also fire shrapnel or case shot against personnel. The force was also equipped with two 5½ inch bronze mortars which fired a 16 pound ball. The mortars were carried in wagons on the march.

All was now ready and the departure date fixed for July 6, but another delay occurred when the Sioux made a raid on St. Joseph, now Valhalla, on the United States side of the border in North Dakota. The commandant of Fort Pembina, just across the boundary from Fort Dufferin, asked the Commissioner to render assistance should the Sioux cross the boundary. The whole force assembled, fully armed and ready for action, but the Indians did not come north. This delayed the departure by a further two days. The *Free Press* in Winnipeg had its own theory about the delayed departure from Fort Dufferin, noting that "desertion is said to be indulged in by the Mounted Police in a wholesale manner. It is reported that twenty-seven of them have taken French leave, including the majority of horse shoers, and the delay in the movement of the force is occasioned by the lack of properly shod horses."[59]

Commissioner French's personnel problems went beyond men deserting. Inspector Charles F. Young, a former British Army officer and one of the first commissioned officers in the Mounted Police, was apparently a staunch supporter of the officers' mess. He did not always see eye to eye with French, and this led to his being summarily dismissed just before the force left Fort Dufferin for "using grossly

- Planning And Preparation -

insubordinate language to the Commissioner when on duty."[60] James Macleod wrote to tell Mary Drever that she would be "awfully sorry to hear that poor old Captain Young has come to grief. He would not keep sober and he had to go. I feel very much for him as I don't know what he can get to do."[61] Perhaps he survived since, a few years later, it was noted that a "Charles F. Young, originally a British Army officer, having fought in the Maori War down under, became a Police Magistrate in Prince Albert, Saskatchewan. When ordering illicit liquor to be destroyed, tears were running down his face at having to destroy such good stuff."[62]

When Ottawa originally approved the concentration of the force at Fort Dufferin, the plan was to proceed to Fort Whoop-Up, and leave two troops there. One of the remaining troops would move on to Fort Edmonton, while the other two would return to the new headquarters at Fort Ellice. The force was to move directly west from Fort Dufferin, using the Boundary Commission trail. Lieutenant Governor Morris opposed this plan, preferring the expedition move by the traditional cart route to Fort Edmonton then south to Fort Whoop-Up. He based his concern on information that a large number of Sioux, who were moving toward the boundary, were unhappy about the activities of the Boundary Commission. He also thought part of the force should remain in the Bow River area near "Stand Off" to prevent liquor being imported and to maintain order.[63]

Just before their departure the government instructed Commissioner French to keep as far north of the boundary as feasible to avoid contact with the Indians. He was also instructed to leave no men at the Bow and Belly Rivers but to have one half "continue on to Fort Edmonton for the winter, the other half to return eastwards to the headquarters at Fort Ellice."[64] Lieutenant Governor Morris wrote to Prime Minister Mackenzie to tell him he had several interviews with French and went over the proposed route with him on the map. He expressed the opinion that "owing to the change of route he will pass through a favorable country and avoid much of the Indian country, evading the Sioux altogether."[65]

- A Double Duty -

The plan to establish headquarters at Fort Ellice failed to impress Commissioner French and before leaving for the west he informed Ottawa that he was arranging to winter the returning portion of the force at Winnipeg and Fort Garry and showed every intention of carrying out this plan. When he came west with the troops who had trained in Toronto, he brought his family with him on the train. They travelled from Fort Dufferin to Winnipeg, where Paymaster Dalrymple Clark rented a house, as the residence for the Commissioner of the North West Mounted Police. As with virtually everything else that the Commissioner did, word of this quickly reached Ottawa and Hewitt Bernard, wrote to French pointing out that "no parties of the force (except the few who may now be in charge of stores) shall winter or be quartered in the Province of Manitoba."[66] By the time that this letter was written, French was trekking west in search of Fort Whoop-Up.

- 4 -

Fort Dufferin To Roche Percée

The force that pulled out of Fort Dufferin late in the afternoon on July 8, 1874 was an impressive sight. The 274 members wore scarlet Norfolk tunics, white cork helmets, white gauntlets, grey breeches and black riding boots. They were armed with obsolescent Snider-Enfield carbines and Adams revolvers. The force was organized into six troops, each mounted on horses of the same colour; "A" Troop on dark bays, "B" on dark browns, "C" on chestnuts, "D" on grays, "E" on blacks and "F" on light bays. Two 9-pounder field guns, the brass mortars and the munition wagons were with "C" Troop. Behind the uniformed troops came a two-mile column of 114 Red River carts with their Métis drivers, still nursing hangovers from the farewell celebrations. Behind this was a string of agricultural implements, mobile forges and field kitchens, with ninety-three cattle on the hoof bringing up the rear of the column.

In his later report Commissioner French wrote that "to a stranger it would have appeared an astonishing cavalcade; armed men and guns looked as if fighting was to be done; what could ploughs, harrows, mowing machines, cows, calves &c., be for? But that little force had a double duty to perform: to fight, if necessary, but in any case to establish posts in the far west."[1] Not everyone was as impressed. The *Free Press* commented that "Colonel French left for the Saskatchewan yesterday with four troops of the Police, the fifth having nearly all deserted." It also reported that "many experienced plains hunters say the police horses are too poor to reach the Saskatchewan this fall."[2]

This first day, July 8, was a shakedown or Hudson's Bay start, so termed because the fur brigades always left in the late afternoon which gave the Métis drivers both a chance to sober up and the opportunity to go back for forgotten items or to get rid of useless cargo. The column went two miles to Lake Louise, a small lake north-west of Fort Dufferin, after having considerable trouble getting started due to "baulky horses placed in the hands of inexperienced drivers and there were quite a number of runaways

- *A Double Duty* -

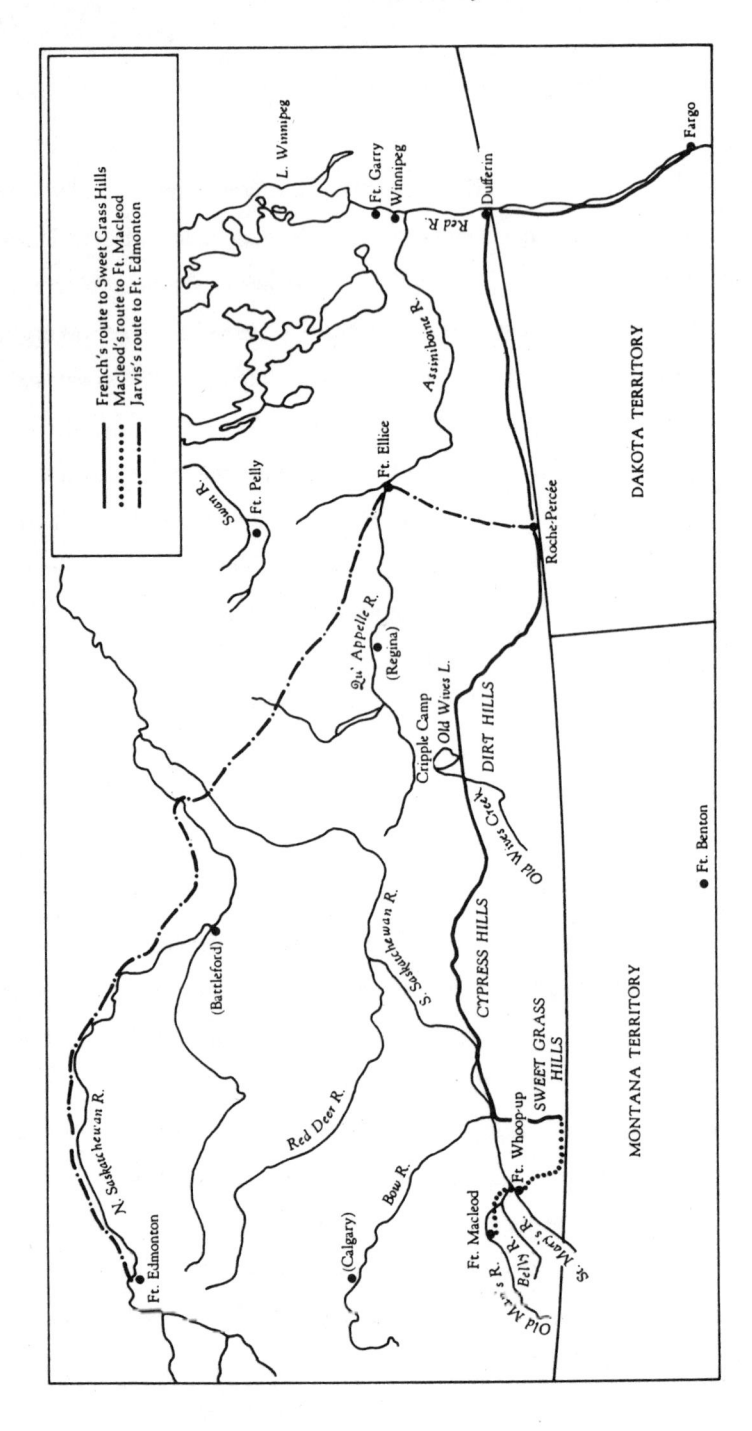

among the horses and oxen. Many men were thrown from their saddles, but none were injured."[3]

At this first camp there was a general sorting out and rearrangement of loads. Two wagon loads of non-essential items such as syrup were sent back and replaced by two loads of oats. It is difficult to understand why there were any oats left in Fort Dufferin when there was a known critical shortage in the column. At this stop the men were also supposedly required to turn in all of their clothing other than the garments they were wearing.[4]

A distinctive feature of this column was the Red River carts, labelled by Commissioner French as "one of the impositions of the country."[5] In describing the carts Sub-Constable D'Artigue was of the opinion that "a den of wild beasts cannot be compared to it in hideousness. Combine all the discordant sounds ever heard in Ontario and they cannot produce anything so horrid as a train of Red River carts."[6] While not enamoured of the Red River cart, Commissioner French had high praise for the wagons, noting later that, "the waggons were splendid, not a wheel or axle broken on the whole trip; a few reaches and single trees were broken, the latter mostly by baulky horses."[7]

Sub-Constable William Parker, much to his disgust, found himself detailed at the last minute to drive oxen pulling a covered wagon loaded with ammunition. His instructions were simply to shout "Gee" if he wanted them to go to the right and "Haw" if he wanted them to go to the left, and he had a stick with a small spike at one end to prod them. He hardly started when the oxen ran away, galloping over the prairie until two Métis spotted and stopped them. Parker went back to a horse.[8]

With all the adjustments necessary after the first short march, things started so slowly the next day that the column did not move off until 4:00 p.m. and camped at dusk, after covering only four dusty miles, amid numerous complaints about the food. The column had to backtrack two miles when no water could be found. This was an early indicator of how little the guides knew about the route and the problems inherent in inadequate reconnaissance.

- *A Double Duty* -

Commissioner French had ordered each troop to provide the horses needed for pulling wagons and machinery, and several officers were unhappy at this use of quality saddle horses. A team provided by "F" Troop bolted when hitched to a mowing machine and ran away on the open prairie, damaging the machine. French rebuked Inspector Richer, the officer involved, for disobeying his order to provide quiet horses. Richer did not agree with using saddle horses for such work and they became involved in an argument that ended with French placing him under arrest for gross insubordination.

The arrest of Richer and the previous dismissal of Inspector Young, shortly before leaving Fort Dufferin, must have had an impact on morale. Both gentlemen made the error of ignoring the first rule of survival in an autocratic organization - don't annoy the autocrat! E.H. Maunsell relates that a relative of Richier [sic] was in the same troop and decided not to stay after this incident. He was driving a two-horse covered wagon on a part of the Boundary Commission Trail running right along the boundary line. He apparently took off his uniform, put on civilian clothes, jumped out of the wagon when passing a boundary marker, and ran a few yards into the United States. Being safe from arrest, he allegedly told Commissioner French to go to Hell.[9]

There was a very slow start again the next day due to horses stampeding and oxen straying, so the column only travelled ten miles, with hay being cut along the way. Camp was made near the present town of Gretna, Manitoba. Since there was no water, the men had to take the horses across the border into the United States to water at the Pembina River, leaving their weapons and ammunition on the Canadian side. Constable McKernan later claimed that at this point Commissioner French, realizing there was a problem with water, placed him in charge of water supply on the line of march.[10] McKernan's admission is surprising since, given all the subsequent problems with water supply, most people would not be anxious to admit being responsible.

Assistant Commissioner Macleod wrote to Mary Drever, his future wife, that evening describing the difficulties of the situation after two days on the trail: "I have not had a moment to myself, what with boards, investigations and general duty which

- Fort Dufferin To Roche Percée -

I am stuck on by the Commissioner. I hardly know when the day ends or commences. We have started and have found it a most difficult business to accomplish. We have not nearly enough transport and all the wagons are so heavy that the horses can hardly draw them along."

Macleod, who had been in charge of the rear guard, bringing in the lost, broken down or just plain slow carts and wagons told her, "I wish you had been here last night. I was left behind to see everything off and as I came along in rear of the train a young officer came galloping up to say that there were three ox trains stuck and could not pull an inch further, so off I had to go, sent my horse on to camp and took the oxen with my own hands. I managed to get two of the teams into camp all right and sent a pair of horses to the assistance of the third. You ought to have heard me 'geeing and hawing' till I was quite hoarse. It was long after dark when I arrived. The half-breeds were awfully tickled when I marched in among them."[11]

Evening Parade   NLC C62549

- A Double Duty -

On July 11, shortly after starting, the column met some Métis who informed the Commissioner that the Sioux had killed some people in St. Joe (now Valhalla) just south of the international boundary, so he ordered ammunition readied and put out an advance guard.[12] Henri Julien reported that "we halted at Grant's solitary log house, where a sturdy Scotchman, with his Indian wife and children, sells liquor to wanderers along the border. The officers of the staff bought some milk from him, and, if the truth must be told, took a stray glass or two of whisky. But they gave positive orders that no beverage of the latter description should be given to the men."[13] Sub-Constable Finlayson refers to Grant's Place as "a very nice building for the western country" and said "there was a dread of the Indians by the inmates and others assembled there. Many were delighted at seeing us and regretted we were not going to stop longer."[14] Having purchased two yoke of oxen and some firewood, the column moved on with few of the men realizing that this was the last substantial dwelling they would see for many weeks.

The force adopted a routine of making a very early start in the cool of the morning, resting in the heat of the day, and continuing the march late in the afternoon until they made an evening halt, with any luck by a wooded stream with good pasture. As the march progressed, the oxen and horses became tired and wagons and carts lagged behind, often strung out for several miles. Since the column was now on the Boundary Commission Road, Commissioner French optimistically believed that "having a good sketch of the route, our marches could be arranged with a certainty of finding wood, water and grass at definite points."[15] This "certainty" lasted about one day. On the evening of July 11 Robert Finlayson noted, "water scarce and very bad"[16] and John Peter Turner wrote, "nearest water said to be 15 miles away."[17]

On July 12, just four days after leaving Fort Dufferin, the column made an early start, without breakfast and with no water. An ox died on the march, an occurrence that would be often repeated. The column reached the Boundary Commission's Pembina Mountain Depot where there was water in the Plum River below Allard's Point, and stopped to eat before moving on. This disappointed those who had anticipated staying longer and Sub-Constable D'Artigue, somewhat sarcastically, recalls that "we naturally

- Fort Dufferin To Roche Percée -

expected to rest there for a day or two but the Commissioner decided that the march should be resumed immediately after dinner. Probably he compared himself to conquerors like Alexander and Caesar, and wanted to leave in the shade the marches of these illustrious men."[18]

Despite the wishes of Sub-Constable D'Artigue, the column moved on, tormented by mosquitoes and masses of grasshoppers, which came in huge clouds like a storm in the sky, devouring anything green in their path. There were so many grasshoppers on the ground that wagons running over them skidded around on the layers of crushed insects. To add to their misery, a heavy thunderstorm, with hailstones the size of walnuts swept down on them. The force camped early in the afternoon on an open plain with plenty of wood and water and the cooks baked bread.

Mosquitoes plagued both men and animals all through the march. Henri Julien, the artist and correspondent, left a graphic description of a mosquito attack: "As soon as the twilight deepens, they make their appearance on the horizon in the shape of a cloud, which goes on increasing in density as it approaches to the encounter. At first, a faint hum is heard in the distance then it swells into a roar as it comes nearer. The attack is simply dreadful. Your eyes, your nose, your ears are invaded."[19] The Commissioner's practice of frequently camping near sloughs made men, horses and oxen even more vulnerable.

It was a beautiful day on July 13, and the troops attempted an early start, although once again there were numerous delays due to wagons and carts breaking down. The column moved on, travelling until 8:00 p.m. when they camped at Calf Mountain, an ancient burial mound which contained a number of skeletons of unknown origin, buried in a sitting position. Grasshoppers were still thick and water was very scarce. The halt afforded the opportunity to cut hay for the horses.

On July 14 the column crossed over Pembina Mountain and into the deep valley of the Pembina River to the ford at Pembina Crossing, south of the present location of Manitou, Manitoba. The steep banks of the river were a formidable obstacle and there were long delays getting the heavily loaded wagons and carts across, particularly in

- *A Double Duty* -

Divine Service   NLC C62571

getting up the bank on the far side. The grade was too steep for the horses so "in ascending the bank we found the oxen of great service. Taking a yoke of them in front of the horses, we would hook the chain in the end of the wagon tongue and with this double team, take the loads up the steep bank very easily."[20]

Following this hard work the column marched until 9:00 p.m. then camped on an open plain near a swamp. The men and horses were tired. Exhaustion was starting to take its toll on both the men and the animals, especially the eastern horses that had difficulty foraging on prairie grass. When the failing horses refused to eat some old hay left on the trail, Henri Julien observed that "government horses, like government men, being used to feed well, are apt to become too dainty."[21] Sub-Constable Finlayson noted, "no water, no wood, no supper. The bull train did not get in till after midnight therefore no provisions."[22] Pierre Léveillé, the Métis chief guide and interpreter, joined the column here along with five other Métis and six carts of presents for the Indians.

64

- Fort Dufferin To Roche Percée -

The force stopped at noon on July 15 in the valley of Badger Creek, about two miles north of the current town of Cartwright, Manitoba. Here they watered the horses and the men bathed. When the march resumed they saw many antelope and several Boundary Commission wagons were encountered heading east. Sub-Constable Finlayson, who should have been getting quite slim by now, recorded, "for supper - *nothing!*" and slept out all night with the sky for a covering.[23]

After a 4:00 a.m. start on July 16, the column marched twelve miles before breakfast which Finlayson describes as, "one *Slap Jack* per man for breakfast. Lucky to get that." He also wrote that "many of the boys who came in late last night were put under arrest for not turning out at roll call." After breakfast the column travelled on to the Boundary Commission's Turtle Mountain Depot at the Long River ford, arriving after dark. The weather was hot and the long hours, hard work, lack of water and poor food beginning to take their toll on the men, horses and oxen. In his notes on the cuisine for this day, Sub-Constable Finlayson reported that, in addition to his single "Slap Jack" for breakfast, he "had for supper the same as I had for dinner, namely *Nothing!*"[24] The *Free Press* of July 16, 1874 described widespread damage from grasshoppers and also noted that the Mounted Police were doing well, making 25 miles per day.[25]

Sergeant Major J.B. Mitchell of "E" Troop became friendly with the Métis guides, especially Pierre Léveillé, and in the evenings he would find out what the trail would be like the next day. If it was good he would try to have "E" Troop ready to leave first to take advantage of a beaten trail and they would often be in evening camp, their meal over and horses out to pasture by the time the rear guard arrived. When the trail was bad "E" Troop would delay, letting others beat the trail. Their horses finished the trek fresher than any others.[26]

The column was on the move at 3:00 a.m. on July 17 and travelled twelve miles without water. Part of the column was delayed due to difficulty finding horses that had been turned out for the night. Sub-Constable Finlayson recorded that "shortly after starting one horse dropped down, played out. My bull played out today so I did not get

- A Double Duty -

up to the command for two days."[27] The main body made camp at Turtle Head Creek, south of the present town of Deloraine, Manitoba.

Commissioner French was now becoming concerned at the slow progress of the march and noted in his diary that the Métis could not be got to start on time and there appeared to be no system among them. The column stretched out for a long distance due to continuous problems with carts and the slow pace of the oxen, all of which could have been foreseen. French complained that the "oxen did not start with us, and I saw nothing of them all day."[28] He concluded that the reason that the Métis were so late in reaching camp every night, was that each of them had to drive four carts, so he ordered that each Troop should provide a certain number of men to assist them.

Sub-Constable D'Artigue, being one of the chosen, commented, "it is useless to mention how we greeted such an order, and I believe had we not been a long distance from any settlement, the Colonel would have had to make the expedition alone."[29] Young Fred Bagley said, "I was one of the several unfortunates detailed to drive and be responsible for three oxen and carts. This was the most severe jolt Romance had been dealt since we left Toronto."[30]

The column made camp that day at Turtle Creek, with no water and no pasture. The exhausted men pitched no tents and many had nothing to eat. The distance travelled from Fort Dufferin was only 153 miles. Commissioner French realized that due to the slow rate of progress the journey would take longer than anticipated so rations were cut down at this point. One member wrote that his meagre ration of half a pound of flour would largely disappear in a cloud when baking in the open on windy days.

The column stretched out over a long distance again on July 18, horses gave out all along the trail and several men got sick from drinking contaminated water. By evening the head of the column had reached the first crossing of the Souris where they crossed on a bridge built by the Boundary Commission and made camp. After only ten days on the march, the animals had exhausted the supply of oats but, fortunately, there was an abundant supply of wood, water and grass at this site.

- Fort Dufferin To Roche Percée -

The disorganized, straggling column made conditions difficult for the men. The rear guard was miles behind the main body and had to camp out in the rain all night with no water for the horses and oxen and no food for the men. Sub-Constable D'Artigue, noted that "our oxen being tired out, we were obliged to camp out of sight of our comrades; and not only this, but our provisions and blankets being on the waggons of the main column, we had to lie down supperless on the bare ground, and in that manner pass the night."[31] Sub-Constable E.H. Maunsell, given the job of herding cattle as punishment for falling asleep on guard duty, wrote that he was once without food for thirty-six hours until he caught up with some Métis drivers four miles behind the main column. He later wrote that "afterwards during my ranching days I often thought how completely ignorant the Colonel was of the travelling capacity of cattle - thinking cattle could keep up with troops."[32]

With many horses physically unable to proceed, the force rested at the Souris River on July 19 and 20, which allowed the oxen and carts to catch up by the night of July 19. Two horses had been left behind and two more had died. One horse was left behind by an imaginative Sub-Constable, Pierre Lucas, who said that when the horse had refused to move, five Indians pursued him and he had to fire at them. For some reason Commissioner French did not believe him. Tall tales make people think of fishing so, at this camp, fishing tackle was issued and Sub-Inspector McIllree, among others, tried his luck in the clear, rapid water of the Souris River. He did not see a fish and did not think there were any caught.[33]

On July 21, after covering fourteen miles over open country, a noon halt was made at North Antler Creek. The weather was very hot, pasturage was poor, and many horses were played out. The Commissioner assigned five men and an ox to bring in played out horses but fifteen sick horses failed to reach camp that evening at South Antler Creek. The force was now 206 miles from Fort Dufferin, probably about one quarter of the distance to Fort Whoop-Up, with horses and men failing rapidly. On July 22 the column covered 15 miles, camped until 3:00 p.m., without wood or usable water, then went another ten miles to the second crossing of the Souris. There was no bridge here and the crossing was quite difficult, particularly on the west side where the bank was very steep so, while the main body camped on the west side, the ox carts did not get across until morning. The column met some Boundary Commission workers on their way to Fort Dufferin and were able to purchase some of their surplus bread supply. The men had food but there were no oats left for the animals.

Due to the horrendous condition of the horses, the Commissioner now issued orders for the men to dismount and walk every other hour to relieve their exhausted mounts. One man on each wagon was to walk while the other drove. Commissioner French would occasionally ride up and down the column to ensure that the men obeyed his orders. Sub-Constable D'Artigue relates that "Sergeant Smith, disobeying the order, was spotted riding in a cook waggon by the Commissioner and being threatened with arrest said, 'I joined a mounted Force, not a foot one, and as I am not feeling very well today, I must ride on something.' He was left among the pots and pans."[34]

It was intensely hot on July 23 and the heat took its toll again when another horse died. In the morning the Commissioner held back three troops until some oxen, cattle and 12 missing horses could be found. Then, at the noon halt, more lost horses had to be found, delaying progress even more. That evening they made camp at Rivière Des Lacs near the Hill of the Murdered Scout. This feature got its name from the legend that at this place a native scout murdered an Indian from another tribe with a stone then cut an outline of his victim in the turf.

"A" Troop was out at 3:30 a.m. on July 24 and, after a long march, reached St. Peter's Springs, a dirty mud hole. Horses and men desperately needed water so the men sank a barrel packed round with stones in the spring to make a serviceable watering place. Fred Bagley observed that "in spite of the sanctified name the 'Springs' proved to be a mere dirty hole reflecting little credit on the name of the great Apostle."[35] Sub-Constable Finlayson was either less critical or the work of "A" Troop had done wonders since he referred to it as "a beautiful spring called 'St. Peter's Wells.'"[36]

- Fort Dufferin To Roche Percée -

By this time diarrhoea was getting worse, mosquitoes were causing much annoyance and the dust cloud along the line of march gave the men sore eyes and catarrh. The wagons and carts stretched out for five miles on the move and stragglers often caused the column to extend out so far that when the head of the column stopped for the night there would still be wagons, carts, machinery and cattle along the trail for miles. The Assistant Commissioner took up the rear and nursed these stragglers into camp.

The main body reached Roche Percée and camped on the banks of the Souris River at Short Creek, where water, wood and grass were all plentiful. Several horses that had lain down were unable to get up again. The men were a far cry from the immaculate troops who had marched out of Fort Dufferin in splendour less than three weeks before. They were ill, their clothing was in tatters and food supplies were low. Sub-Constable D'Artigue reported that "on our arrival at Roche Percée the column resembled a routed army corps. For several miles the road was strewn with broken carts and horses and oxen overcome with hunger and fatigue."[37] A member of the force using the pseudonym "Peeler" wrote to the *Free Press* on July 28 stating that "we made some very forced marches," and "a number of our horses died on the way being over-driven."[38]

When turned out to graze most of the horses improved on the good pasture, although one died. Commissioner French had written to Inspector Shurtliff, in charge of the detachment at Fort Ellice, ordering him to come to Roche Percée with all the horses he had in good condition. Inspector Shurtliff's party arrived on July 26 but, unfortunately, could only bring six horses, the others having gone to Winnipeg for supplies. Why the provision of fresh horses had not been preplanned is an unanswered question. When part of the Palliser Expedition travelled west along the boundary in 1859 they sent several horses over the Fort Garry-Edmonton cart track to Fort Ellice so they could gain strength from the good pasture there in readiness for the next stage of the journey.

- *A Double Duty* -

The force rested at Roche Percée for several days while Commissioner French revised his plans, reorganized his force, made necessary repairs and rested men and animals. Faced with the unanticipated burden of sick men, horses and cattle, he decided to send those least likely to stand the march, directly to Fort Edmonton via the established cart trail through Fort Ellice and Fort Carlton. He anticipated that this route would be easier on men and animals. Surplus stores and animals were to be left with the detachment at Fort Ellice, which was on their route.

On July 29 Commissioner French divided the best horses of "A" Troop between the other troops and assigned 55 of their weakest to "A" Troop for the trip to Edmonton. Inspector Jarvis also got "six men from other troops, 12 half-breeds, 24 wagons, 55 carts, 62 oxen and 50 cows and calves as well as agricultural implements and general stores (including 25,000 lbs. of flour) not essential to the main body."[39]

North West Mounted Police Camp At Roche Percée   NLC C61449

- 5 -

Roche Percée To Fort Macleod

The force moved a short distance to Wood End and stayed in camp on July 30 while the cooks baked a three-day supply of bread and the men cut firewood. Sub-Inspector McIllree again took the opportunity to go fishing and this time, although he saw fish, he again had no luck in catching any.[1]

Commissioner French's original instructions had been for the force to move straight west, using the camps and depots of the Boundary Commission. Just before leaving Fort Dufferin he received instructions to keep as far to the north of the boundary as feasible to avoid any conflict with Indians, reported to be restless just south of the boundary. French told Ottawa that he intended to follow the Boundary Commission Road as far as Wood End, swing northwest for a distance then, before reaching Fort Qu'Appelle, turn straight west. The ox teams of the Boundary Commission, stocking their depots, travelled by a trail along the Missouri Coteau for about forty miles then turned west to Willow Bunch and Wood Mountain. From Wood Mountain there were trails both north and south of the Cypress Hills. It is difficult to understand why Commissioner French did not use this route.

It required a lot of hard work to prepare a road to get the wagons and guns across the West Branch of the Souris River on July 31, after which the column crossed Long Creek and made camp. The next morning they left the Boundary Commission Road and headed northwest on a course parallel to Long Creek and in sight of the Missouri Coteau, the escarpment that runs north west from near the present day Estevan toward Moose Jaw. It was rough going. Despite their respite at Roche Percée, the men were weary and the animals were in no condition for what lay ahead.

Commissioner French did not trust the guides and made an entry in his diary; "On Monday my sketch of the Boundary Commission Road will give out, and I shall be completely in the hands of guides who will, doubtless, make marches in accordance with their lazy idea of a day's work."[2] French appears to have been badly let down by

- A Double Duty -

Lieutenant Governor Morris who assured him that his route would take him into "good country in which he would find adequate feed for his livestock."[3] Morris had also provided the guides who were now proving to be totally inadequate. Paul Sharp says "the guides proved so incompetent that the force wasted valuable time finding passages around sloughs and lakes and seeking suitable fords across rivers" and that "this inexperience in western ways led to blunder after blunder, causing costly delays and unnecessary hardships for the men."[4]

August 2 being a Sunday, Commissioner French kept the column in camp and held a church service in cold, wet weather. There were two major concerns on his mind this day. First, the fact that the Métis were no longer useful as guides and, second, a long sick list, including dysentery and two mild cases of typhoid. Of the 22 men on Sick Parade, five were unfit for any duty, nine received "light duty" and the remaining eight, "Medicine and Duty". French had genuine cause for concern since seriously ill men are not only unable to do their work but are also a burden on the others and any large number are a worry for a commander far from medical facilities of any kind. Many of the animals were also very sick and Sub-Inspector McIllree said, "I don't know how we are going to get through with the horses we have."[5]

Since the column was now in an area unfamiliar to their guides, Commissioner French navigated by compass and took sun and star shots which he attempted to relate to Palliser's map, described by William Pearce as amusing in its lack of data.[6] It is unlikely that French was amused. It was fortunate that he was an Artillery officer and as a "Gunner," with training in survey, could determine their position and was also able to compute distance from an odometer attached to his wagon. The next morning, the column made an early start on a long march in sultry weather between the Coteau and Long Creek. When the exhausted men camped that night a violent thunderstorm blew all their tents down and soaked everyone, making their lives sheer misery. Sub-Inspector McIllree described the night's events as follows: "I had got to sleep when I was woke up in a short time by the wind which was blowing a hurricane. The first thing I knew was, the curtain of the tent blew up and I nearly got smothered with a

The Storm of August 3, 1874.   NLC C62572

cloud of dust and gravel. The next thing was the tent went bodily up into the air, followed by my helmet and sundry tin plates, blankets, etc. I grabbed my clothes and got some of them on, and went about camp. I could not help laughing. Nearly every tent was down, and the men were rushing round in their shirt tails or other equally classical costume trying to find their raiment. It blew and rained and hailed for some time and then it quieted down, and the clouds broke, and the moon came out and revealed our misery in full."[7]

The storm continued the next day and the column moved off, without breakfast, headed northwest over the rough country. They now descended the Coteau which they "need not have ascended if the guides knew the country properly."[8] They used their last firewood and that evening cooked supper on buffalo chips. Assistant Commissioner Macleod took several carts to Willow Bunch to procure pemmican and meet the column farther down the route. The following day there was a lot of trouble with failing horses

- A Double Duty -

Crossing The Dirt Hills   NLC C62596

so the Commissioner cancelled the afternoon march to allow wagons and carts to catch up. Henri Julien, the artist from the *Canadian Illustrated News,* went hunting and got lost in the hilly country. The camp fired a field gun and sent up rockets to guide him back. This must have been popular with the gun crew who had to clean the gun.

On August 6 the column crossed the Dirt Hills, the highest part of the Coteau, in a winding ascent of four or five miles, manhandling the heavy field guns up the steep slopes. Inspector Denny wrote that "these guns gave us more trouble and crippled horses than all the rest of the transport."[9] Henri Julien, who could possibly be considered an ingrate since one of these guns had been fired to help him when he was lost, wrote that "they were always in the way, retarded our march, took up the time of several men and the service of several good horses. . . . But I suppose they looked military and had therefore to be dragged along with us, as much for show as anything else."[10] In any case, the guns proved too much even for teams of six horses on the steep

- Roche Percée to Fort Macleod -

slopes of the Dirt Hills so, on the following day, August 7, a party of men with oxen went to bring them forward while the rest stayed in camp and stocked up on firewood.

Commissioner French, without competent guides, led his force across the worst possible terrain. To the south they could have taken the trader's road to Wood Mountain and further north they would have been on the plains, thus avoiding the rough terrain of the Dirt Hills. This exhausting diversion was unnecessary. By this time, to the west of them, a Boundary Commission party from Fort Dufferin, travelling along the international boundary, reached the base of Chief Mountain in the Rockies without encountering hostile action along the border, despite the warnings given to French about the Sioux.

On August 8 the column, descending the Coteau by a bad hilly trail, could see Old Wives Lake. Having no water they pushed forward only to find the lake water was alkaline and of no use. The massive effort completely played out the horses so carts and wagons which were left behind straggled in throughout the night. There were lots of ducks and geese, which offered some change of diet and augmented fast diminishing food supplies. After a day of rest, which let the men do laundry and bathe, the column moved a short distance in an attempt to find better pasture and water. Assistant Commissioner Macleod arrived with 4,700 pounds of pemmican which the men put in their pockets and chewed all day. Fred Bagley said "it was pretty dry chewing . . . we found it both filling and nutritious."[11] By this time his lips were so swollen and blistered by thirst and heat that when Commissioner French ordered him to sound a trumpet call he could not do it.[12]

August 11 was a day of hard going, especially for the animals. Sub-Constable Finlayson's horse gave up and he had to unharness him and let him feed for two hours before he could get into the noon camp.[13] The following day the terrain became much more difficult so an advance guard laboured to cut a slope the carts and wagons could negotiate. The force camped at Old Wives Creek where there was good pasture and the animals recuperated for a few days. Some Sisseton Sioux, part of the tribe that had come to Canada after the 1862 Minnesota Massacre, visited the camp for a "powwow."

- A Double Duty -

When they asked why the force was coming through their country, the Commissioner gave them calico, powder, balls and flints, but may have had some difficulty providing a satisfactory answer to their question.[14]

By this time rations were cut to ½ pound of bread per man daily, the sugar was all gone and Assistant Commissioner Macleod was off again to Wood Mountain to obtain more oats. On August 15 the police searched a wagon and eleven Red River carts enroute to Winnipeg with a load of buffalo robes but no liquor was found. The Commissioner purchased seven ponies and carts loaded with pemmican to augment the rations.

A new guide, Frances Morriseau, turned up on August 16, claiming to know the country but Commissioner French had serious doubts about him, noting that "he is a hardlooking case, describes himself as a trapper, and says he trapped on the Bow River 3 years ago. Many think him a spy of the outlaws."[15] He left camp the next day, ostensibly to retrieve some ammunition he had hidden. When he did not return on time, Inspector Carvell and Corporal Latimer prepared to go to Wood Mountain to arrest him but he returned before they left. One can only wonder on what possible grounds they proposed to arrest him.

Commissioner French now realized that the majority of police operations would take place in the Blackfoot lands and that this region could not be effectively policed from Fort Edmonton, so he sent a despatch urging that part of the force be left near Fort Whoop-Up. He asked Ottawa to telegraph their reply to him at Fort Benton. On August 18 Assistant Commissioner Macleod returned to Old Wives Creek with a large quantity of oats obtained at Wood Mountain. He was accompanied by Lawrence Herchmer, the Supply Officer for the Boundary Commission. As soon as the ox carts arrived with the oats the men immediately fed the horses.

Commissioner French, having been stationed in Kingston, probably knew Herchmer since his family also lived in Kingston and both were friends of Sir John A. Macdonald. Herchmer had just been to Fort Benton, dealing with a contract for oats, and in his *1874 Annual Report* French notes that "before leaving Cripple Camp I heard

- Roche Percée to Fort Macleod -

from a Boundary Commissioner official, who had been at Benton, there were a number of whisky traders there, and that they stated to him that as soon as the Mounted Police left the country they would return."[16] He noted that "a post at or near the Boundary Line will spoil their little game."[17]

The trek resumed on August 19, moving several miles to establish a camp called Cripple Camp under Sergeant Sutherland for seven sick men, 12 wagons, 26 sick horses and some exhausted cattle. Having established the camp, the column moved on in sultry weather bothered by flying ants. They moved along slowly, over country stripped of grass by buffalo. Sergeant Major J.B. Mitchell described the monotony of the march; "There beneath us was the earth with the grass becoming brittle and there, day after day, was the sky. That was all, Earth and Sky."[18]

On the trail they met a party of Métis including Louis Léveillé, brother of the chief guide Pierre Léveillé, who agreed to join the column as a guide. On August 22, Assistant Commissioner Macleod was off again, to the Boundary Commission Depot on the White Mud River, for more oats. The Commissioner, considering they might now be in hostile territory, increased the night guard and sentries were issued ammunition. He also ordered the troops not to turn horses out to graze before daylight. The men were finding it difficult to work hard all day then go on guard every other night.[19]

The march continued across the plains until, on August 25, they reached the Cypress Hills and camped by a small lake to prepare for the final phase of the trek and wait for Assistant Commissioner Macleod to return with the oats. On August 27 it started to rain so it became necessary to move the camp. The rain continued for the next two days. On August 29 the storemen issued out the last bacon and two days later Macleod returned with several cart loads of oats. That day Constable Chapman left to take letters and reports back 600 miles to Fort Dufferin and the following day the column marched on in the dismal rain.

There were old buffalo trails and bleached bones everywhere, but none were sighted until September 2 when the first buffalo herd was encountered and Commissioner French, Pierre Léveillé, Morriseau and Henri Julien each killed one. As

- *A Double Duty* -

The Great Buffalo Hunt   NLC C62665

one trooper commented, it was lucky the buffalo turned up when they did, since food was running short and buffalo meat became their main food. Sergeant Major Mitchell learned buffalo could be dangerous to hunt. He and a companion had "ridden ahead and came upon two grazing buffalo. Advancing stealthily each man selected a target and fired together. Mitchell's animal fell but the second, though badly wounded, raced away, closely pursued by the other hunter. Mitchell dismounted and walked leisurely toward his prize. As he knelt on one knee beside the huge head, the beast suddenly came to life, reared up and lunged at him. Fortunately, Mitchell still held onto his horse by means of a 20-foot lariat, one end of which was wrapped around his left wrist, and the terrified animal dragged him to safety from the first mad onrush. Mitchell regained his feet in time to dodge succeeding charges, working his way hand over hand and jumping from side to side he regained the saddle. Finally, drawing his pistol, he shot the charging buffalo between the eyes, thereby settling an old argument among the men as to whether a bullet in the forehead would prove fatal to one of the great beasts."[20]

- Roche Percée to Fort Macleod -

As the march progressed the terrain became rougher. On September 4, while negotiating stony, hilly terrain, the men locked the wagon wheels on the way down the steep hills and then had to prepare a road to get up the other side. This work of cutting the banks of the ravine occupied an officer and 25 men. Sub-Constable Finlayson wrote that going down the hill, "the back of one my wagon wheels broke and the driver barely escaped with his life."[21] Some ox carts were upset.

Horses were now dying daily and the outlook was ominous. By September 6 the officers and men of the force began to realize that they were lost. Finding that the guide did not know what he was doing, Commissioner French commented, "there is not a soul in camp that knows this place and the Scout has brought us nearly a day's march out of our road during the last two days, and he would make it still worse tomorrow. I am not quite certain whether his actions are due to ignorance or design. He is the greatest liar I have ever met. He is suspected of being a spy of the whoop-up villains but there is nothing definite or tangible to show this. Although I have never been here, I will do the guide myself tomorrow. If I could have relied on Palliser's map, I would have taken this duty sooner."[22]

The column only covered 20 miles on September 8 because the horses were too weak to go further. Sub-Constable Carscadden, becoming increasingly disillusioned, noted in his diary that, "if some of the M.P.s who passed that good bill for prevention of cruelty to animals saw the way these poor horses are being killed by the Commissioner, I think he would be deposed." Further expressing his disdain for Commissioner French, Carscadden wrote that "from what I have seen of our Commissioner I must say that I find him wanting in human feeling and without honor. This is hard to say of anyone but I assert that it is true."[23]

The march continued in the cold and rain, through country with poor grass and water and with many of the horses in very serious condition. When the weather grew colder, some horses, herded into a ravine for protection from the wind were too weak to reach the high ground. Five of them were abandoned while three others required assistance to get out of the ravine. Sub-Constable Carscadden observed that "it looks

- A Double Duty -

very much like starvation, so much so that we must keep moving ahead or sure death awaits us."[24] The Commissioner ordered that every officer and man give up one of their blankets to help protect the horses from the bitterly cold wind. The horses were chilled in the cold rain, weak from lack of feed and dying. That night, in the cold, a spasm of the muscles of the neck and face attacked a number of the horses and some of them died.[25]

While his men shivered in the cold, without fuel to cook food or warm themselves, the Commissioner refused to let them burn surplus carts since this would be destroying government property. There was a shortage of food and many of the men were miserable and dejected. On September 10, "B" Troop refused to leave camp until they had breakfast because they had had no dinner or supper the previous day.[26]

The situation was now getting really desperate. By the Commissioner's calculation, they were very close to the junction of the Bow and Belly Rivers, supposedly the site of Fort Whoop-Up. French sent scouts out but they found nothing other than three deserted log cabins without roofs. The force had come 781 miles and after the first 18 miles had seen no human habitation other than tepees. Winter was coming and the Commissioner knew that a year previously an early storm on September 20 had left a foot of snow on this region. Several oxen had died of starvation and clearly pasture had to be found before all the horses perished. Survival now took priority over everything else. French wrote in his diary, "I begin to feel very much alarmed for the safety of the Force. If a few hours cold and rain kills off a number of horses, what would be the effect of a 24 hours snow storm."[27] The column started south toward the Sweet Grass Hills. Joseph Carscadden noted "even the Commissioner who usually has so impassive a countenance and who can fine any individual without the slightest change of countenance or features, begins to look more down mouthed. He feels his responsibility in bringing a lot of Troops and animals into a position when he cannot see his way out of it."[28]

Sherill MacLaren noted that morale had become the critical factor in the survival of the force, with Commissioner French and Assistant Commissioner Macleod taking

- Roche Percée to Fort Macleod -

very different approaches, one by stiff discipline and the other by inspiration. She compared French to Captain Bligh and saw Macleod as the Fletcher Christian of the trek, who periodically appeared with loads of oats or pemmican and nursed weary stragglers back into camp.[29]

Sub-Constable Carscadden relates that Commissioner French somehow learned that some biscuits disappeared one night from a barrel on a cart. He paraded the men who were on guard in the night and checked the pockets of their greatcoats. No biscuits were found but two men had crumbs in their pockets. Since carrying biscuits in greatcoat pockets was a common practice there was no real proof that the two had stolen biscuits. French is reported to have had the men placed in irons until Assistant Commissioner Macleod interceded and had them released. The men were freed on the charge of stealing biscuits but French would not accept defeat. He had one of the men charged for allowing the biscuits to be stolen and the man was fined $15.00. Carscadden called this "the most damnable perversion of Justice."[30] Carscadden was the only source found describing this incident although others such as McIllree, Finlayson or Denny were with the column at the time. If, as Carscadden states, the Assistant Commissioner openly interceded and told the Commissioner in front of the men that he could not place the prisoners in irons this would be an open rift between the two senior officers in the force. French, who prided himself on being a strict disciplinarian, would not easily forgive or forget an action which he would see as diminishing his authority.

On September 11 the column moved four miles and reached the South Saskatchewan (Belly) River but could not find a ford. Commissioner French sent out two patrols. One under Sub-Inspector Welch investigated the South Saskatchewan to the west. The second, under Sub-Inspector Denny, with three Métis, went up the west side of the Bow River to see if there was any sign of a trading post or human activity. In the afternoon Denny and his companions saw two Indians who ran into a ravine. They followed them, only to find themselves facing about 50 Indians with rifles. When the Métis could not make themselves understood Denny fell back on the old dictum that

- *A Double Duty* -

discretion is the better part of valour and quietly withdrew and bypassed the spot. The patrol went another forty miles and saw no trail or habitation but witnessed thousands of buffalo swimming across the Bow River.

On September 12, Commissioner French called a Council of Officers. Lost, alarmed for the safety of his men and with his animals starving to death, he appeared to have been convinced by Lawrence Herchmer, during their meeting at Old Wives Creek, that there was nothing sinister or illegal going on at Fort Whoop-Up and that it was " . . . principally a trading post of the firm of Baker & Co. of Benton, highly respectable merchants who do not sell whiskey or spirits."[31] He was also informed by Herchmer that the whisky traders who had been at Fort Whoop-Up were now at Fort Benton and would stay there until the Mounted Police left. If there were no heavily armed whisky traders in Fort Whoop-Up, the whole of the force was not required near the Sweet Grass Hills. French was now free to return east with two troops as originally planned. The remainder were to establish a post near the international boundary. This would spoil the whisky traders plans of returning. French decided that he would send one troop to Edmonton, move two to the Sweet Grass Hills and, after going to Fort Benton for supplies and to contact Ottawa, would return east with the remaining two troops.

Cruise and Griffiths state that the officers did not know where Commissioner French's information about Fort Whoop-Up came from.[32] Carscadden questioned why the force did not go to Fort Whoop-Up and finish the job they set out to accomplish, noting that this was a question that none of the Mounted Police could solve.[33] He believed that the guide Piere Léveillé won the Commissioner's confidence and guided the force away from Fort Whoop-Up. It is difficult to understand why French would not have told his officers about the information he obtained from Lawrence Herchmer. It is much easier to understand why Carscadden was in the dark, since he was possibly the last man in the force in whom French would confide. It is unlikely that the guides influenced the decision since French did not trust the guide, Morriseau, who was the

- Roche Percée to Fort Macleod -

only person with the force who was familiar with Fort Benton and Fort Whoop-Up and the other guide, who was trusted, Léveillé, was allegedly unfamiliar with the area.

The patrol under Sub-Inspector Welch returned on September 13, having seen no signs of trading posts or trails. Sub-Constable Finlayson wrote in his diary, "we are lost on the prairie. No one knows where we are. A circle of officers was held and decided to make for the Three Buttes on the Boundary Trail. Horses and oxen are dying fast. Provisions are getting scarce. Things look dark. Very cold."[34] The feature of the Three Buttes was visible on the horizon, perhaps 60 miles away. Ironically, on the same day, there was a Boundary Commission party at the Sweet Grass Hills with surplus cattle on the hoof which were to be herded back to Fort Dufferin.

The following day, September 14, it got much colder with a weakening effect on the horses and oxen and two more died, bringing the total to nine within 36 hours. This could not go on. Commissioner French ordered Inspector Walsh with 70 men and 57 horses of "B" Troop to ford the South Saskatchewan and camp on the opposite bank, ready to go on to Fort Edmonton. When Sub-Inspector Denny and Pierre Léveillé returned, having seen no trails or human habitation, Léveillé advised the Commissioner that "B" Troop would never make it to Fort Edmonton with their weak animals. French then instructed Walsh to return across the river and follow the main body to the Sweet Grass Hills, rounding up any abandoned horses and oxen on the trail. The Commissioner watched the main column move out and, bringing up the rear, found a stalled ox wagon which he brought in by using his own and Inspector Carvell's saddle horses.

It was hard to imagine that conditions could get worse but they did. On September 15, in miserable, wet weather the column marched six miles to Grassy Lake where they abandoned more oxen. The force then continued a hard afternoon march across the sage brushland. People were marching by rote. Men, horses and oxen were stumbling blindly onward, with the men's hopes only kept up by the thought of better conditions at the Three Buttes. The Commissioner, already planning his return to the east, sent a message to Sergeant Sutherland at Cripple Camp to take all the oats and hay

Crossing The Belly River   NLC C62677

possible to a rendezvous on the Boundary Commission Trail and wait for the returning portion of the force.

Conditions continued to deteriorate; "Always, there were exhausted animals dropping to the ground to die. Not even mediocre pasturage could be found, and whatever water occurred, it had been trampled into mud and contaminated by buffalo."[35] In "B" Troop, bringing up the rear, Constable Thornton went hunting and got lost. At night the men in camp built a fire and sent up rockets as a signal for him. When he was still missing the next day an officer and three men went out to search for him with no success.

Running out of time, food and stamina but not courage and determination, the force pressed on in a penetrating north wind and rain that devastated men and animals. When the column made camp under the shelter of a ridge north of the Milk River, the men drew the wagons up to form a corral and draped tents over the windward side to break the wind. Inside the corral men covered the horses with blankets and fed them the very small ration of oats available. Ominously, snow could now be seen on the summit of the Sweet Grass Hills.

John Peter Turner, described the final march to the camp at the Sweet Grass Hills extremely well; "Drenched by driving sleet, chilled from swirling snow, haggard, tired and thirsty, the dismounted, weary horsemen fought back the oppression of the last cheerless miles. Blankets revived many a favoured mount, trembling and exhausted by cold and hunger. The Three Buttes, snow-capped and sparkling in the lessening distance, stood out in bold relief, and hope revived as the advance scouts reported ample pasturage not far ahead. Lifted as by magic from its drudgery, the Force responded. Even the suffering animals seemed to sense relief. Stretched out for eight miles or more, the tattered division of the once brilliant array strained forward. Shouldering and pulling at the labouring wheels, stumbling and lurching, swearing and cheering with the rigid determination of its right to triumph, the vanguard of ordered sovereignty on the plains lashed its dying energy to a final effort."[36] The main body established camp at the West Butte.

On September 19 the Assistant Commissioner went to locate the Boundary Commission Trail and some Boundary Commission men visited the camp. The force had left the railway at Fargo 97 days before and had travelled 1,009 miles, although at great cost in horseflesh and oxen. The Veterinary Surgeon, John L. Poett, reported that "while marching from the South Saskatchewan River to the Three Buttes, over those desert and arid plains some 12 of our cattle, who were very weak and emaciated, died, and the cause of their death was to be attributed to nothing but want of feed and water." He reflected the thoughts of many when he said that "the debilitated state of horses generally at this place was a sight that will not soon be forgotten."[37]

While no men had been lost, many of them had suffered incredible hardships on the march, but their arrival at the Sweet Grass Hills seemed to infuse them with new spirit. Anyone who had seen them leaving Fort Dufferin two months previously would not have recognized them. Sub-Constable Fred Bagley noted that "if by some hocus pocus of sorcery a stranger unaware of our identity were to drop into this camp and

- A Double Duty -

view our tatterdemalion mob he would surely wonder by what means, or under what miraculous circumstances so many tough looking armed bandits and outlaws could have gotten together in one place."[38] Sub-Inspector McIllree wrote that the "men are very badly off for boots and I saw a man walking the whole of one very cold, rainy day with no stockings and an old pair of carpet slippers down at the heel."[39] In the same vein, Sub-Constable Carscadden wrote, "to add if possible to our pitiful condition most of the men's boots were worn out and you may see many limping about with half the soles of their boots gone and a good sized blister filling up the vacancy."[40]

Meanwhile, back down the trail "B" Troop, (acting as rearguard), had two of their horses die and passed three more dead horses on the trail. Sub-Constable Finlayson recorded that they passed six dead horses on the trail on September 19. The missing man, Thornton, had still not turned up and the troop camped overnight then joined the main body on September 20 without him. On the morning of September 21 Constable Thornton came into camp after five days of being lost and without food. When he became lost and his horse played out he knew that the force had gone to the clearly visible West Butte so he headed for it on foot.

Since "B" Troop would not be going to Edmonton, the Commissioner now decided that "B", "C", "F" and the remainder of "A" Troop would stay in the west under Assistant Commissioner Macleod while he would take "D" and "E" Troops back to Fort Ellice to establish headquarters. At midday they mustered all the horses and the two troops returning to the east with Commissioner French got the best of them. On the afternoon of September 21, "D" and "E" Troops, under Inspector Carvell moved south to the Boundary Commission Trail with orders to move slowly eastward to Wild Horse Lake and wait there for French who would join them on his return from Fort Benton.

September 22 was Fred Bagley's sixteenth birthday! As a birthday surprise, he and the rest of the force found that they had pitched their tents on an old camping ground and had become infested with vermin. Washing, either clothing or bodies, seemed to have little effect. The Surgeon concluded that Juniper Oil would be effective against lice. He had five gallons of the oil so "every man was paraded and undressed

- Roche Percée to Fort Macleod -

and well rubbed with the oil; the clothes and blankets were next well sprinkled with the same; not an article that could harbour this pest remained unsprinkled."[41] The Surgeon reported the cure a success and said the lice had disappeared. Others had their own methods and Sub-Inspector Walker considered that "his best antilouse tip came from the Métis, who were seen removing their shirts and spreading them over ant hills."[42] To avoid further infestation, the camp moved a few miles. Vermin infested, feet blistered, shivering from the cold, and often hungry, Fred Bagley must have taken time on his birthday to think of the sun, sand and sea in St. Lucia where he was born.

On September 22 Commissioner French, Assistant Commissioner Macleod, and a small party left for Fort Benton, about 100 miles away, in Montana. They made very good time and by noon on September 24, they were in Fort Benton, a former American Fur Co. post, named after one Thomas Hardy Benton who, allegedly, saved the company from prosecution for selling whiskey to the Indians. Macleod described it as "a miserable hole, nothing but two stores and a collection of whisky shops." He took the opportunity while in Fort Benton, to write to Mary Drever that he was "all safe and well, the only things that have suffered are the horses and oxen and the amount of frost and cold played sad havoc amongst them. Just think, the first cold night there were ten horses died and in all we have lost about 40."[43]

A telegram was waiting for Commissioner French approving his plan to leave a force on the Bow River and instructing him to return with the remainder to a new headquarters in the vicinity of Fort Pelly where Public Works was erecting a barracks. The reason given for this change was that "subsequent enquiry and consideration have induced a conviction that Fort Pelly, lying about ninety miles to the northward of Fort Ellice and connected therewith by a good road on the west bank of the Assiniboine River should be adopted in lieu of Fort Ellice."[44] French, in acknowledging these instructions, expressed regret at the choice in a somewhat intemperate reply. He was not alone in his questioning the choice. The *Free Press* said, "Why Pelly should be selected as the headquarters for the peelers does not at once strike a person. In fact it doesn't strike a person after some thought."[45]

- A Double Duty -

In Fort Benton, Charles Conrad of I.G. Baker & Co., a former Confederate cavalry officer, befriended and assisted Commissioner French and his party. Conrad introduced them to Jerry Potts, who did not make an immediate good impression but, since there wasn't much choice, French hired him as a guide. I.G. Baker & Co. arranged to send supplies northward to the troops in the Sweet Grass Hills and, on September 26, travelling light, French left Fort Benton to catch up with Inspector Carvell and his men at Wild Horse Lake.

Back at the Sweet Grass Hills, those men who were not returning east remained in camp to rest and catch up on their domestic chores. Sub-Constable Finlayson reported that he "washed clothes and had to go in my drawers and no shirt until my clothes dried. If the people of Canada were to see us now with bare feet, not one half clothed, half starved, picking up fragments left by American troops and hunting buffalo for meat, and have to pay for the ammunition used in killing them. I wonder what they would say of Colonel French."[46]

Inspector Winder received a message from Fort Benton on September 28 instructing him to move to the Whoop-Up Trail and wait for Assistant Commissioner Macleod. The messenger said "the country to the west was well wooded, with many rivers and quantities of game." He said there were few traders left, the remainder having returned to Fort Benton.[47] The troops marched to Spring Creek and the next morning horses and men went back for the guns and balance of the wagons since there were not enough horses to move them all at once. Sub-Constable Finlayson commented that "if Canadians knew what this expedition will cost, I think Colonel French would very soon get his discharge. He left here with the best wishes of the men, that he may never come back. The guns came into camp at 5:00 p.m."[48] On the day Finlayson penned this entry in his diary, the subject of his ire forded the Milk River and rejoined Carvell to start the trip eastward to Fort Pelly.

On September 30 the men made 15 miles but hard driving used up the horses and the guns had to be left behind again. They camped overnight without water and had no supper. The next day they reached the Fort Whoop-Up Trail at Rocky Springs and

- Roche Percée to Fort Macleod -

made camp. On October 2 they marched six miles to camp at the Milk River where they were surrounded by thousands of buffalo. Once again horses and oxen were sent back to help relay the guns and wagons. At Milk River the men had a visit from an entrepreneurial Fort Benton merchant, John Glenn, who had his wagon loaded with flour, sugar, canned fruit, and other items which he quickly sold at inflated prices. That evening Assistant Commissioner Macleod returned from Fort Benton accompanied by Charles Conrad of I.G. Baker and Jerry Potts, the new guide.

The wagons and guns were moved forward in relays due to the hard going, particularly across the Milk River Ridge. John Peter Turner says that Assistant Commissioner Macleod left Sub-Inspector Denny with twenty men and some weak horses to wait for the I.G. Baker bull train bringing supplies from Fort Benton while he pushed on, presumably with the men, the wagons and the guns.[49] Denny says that he was left at Milk River "with my troop horse, many wagons, the nine-pound guns, and loads of ammunition, for none of which transport was available. I had, besides, several sick men, a corporal, and a few others - about twenty in all."[50] The bull teams were to haul these wagons and guns for which there were insufficient horses. Most descriptions of the "capture" of Fort Whoop-Up mention deployment of the guns but few of these come from actual participants. Denny says the guns were three days behind the force and, if this is true, they could not have been deployed at Fort Whoop-Up.

Fort Whoop-Up was a formidable log structure built in the form of a hollow square with ramparts, loopholes and bastions on opposite corners. "There were small wickets that allowed the passage of buffalo skins and the outward passage of trade goods and 'whisky.' There were loopholes for firing weapons and iron bars across the windows and chimneys to prevent entry. . . . Through a narrow wooden gate, too small for an irate Indian to reach the trader, the goods appeared in exchange for furs."[51]

The police lined up and prepared for an assault but there were no signs of life. Assistant Commissioner Macleod approached the gate and knocked. Eventually the door was opened by one Dave Akers, an old man who claimed to be a veteran of the American Civil War. He invited all to come in for a meal of buffalo meat and fresh

- A Double Duty -

vegetables. Although the police accounts say that the only inhabitants were Akers and some Indian women, the *New North West*, a weekly published in Deer Lodge, Montana, published a letter from Charles Schafft, a gold prospector who claimed to have been present when the Mounted Police arrived at Fort Whoop-Up. Schafft said he was "convinced the search was made for liquor to drink not confiscate" since "all appeared dry after four months march on the arid plains . . .."[52]

Assistant Commissioner Macleod supposedly offered Dave Akers $10,000 for Fort Whoop-Up but he held out for $ 25,000 which was too much and the force moved on. Three days later Jerry Potts led them to an island in the Old Man's River where they built their new home, Fort Macleod, from twelve inch cottonwood logs.

- 6 -

Sweet Grass Hills To Fort Dufferin

When the Mounted Police reached the Sweet Grass Hills in September 1874 Commissioner French directed that "D" and "E" Troops would return east with him to establish headquarters. He instructed the two troops under Inspector Carvell to move slowly eastward on the Boundary Commission Trail to Wild Horse Lake, about 70 miles east of the Sweet Grass Hills and wait for him to return from Fort Benton. The men and horses got some rest while waiting, although wolves, which gathered quite close to the camp, were a bother at night. On September 29, the Commissioner forded the Milk River and joined Inspector Carvell and his party.

The column moved off and made good time for a few days, stopping where suitable pasture and water were available and covering better than 20 miles each day. On October 4, a Sunday, the column had an early halt and a church service was held. Sub-Inspector Walker rode out to locate Sergeant Sutherland and the Cripple Camp party and brought them into camp. Sixteen of their horses had strayed two nights previously but three were found while the column was on the move. The next day, October 5, Louis Léveillé found twelve more of the missing horses.

On October 6 Commissioner French took a spring wagon and some spare horses and travelled 43 miles to Wood Mountain Post, while the main column continued northeast toward Cripple Camp on Old Wives Creek. In Wood Mountain French arranged for a few of the weakest animals to be cared for over the winter and, realizing that there was a need for a police detachment in this region, purchased the Boundary Commission Depot, two corrals and eight tons of hay for $100. This sale later became the subject of an acrimonious dispute when Captain Cameron inaccurately alleged that Captain Herchmer had failed to properly credit the proceeds to the Boundary Commission.[1]

Commissioner French left Wood Mountain Post early on October 8, travelling forty miles to Cripple Camp that day. He found the animals left with Sergeant

- A Double Duty -

Sutherland on the way west were doing well and the sick men had recovered. They repacked the wagons and sent several loads of surplus equipment to Wood Mountain Post, along with the weak horses and an ox. The ox had been left on the trail by Inspector Carvell and when Commissioner French sent two men, Sub-Constables Thomas Mooney and John Richardson, to bring it in they got lost. Louis Léveillé went to search for them and found them, headed in the wrong direction, back toward Milk River. Since their horses were exhausted and the two men obviously needed some time to learn their way around this part of the country, French assigned them to be the first members of his new Wood Mountain Post detachment and left them there.

The column moved on in conditions that continued to deteriorate. At the Old Wives Lakes, the water and grass were poor so the men fed hay to the horses. The poor conditions continued and on October 11 they had to travel 20 miles before finding water. As they crossed the rough terrain of the Missouri Coteau and descended the eastern side, the column entered a vast expanse recently swept by prairie fires. They were fortunate to find grass and water at Moose Jaw Creek.

The column now made a long, tiresome march across the plain toward Fort Qu'Appelle, still pushing 20 miles or more a day. At Boggy Creek, with smoke from prairie fires filling the air, five traders' carts were searched for liquor but none was found. The march was now through completely burned over country, with no grass or water. The oxen, unable to keep up the pace, lagged far behind. As the column neared Fort Qu'Appelle, Commissioner French went ahead to arrange for their reception. The rest of the column straggled on. They arrived at Fort Qu'Appelle after dark having covered 31 miles that day. The exhausted oxen had been left at the noon campsite to be retrieved later.

Because of the grasshopper plague, there was only very poor quality hay available in Fort Qu'Appelle. Operating like a modern day automobile dealer, the Hudson's Bay Company Chief Factor sold Commissioner French two oxen and took in six played out oxen in trade for four in better condition. Presumably there was no

- Sweet Grass Hills to Fort Dufferin -

warranty offered. The Hudson's Bay Company also took in three worn out horses, two empty wagons and a cart for safekeeping. One sick horse died.

Leaving Fort Qu'Appelle on October 17, the column crossed the File Hills and moved through the Beaver Hills with fires burning all around them. After a couple of days their progress was slower, in completely burned off country, under a dense cloud of smoke. On October 21 Commissioner French moved ahead of the column to the Hudson's Bay Company post at Fort Pelly, then on to the junction of the Snake and Swan Rivers, the site of the new headquarters for the Mounted Police. While variously called Fort Pelly, from the Hudson's Bay Company post ten miles away, or Fort Livingstone from the proposed telegraph repeater station, the Mounted Police referred to the location as Swan River Barracks. Commissioner French, to his consternation, found Swan River Barracks to be a barren area strewn with huge granite boulders, no sheltering trees, and the newly erected barracks stretched out on the crest, exposed to the prevailing north wind. Fires had burned within 20 feet of the buildings, which had very nearly been lost. To add woe to misery, Inspector Shurtliff arrived from Fort Ellice with the news that fire had destroyed half the winter hay supply and that the Hudson's Bay Company post also lost a large quantity.

Commissioner French, who never liked the idea of a headquarters at Fort Ellice, had already made preliminary arrangements to use Lower Fort Garry, the immigrant sheds at Winnipeg and Fort Dufferin instead. When he learned at Fort Benton that the headquarters was to be near Fort Pelly he had been equally negative to that idea. Conditions on the ground now reinforced his earlier predisposition against the location.

The location for Swan River Barracks was chosen because it was on the surveyed line for the proposed Canadian Pacific Railway and the telegraph. The selection of this general area was not completely illogical, as the railway and telegraph would have provided communications both east and west. However, the choice of the specific location, on an exposed hill covered in large granite boulders on top of a denning area for garter snakes, was not a brilliant move. Public Works received instructions to build the barracks on July 9, 1874, well into the summer season and then

- A Double Duty -

had to bring machinery and supplies in from Ontario, recruit men and move them to Fort Pelly, where they arrived on September 10. About the time construction work should have been finishing it had just started from scratch. Trees were cut then run through the sawmill to make boards and shingles, which were used immediately, without drying, to erect buildings. Anticipating that the police would arrive by November 15, and with the winter fast approaching, the crews worked night and day but the buildings were far from ready when Commissioner French arrived earlier than had been anticipated.

When he saw the state of the buildings, Commissioner French immediately realized that they were too incomplete to provide accommodation for all his men. He sent a message back to the column to go into camp at any good pasture they could find near Fort Pelly. He then convened a Board of Officers to look into the situation. The Board of Officers approved a plan, proposed by the Commissioner, that most of "E" Troop would winter at Swan River Barracks under Inspector Carvell, while "D" Troop, the rest of "E" and the headquarters staff moved on.

On October 24 the column started down the Assiniboine toward Fort Ellice, intercepting and turning back some carts found enroute to Swan River Barracks with supplies. Why they turned back supplies is a mystery since the men left at Swan River Barracks were short of virtually everything throughout the following winter. The weather now turned colder and there was freezing rain that chilled both men and animals to the bone. At the end of the day the men fed the horses oats and hot bran as well as some hay obtained at Fort Pelly. The men put blankets on their horses for the night and huddled over fires that were kept burning. On October 28 Commissioner French rode ahead into Fort Ellice and sent back hay for the horses in the column.

The Commissioner arranged to leave some horses and oxen at Fort Ellice. The weather was very unpleasant on October 29 with blowing snow so everyone gladly stayed in camp, with the animals well fed and cared for at the post. The Surgeon attended a case of typhoid fever while at Fort Ellice and a few days later, unfortunately, came down with the disease himself.

- Sweet Grass Hills to Fort Dufferin -

The march resumed on October 30 in very cold weather, making good time under difficult circumstances. On November 1 they met Paymaster Dalrymple Clark on his way from Fort Dufferin to Swan River Barracks with a small party which turned around and joined the column. By this time the column straggled out for two or three miles, with most of the men on foot, their thin horses walking along unsteadily and occasionally collapsing. The men's clothing was in tatters, most had no hats and their boots had been replaced by moccasins.

The column moved on in increasingly cold and unpleasant weather, having some difficulty in crossing the Little Saskatchewan River due to the steep banks which made it necessary to haul the horses up by hand. On November 3 they reached the government depot at Beautiful Plains, now Neepawa, Manitoba, and started to see signs of civilization - settlers and homesteaders. Commissioner French, using Paymaster Clark's fresh horses, pushed on ahead and arrived in Winnipeg on November 4 while the main column, moving at a much slower pace, arrived on November 7 when stables and accommodation were found for them. The *Free Press* commented that "for physique and military bearing the troop will hold its own with any other corps in the country and their appearance after the hardships undergone was very satisfactory."[2] This is high praise indeed, since none of them had full uniforms. The men stayed in Winnipeg for some time until ordered by Ottawa to move to Fort Dufferin, sixty-five miles south, to winter in the Boundary Commission buildings.

- 7 -

Roche Percée to Fort Edmonton

At Roche Percée most of "A" Troop, under Inspector Jarvis, left the main body and proceeded, via Fort Ellice, to Fort Edmonton, a distance of 875 miles. They had 55 sick or tired horses, 24 wagons, 55 ox carts with 12 drivers and 62 men, five of them sick, 50 cows and 50 calves. The horses were so weak that even taking turns they could only do about eight miles a day. When the rest of the force left, Sam Steele commented that "A" Troop "were a disconsolate lot when we saw the force depart on their long trek, but we had a much harder time before us than any experienced that year."[1] One constable remarked that their "comrades laughed when they saw the skeletons and the animal zoo we have in charge."[2]

The column left the Souris River the morning of August 1, heading northeast toward Fort Ellice, where they would join the established cart track between Fort Garry and Fort Edmonton. Between Roche Percée and the Moose Mountains there was a lot of rain and thunderstorms, which sometimes lasted all night and in a few days the horses and cattle were beginning to show increased signs of fatigue. On August 4 there was some apprehension in the column when it was found that a band of Sioux was on a parallel course to their east so the guard was doubled and everyone warned to remain vigilant with weapons ready, but nothing came of it.

Progress was difficult. At the head of Moose Mountain, five wagons spent the night out in the rain because they were unable to get into camp. A few days later, with the wagons lagging, they abandoned two horses. At Calumet Creek on August 9, oxen hauled the wagons over two bad hills. The men manhandled five of the horses out of the muddy banks of the creek when they collapsed. The next day six horses arrived from Fort Ellice to help.

The weary column struggled into Fort Ellice where the troops had an opportunity to recuperate from hardships already suffered and to prepare for those ahead. Fort Ellice was a large Hudson's Bay Company post, built high on the south bank of the

- Roche Percée To Fort Edmonton -

Assiniboine River near its junction with the Qu'Appelle. The column stayed here until August 18, making repairs, sorting supplies, repairing equipment and resting. The only excitement during their stay was on August 13 when they pursued and captured one of the Métis who had deserted. He was fined ten dollars.

Superintendent Jarvis left some sick men, cows, calves, sick horses, wagons and some supplies at Fort Ellice then moved out on August 18, heading west, just south of the Qu'Appelle River. After a time the column crossed the Qu'Appelle with some difficulty due to the steep descent which was slow for the ox carts. Inspector Jarvis now became the guide since he had travelled this route the previous year and his knowledge helped them find good locations for camps. In his report he wrote that "after leaving Fort Ellice I found pasture and water so bad that I had great difficulty in procuring enough to keep life in the horses and oxen."[3]

The column moved on slowly giving time for the lagging ox carts to catch up. Water was generally scarce and campsites had to be selected carefully. After some very hot weather the rain and fog returned and mud made the trail sticky delaying the march. On August 28 a group of eastbound travellers appeared, including the Reverend McDougall who had carried the message of the coming of the Mounted Police to the Indians. While the difficult travelling was hard on both the men and the animals, there were also some enjoyable moments. Sam Steele recalls that "the evenings were fine, and the half-breed drivers had great fun after supper. One of them had a violin, and to its music the remainder in turn danced a Red River Jig on a door which they carried in their carts for the purpose."[4]

By September 1 the weather was turning cold and finding good water was becoming more of a problem. On the morning of September 2 there was ice on the water buckets and for the first 20 miles of travel there was only alkaline water. The column finally found a campsite with good water and grass that evening but on the following two days they travelled fourteen and fifteen miles without water. Thankfully, on September 5 the weather improved and there was an ample supply of good water.

- A Double Duty -

On September 6 the column met several brigades of Red River carts driven by hunters, freighters and traders, laden with buffalo robes, dry meat and pemmican. Inspector Jarvis bought a supply of pemmican to augment the rations. Sam Steele, who was a great connoisseur of pemmican, called it "the best food in the world for the traveller, soldier and sailor, either on the plains of America or in the Arctic regions." He recalled that people cooked pemmican in two ways in the west. One was a "rubaboo," a stew of pemmican, water, flour and wild onions or dried potatoes, if there were any. The other was a "rechaud," which was pemmican cooked in a frying pan with onions or potatoes or alone.[5]

The column reached "Dumont's Crossing" on the South Saskatchewan River on September 7. Fortunately there was a cable ferry in operation since the river was about 250 yards wide and quite deep at this point. The ferry operator was Gabriel Dumont who was later to take a prominent place in Canadian history during the 1885 Rebellion. There was a steep descent down the bank to the ferry which was very slow, so it took two days to get the wagons and carts across and the cattle were forced to swim. The crossing was completed just in time because the weather turned bad on the afternoon of September 9, with rain, hail and a thunderstorm that continued through the night.

The column stayed in camp on a cold and rainy September 10, while the carts caught up and a yoke of lost oxen was found. Inspector Jarvis went on into Fort Carlton to arrange for their arrival. On September 11 there was a long delay in getting started due to the horses, which were now showing their rundown condition. Many had to have help to get to their feet and their limbs rubbed to take out the stiffness, which was additional hard work for the men. They eventually arrived in Fort Carlton after dark, where the men were quartered and the horses stabled in the Hudson's Bay Company buildings. September 12 was a day of rest for the men, who were comfortably housed and well fed in the fort, but the next day was bitterly cold and the horses suffered badly. Jarvis got first hand experience in labour relations on September 14 when the Métis decided they had had enough and went on a strike! After a lot of persuasion, Jarvis coaxed them into returning to work.

- Roche Percée To Fort Edmonton -

The column was ready to move but, first, they had to cross another formidable water obstacle, the North Saskatchewan River. There was a scow ferry of limited capacity which was very slow and moving a force of this size across the river was a major operation. On September 15 and 16 the Métis took the carts across in good weather. On September 17 and 18 the wagons crossed and by September 20 all the horses were over. Most of the cattle got another swim.

From here on the trail started to deteriorate, cluttered with stones and roots and, in places, under water due to recent heavy rains. Wagons often sank in to the axles and it would take two or three ox teams to extricate them. Sam Steele reported that "heavy rains had fallen, reducing the trails to a deplorable state, and the poor horses in the waggons staggered along with marvellous pluck. They suffered much more than the oxen and, as the nights became colder, when they lay down to rest the unfortunate brutes became so stiff that they could not rise without help, and I had to call the men up many times during the night to lift them by main force and rub their stiffened limbs to restore the circulation. This occurred so often that the men themselves became exhausted from fatigue and want of sleep."[6]

While travelling through the areas where there were marshes or sloughs, ducks and geese were plentiful. In one place snow geese were so abundant around the sloughs that Corporal Carr got 11 geese with one shot.[7] The trail now alternated between excellent and terrible, as did the weather. A horse had to be shot on September 24 and the next day they killed an ox with a broken shoulder and cut it up for food, while another was simply left behind. Pere Lestanc, the Roman Catholic priest who had encountered Commissioner French and the main body at Old Wives Creek, came along the trail enroute to Fort Edmonton. He told them that the main party's horses were in no better condition than theirs.

By the end of September the horses and cattle were very tired. In early October the weather turned better but the trail turned worse. The rough going was hard on the animals and exhausted the cattle. Each day was more difficult than the day before and it got harder and harder to make the horses pull. Many teams lagged behind. The trail

- A Double Duty -

was so bad that it needed constant work and the men wielded axes and spades to make it passable. The Mounted Police were no longer mounted, with men walking beside the horses that could no longer carry them. The column wasted an incredible amount of effort when it mistakenly took a side trail toward Fort Pitt past Frenchman's Butte. The going was hard and one horse, dragged to the top, had to descend the steep slope again the following morning to get back on the right trail.

A horse collapsed on October 3 and was unable to rise. Another, unable to move, was abandoned the next day. Jarvis ordered a day of rest on October 8 because the animals could go no further. On October 12 they encountered a long hill that proved so difficult the column travelled only four miles that day and four wagons had to be left behind. A sick ox died this day and another ox died the next day, while they abandoned one that could go no further. The column stretched out on the trail as the cattle lagged.

Starting on October 15, the column encountered extremely bad roads through wet areas with low meadows and sloughs. Oxen went back to pull the slower vehicles through and on many days the wagons did not reach camp until well after dark. The trail crossed several streams, two of which had to be bridged. When crossing Mud Creek on October 18, a wagon became so completely bogged down that it almost disappeared.

After abandoning three oxen and leaving three more wagons behind, the column camped half a mile short of the Hudson's Bay Company post of Victoria, unable to summon enough energy to get over the hill that lay between them and the post. Horses were now dying at the rate of one a day. On October 19 the column crossed the hill and staggered into Victoria, with the last of them not getting in until 10:00 p.m. Inspector Jarvis arranged for the trader at Victoria to have a settler in the Métis village take care of some animals for the winter, paying $15.00 per ox and $10.00 for each calf. The column redistributed loads and left several wagons and some flour in the village.

On October 21 the train set off again, with Sub-Inspector Gagnon and some men travelling ahead to undertake minor engineering tasks to make the road passable. These men built bridges over streams, filled mud holes and, in one place, laid eight miles of corduroy road. The animals were becoming very run down and were moving slowly; horses would frequently collapse and have to be helped to their feet. When the weather turned very cold, the weaker horses were put in tents. Some wagons and men were left far behind.

The column reached Sturgeon Creek at noon on October 26, with all the horses nearing exhaustion. There was a great deal of difficulty fording the creek and one horse died in the stream. Inspector Jarvis, who had gone ahead into Fort Edmonton, sent back a message asking that the column come into Fort Edmonton as soon as possible. Sub-Inspector Gagnon went ahead with the oxen while Sergeant Major Steele looked after the horse teams. The horses were in pitiful condition. Those that could not go on were put in tents with men to look after them, while others had to be helped virtually every step of the way. Sub-Constable D'Artigue recalled that "we took charge of four horses at Horse Hills and walked the last 12 miles, each man holding his horse with both hands, one at the head and another at the shoulders, to keep the poor skeletons on their legs."[8]

At this point, the trail degenerated until it alternated between track and slough, with men and animals up to their knees in black, sticky mud. The men unloaded mired wagons, dragged them out by hand, then reloaded them. Horses and oxen would rush to small frozen ponds to drink, then would break through the ice and men would have to haul them out with ropes. It was backbreaking labour for cold and exhausted men. After 20 hours the column had still not reached Fort Edmonton but they were completely worn out and called a temporary halt at Rat Creek, four miles from their goal.

On October 27 Sergeant Major Steele pitched tents, started two rows of fires and had the horses washed, dried and turned out to pasture for a time. After only three hours of rest, the column was ready to move again. By a tremendous effort the horses made it the four more miles into Fort Edmonton, with the column spread out over the whole distance. Sub-Inspector Gagnon struggled in the next day with the ox teams, having left

- A Double Duty -

behind several men, loaded wagons and carts. On October 29, and for the next few days, the remnants came straggling in. By November 1 the entire column had reached its destination. Of the ten wagons drawn by oxen that left Fort Carlton only four completed the journey. "A" Troop had travelled the 960 miles from Roche Percée in 88 days - 60 of them travel days.

Inspector Jarvis, given the men and animals in the weakest condition, had overcome the adversity of weather and terrain to bring them to their destination at Fort Edmonton. At least the exhausted men of "A" Troop did not have to build their own quarters, as their colleagues at Fort Macleod were doing at this time, since the Hudson's Bay Company assigned quarters within the palisade of the large fort, situated on a wooded bank above the North Saskatchewan River.

- 8 -

Flawed Planning, Intelligence and Logistics

The great "March West" was now over. It has become part of Canadian folklore and is surrounded by mythology. As Paul F. Sharp describes it, "the achievements of the westward march, like the epics of ancient Greece, suffered distortion by false legends and unbelievable exaggerations."[1] The great achievement was not in crossing the plains but that the men involved overcame the formidable obstacles and tremendous difficulties inflicted on them, not only by nature, but to a large degree by the ineptness of their professional and political masters. The march was essentially a military deployment, plagued by flawed planning, inadequacies in the acquisition and analysis of intelligence and a breakdown in logistics which was responsible for the loss of many horses and oxen. The fact that no men died is probably attributable more to luck than to management.

Any successful operation of this type must use the best available intelligence and reconnaissance. Since the immediate objective was to close down Fort Whoop-Up, Commissioner French should have had accurate information on its location, structure, occupants and their armaments. French appears to have accepted exaggerated reports about Fort Whoop-Up without any serious attempt to confirm them. The Mounted Police had a wildly inflated idea of what was awaiting them in the west. They were also unable to even locate Fort Whoop-Up and got lost on the plains in an embarrassing debacle that was completely unnecessary. Considering that the force was led by a professional Army officer, the shortcomings in the intelligence field were surprising. It would have made sense for French to have appointed an Intelligence Officer, just as Captain Cameron did in the Boundary Commission, responsible for the collection, collation and confirmation of the intelligence needed for the deployment.

Why Commissioner French did not have a reconnaissance made to confirm both the location of Fort Whoop-Up and the number of occupants is curious. Determining the location of Fort Whoop-Up should not have been a major problem. In the previous

- A Double Duty -

year, 1873, the Reverend McDougall was at Fort Kipp, heading for the Missouri River. One of the men there drew him a map, then the Fort Kipp traders escorted his party to Fort Whoop-Up. Early in 1874, while making his visits to the Indians to tell them that the Mounted Police were coming, McDougall again stopped at Fort Whoop-Up, presumably to tell the sinners that their days were numbered. The Boundary Commission personnel also knew the location of Fort Whoop-Up since they purchased their refreshments from the traders there and visited back and forth.[2] Had an experienced officer, perhaps Inspector Jarvis who had travelled in the west, been appointed as Intelligence Officer and pursued his duties with vigour, many of the difficulties encountered on the march could have been avoided.

Much emphasis has been placed on the error made in marking the location of Fort Whoop-Up on Palliser's somewhat inaccurate map which Commissioner French used on the march. This, in turn, was blamed on an error in the published report of Colonel Robertson-Ross. The location is much more accurately shown in Robertson-Ross' actual diary. In addition, Colonel Robertson-Ross was probably available for consultation, but there is no indication that these sources of intelligence were considered.

It is almost impossible to believe that Commissioner French did not order a reconnaissance made. There were Boundary Commission officers as far west as Wood Mountain by June 20, 1874, well before the force left Fort Dufferin, and by the end of July they were at the Sweet Grass Hills. There is no apparent reason they could not have had a Mounted Police officer with them. Since French and Assistant Commissioner Macleod had no difficulty learning all about Fort Whoop-Up when they eventually arrived in Fort Benton, an officer on a reconnaissance would probably have done so much earlier. If, for some reason, a Mounted Police officer could not go west prior to the march it seems reasonable that the Boundary Commission could have been tasked to provide the intelligence.

Although Commissioner French, in his Annual Report for 1874, acknowledges the assistance provided by Captains Cameron and Anderson, it appears the Boundary

- Flawed Planning, Intelligence & Logistics -

Commission officers were in a position to provide a great deal more information than seems to have been forthcoming. The Boundary Commission was in a position to give extensive advice and assistance to the fledgling force. They had guides who were familiar with the area, they knew the exact location of Fort Whoop-Up, they had experience with horses imported from Canada, they knew the location of water and forage on the route and they had an established supply line. It appears that the Mounted Police were not given the benefit of this experience or chose to ignore it. The Commissary Officer, Lawrence Herchmer, provided valuable information to French when they met at Cripple Camp but this appears to have been serendipitous.

There also appears to have been no consideration for the manner in which the "forts" or trading posts were operated. They were active in the period from autumn to spring, about eight months, and unoccupied for about four months in the summer. However, one the size of Fort Whoop-Up might have had a caretaker. The Mounted Police expedition was made at the time of the year when there were no prime furs to trade and there would normally be few, if any, personnel at the post. In actual fact, Fort Whoop-Up was virtually unoccupied when the force arrived.

The planning for the march included estimates of the stores required and the transport necessary to move them. The figures appear to have gone through several iterations and ultimately the grossly overloaded wagons played havoc with both horses and men. This problem was compounded by all of the horses having been purchased as saddle horses, not draft animals, although in his initial planning in early 1874 Commissioner French clearly realized the need for horses suitable for pulling heavily loaded wagons and guns.

There is documentary evidence that large numbers of animals died due to lack of feed. If the march were repeated today and the same number of animals perished from lack of feed, the organizers would doubtless face criminal charges. A large quantity of oats was lost when a barge sank on the Red River and additional quantities were ruined when carried as deck cargo on a river steamer. Since waiting to replace these oats would make it impossible for the expedition to take place in 1874, those in charge took a calculated risk that the horses would survive. A report to the Colonial Office acknowledged that "the Force had therefore to leave with a very trifling supply of oats or the expedition could not have been made in this year."[3] Rather than having overcome adversity on the march due the shortage of oats, Commissioner French appears to have gambled with the lives of his horses and lost.

There is also overwhelming anecdotal evidence in diaries and reminiscences to show men often missed meals and went hungry. It was also necessary to put the force on half rations shortly after leaving Fort Dufferin, when they were supposedly carrying six months to a year's supply of food. Although soldiers griped about rations almost as a matter of routine, there was not one positive comment about the quantity, quality or cooking of rations, other than those of Commissioner French. This could have been attributed to the conditions under which they travelled except that memoirs of personnel of the Boundary Commission, operating under the same conditions, describe their food as "of the very best, and the amount more than could be used, even when we were many hundred miles from semi-civilization."[4] There are references to Crosse & Blackwell's potted meats and pickles, anchovies etc. delicacies unknown to the Mounted Police.

Commissioner French reacted angrily to reports of men being hungry or starving, describing them as absurd. He asserted that "the whole force had their three meals a day as regularly as if they were in barracks. All ranks had the same rations, from Commissioner to sub-constable, all had the same."[5] This is so patently untrue that it reflects badly on the credibility of Commissioner French. While all ranks may have been on the same ration scale and it may have provided for three meals a day in theory, there is just too much evidence to the contrary to accept the absurd contention that they actually had three meals a day just as if they were in barracks. Feeding was based on cook wagons and when the column was strung out over many miles those who were with the wagon at the halts sometimes got fed, while those who were not there usually did without. Food preparation depended on the availability of fuel and water and the frequent absence of one or both would prevent preparation of a hot meal. The meat

- *Flawed Planning, Intelligence & Logistics* -

supply was on the hoof and the long marches meant that butchering could only take place at halts where there was sufficient time. These were few and far between.

There is no documented explanation of why Commissioner French insisted the force carry its own supplies and should not rely in any way on the Defence Department or others. French appears to have been reluctant to have anything done for the force by outsiders, although the force ultimately obtained considerable assistance from the Boundary Commission, the Hudson's Bay Company and the Militia. The decision to have the force carry its own supplies was, at minimum, questionable. The Boundary Commission had operated quite effectively for two years from a system of fixed depots, stocked by supply trains from Fort Dufferin. The Boundary Commission was already contracting for supplies, especially oats, from Fort Benton so this was a known source which was, ultimately, used by the Mounted Police for several years.

The Boundary Commission had a well-established supply line over 800 miles long, based on four principal depots between Fort Dufferin and the Rocky Mountains, with several sub-depots between them. They were looked after by twelve depot keepers and stocked by a fleet of thirty commissariat wagons and seventeen Red River carts. Had a supply train prestocked the Boundary Commission depots on behalf of the force, the march west could have been easier. The tactical elements could have advanced much more rapidly and, hopefully, without the loss in horses and oxen. Even when the force left the Boundary Commission Trail after Roche Percée, they were within access of the depots at Wood Mountain and White Mud River, where they obtained supplies of oats.

For some reason Commissioner French insisted on attempting to move the force as one unit, possibly to keep everything under his scrutiny or to reduce the danger of attack. The failure to separate the tactical from the administrative or support elements of his force reduced the rate of march to the speed of the slowest components, cattle on the hoof, farm machinery or Red River carts pulled by oxen. Any advantage in terms of being easier to defend was quickly lost because, in practice, the column was usually spread out for many miles on the trail.

- A Double Duty -

The area where the failure in logistics planning had the greatest impact was probably in water supply. In Commissioner French's logistics planning there appears to have been no allowance made for carrying water in bulk on wagons or in carts. The force was to depend on rivers, streams and ponds along the route. Another incomprehensible shortcoming was the failure to provide water bottles. Fred Bagley wrote, "it is almost incredible that water bottles, which are rightly considered essential for the well being of the modern soldier, were entirely absent from our equipment. Not one man in the Force possessed one."[6] This is so alien to military practice that it is hard to believe that Commissioner French would have allowed such negligence. His failure to arrange for water supply is even more difficult to understand because he admitted prior to the march that he "feared they would be often without water."[7]

At Fort Dufferin, before departing for the west, the force had at least one water cart, a Red River cart with two barrels mounted on it, pulled by a pony. William Parker wrote that he had the job of hauling enough water from the Red River to supply all six troops so this cart appears to have been one of a kind. There is no evidence whether that cart accompanied the force but it would have been completely inadequate on its own. There is clear evidence that the Boundary Commission had water carts out on the plains.[8] When on the move the Boundary Commission filled their carts from any available source, including rain water and this was sufficient to last several days while moving across the arid plain. The Boundary Commission also had at least "two water carts with zinc-lined boxes instead of the barrels on wheels which served other parties."[9] The force's Veterinary Surgeon recognized the problem after the fact, and suggested "that a certain number of properly made water carts, with barrels, be supplied, as the present arrangement is both imperfect and insecure."[10]

It is interesting to compare what happened to the Mounted Police with other forces that were travelling across the plains in the Summer of 1874. In August 1874 the Provisional Battalion at Fort Garry provided an escort of two infantry companies with a 7-pounder mountain gun for Alexander Morris and David Laird, who held treaty negotiations with the Cree and Ojibwa at Fort Qu'Appelle. This involved 113 military

- Flawed Planning, Intelligence & Logistics -

personnel and four Métis scouts, 12 double wagons, 15 carts and 46 horses. The gunners dismantled the mountain gun and stowed it in a wagon. They carried a very small supply of oats and for 28 days the horses ate grass.

The soldiers carried their personal weapons and equipment, including waterbottles, and marched both ways, via Fort Ellice. In 16½ days they travelled 333 miles under conditions very similar to those encountered by the Mounted Police and had no men or horses lost or injured. The Army used acclimatized horses which required minimal grain supplies and subsisted on prairie grass. In his report on the march to Fort Qu'Appelle, Lieutenant Colonel Osborne Smith, doubtless still smarting from the acrimonious dispute over his encounter with McIllree and Neale at Fort Garry, stated "no horses . . . should be used that are not either country bred or thoroughly acclimatized, where oats cannot be procured; or losses as disastrous as those experienced in a late expedition by a civil force are certain to be met with."[11]

Commissioner French reported "it is an admitted fact that almost all Canadian or American horses fail during the first season they are fed on prairie grass, and therefore it is little to be wondered at that ours should have failed."[12] If this was so well known it raises the question of why the force, using mostly Canadian horses which fail during the first season on prairie grass, did not make provision for extra horses or the necessary supply of oats to keep them in working condition. The initial supply of oats was used in about ten days, well before the force reached Roche Percée.

William Pearce questions Commissioner French's practice of purposely camping near sloughs in the belief that the feed was better. Pearce believes that despite the buffalo having eaten or trampled the prairie grass it would still have been more nutritious than slough grass. He suggests that French probably did not know that they only had to give the horses sufficient time to fill up on grass on the ridges to stay in good condition.[13]

When the work of the Boundary Commission was finished in the summer of 1874, a party of 167 officers and men, with 200 horses and 100 wagons, travelled 800 miles from the Sweet Grass Hills to Fort Dufferin in 40 days. They positioned hay

- *A Double Duty* -

supplies at campsites near water at the likely end of each day's march so the horses had food. At the end of the 800-mile journey the Boundary Commission reported the horses in perfect condition.

Soldiers were not the only ones who crossed the prairies efficiently. The McDougalls at Morley, west of the present City of Calgary, travelled to Winnipeg for their supplies. They carried furs on the outbound journey and supplies on the way back so were heavily laden in both directions but still completed the return journey in five months, including their time in Winnipeg. They did not suffer great losses in horses.[14]

If others could travel across the plains without having their horses and cattle die and their men falling ill or complaining of hunger, what was so different with the Mounted Police? It is impossible to know precisely, but the available evidence suggests that the Army and the Boundary Commission both provided adequate supplies of water and forage and had well-organized supply systems. The Boundary Commission, by reconnaissance, preselected suitable campsites near usable water supplies.

Considering the state of disorganization and the condition of both men and horses on the march, an attack in force by Indians could well have been disastrous. Given the propensity of the police horses to stampede, a large number might have been run off, leaving the force at least partially immobilized. The ox carts and wagons lagging in the rear would have been easy targets and their loss would have included the supplies they carried. Had the force been required to take up a defensive position for any extended period on the open prairie, the lack of bulk water supplies and individual water bottles would have been disastrous.

- 9 -

Establishing Law And Order In The West

Winter was not far behind when Jerry Potts led Assistant Commissioner Macleod and his men to the island in the Old Man's River that was to be their new home. The main column arrived on October 13, 1874 and the first snow fell on October 19. The main priority was now protection of the men and animals from the increasing cold. They built the hospital and stables first, the men's quarters followed and the officer's quarters were done last. This followed the military tradition that officers saw the men and horses fed and quartered before looking after themselves. They built the fort of twelve foot cottonwood logs placed upright in trenches and chinked with clay mixed with hot water. The roof, made of poles covered with a foot of dirt, was not entirely waterproof. Windows and doors came on the bull train from Fort Benton. They named their new home Fort Macleod.

Fort Macleod received supplies by bull trains, traditionally used to haul heavy loads from Fort Benton. Inspector Denny left a good description of them: "These bull trains were an institution peculiar to the plains. Each team of twelve or fourteen yoke of oxen hauled three enormous canvas-covered wagons. There were often as many as eight teams of twenty-four wagons to a train. Loads ranged from seven thousand pounds up to ten or twelve tons to a team. Their rate of travel was slow, ten to fifteen miles a day, but nothing stuck them. A driver went with each team; a night herder and cook completed the outfit. Three or four horses, tied to the wagons when on the move were used for night-herding the cattle. The drivers walked alongside the teams during the day, their heavy bull whips exploding as they swung them in reports like pistol shots."[1]

By December, due to the hard work of the men, the fort was habitable and the force was in quarters. Although the chimneys were only partially completed, they were high enough for fires to be lit. In a good tactical move, most of the officers occupied the kitchen during construction of their quarters. Winder, Jackson and Dr. Nevitt lived

- A Double Duty -

in a doubled tent pitched in the woods and heated by a stove. James Macleod stayed with Mr. Conrad of I.G. Baker, who had a house quickly built outside the fort.

I.G. Baker & Co. built a trading post near the fort and a village quickly sprang up around it with some stores and a billiard room. Inspector Denny recalled that "prices at the I.G. Baker post were high; a dollar a can for fruit or vegetables, for example. As we had received no pay since leaving Fort Dufferin, all purchases were made on credit. Orders were taken on the men's pay, and when money at last came little was left to them after their accounts had been settled."[2] The delay in pay was the source of a great deal of dissatisfaction which was compounded by the need to obtain credit from the traders.

The three troops were isolated and on their own, with no hope of reinforcement in the case of an Indian uprising. The only communication with Ottawa was by telegraph from Fort Benton or Fort Shaw, 200 miles away. Survival of the force was now completely dependent on maintaining good relations with the Indians. The Reverend George McDougall wrote that he had "sometimes heard the Mounted Police swagger about what they would do with the natives in the case of an insurrection, but my opinion is that if the good Lord had not predisposed the red man to look upon the troops as friends, very few of them would have gone back to tell of their adventures in the North West."[3]

While the Mounted Police were building Fort Macleod, the Blackfoot chief, Crowfoot, decided to test the truth of what the Reverend McDougall had told him about the newcomers. After the arrival of the Mounted Police in October, he sent his brother-in-law, a minor chief named Three Bulls, to report that he had exchanged two good ponies for two gallons of whiskey. He said that he had received the liquor from a man named William Bond, based fifty miles north at Pine Coulee. The police immediately prepared to meet this challenge. To prevent word of their activities from spreading, Jerry Potts arranged to meet Three Bulls out on the north trail after dark the next night. The following evening, Inspector Crozier and ten men quietly left the fort with Jerry Potts to rendezvous with Three Bulls. The party travelled north where they arrested

- Establishing Law And Order In The West -

William Bond, Harry "Kamoose" Taylor and three others. The police seized and later confiscated the men's wagons, horses, rifles, revolvers and 116 buffalo robes. It is interesting that the traders had modern Henry repeating rifles while the police had obsolescent Snider-Enfield carbines. The Mounted Police destroyed the alcohol and Bond and Taylor were each fined $200 and the others $50 each. A trader named "Waxy" Weatherwax from Fort Benton paid all the fines except that of Bond who was sent to jail in lieu of payment.

Assistant Commissioner Macleod issued fifty of the buffalo robes to the policemen and gave the remainder to the tailors who made them into caps, mitts, jackets and trousers. There was a roll of red flannel cloth with the Indian supplies and Macleod had it transferred to the Police Stores to use for linings for the garments.[4] The standard dress in the Mounted Police at Fort Macleod was coats and trousers sewn by their tailors from tanned buffalo skins with Indian moccasins for footwear. Inspector Denny said, "on parade, in our uncouth garments, we were a motley crew."[5]

The patrol by Inspector Crozier and his party showed just how poor the condition of the horses was at Fort Macleod. "One of his horses broke down only after having gone a few miles and although it was brought back and treated with every care, died a couple of days afterward from paralysis."[6] The shortage of hay aggravated the condition of the horses so, on October 30, Inspector Walsh and a small party took several of the poorer horses and cattle 214 miles south to the Sun River Valley in Montana where feed was available. Fifteen of the horses were lost on the trail.[7] By the time Walsh returned, hay supplies were even more critical so he went back with more horses and instructions to try to buy good horses in Montana. Hay was available at Fort Kipp, an abandoned whisky fort about 18 miles down the Old Man's River, so Assistant Commissioner Macleod sent a small detachment of 13 men there under Inspector Brisebois. There were rumours that Macleod wanted to get rid of Brisebois since they had some kind of disagreement during the construction of Fort Macleod and he had accused Brisebois of insubordination.

- A Double Duty -

While his men built Fort Macleod, Assistant Commissioner Macleod sent Jerry Potts to visit the Indian chiefs and dispel the rumours being spread by traders that the Mounted Police were there to fight the Indians and would be gone the next year. Potts visited the Bloods, Peigans and Blackfoot late in November and passed the word that Macleod would like to meet with their chiefs. Although he was told that the police were his friends, Crowfoot sent a messenger to obtain assurances before coming into Fort Macleod on December 1 where the police received him with dignity. Assistant Commissioner Macleod was charged with establishing good relations with the Indian tribes. Because the most warlike and independent was the Blackfoot, he cultivated the chief, Crowfoot, and the two men quickly established a feeling of friendship and trust. At the first meeting with Crowfoot and the other chiefs Macleod told them that the police had not come to take their land. He explained that the coming of the police was to their advantage and that they would mete out justice to Indians and whites alike.

While Assistant Commissioner Macleod was establishing friendly relations with the Blackfoot, his men were busy finishing the buildings at Fort Macleod and making their spartan quarters as comfortable as possible. To add a little excitement to the busy life of the fort, the prisoner, Bond, escaped on December 2 and although a sentry fired at him as he fled, no trace of him could be found. Macleod had issued an order that a corporal and two men would guard Bond at all times but when he escaped only one man was on duty. As a result, Macleod reduced Corporal Uniake to the ranks and dropped Corporal Killaly, who came out to Lower Fort Garry in the first contingent with Inspector Walsh in 1873, to the end of the seniority list. The following spring the body of William Bond was found with a bullet between the shoulders. It was impossible to tell if it was the shot fired by the sentry.

Crowfoot   GAI NA-1407-1

- *Establishing Law And Order In The West* -

Commissioner French, on hearing of this debacle, was not impressed and wrote to Macleod asking him to "be good enough to state what steps were taken to reapprehend the prisoner, Bond, as I do not understand (even if horses could not be used) why men on foot could not have traced the fugitive who, having no ammunition or provisions, could not have got very far."[8]

Feeling the incomplete condition of Fort Macleod had contributed to the escape, Assistant Commissioner Macleod ordered an extra fatigue parade on the Sunday before Christmas to strengthen security and prevent another escape. When he returned from a trip to Fort Kipp and Fort Hamilton he found that the men, except the sergeants and two corporals, had refused to turn out for the fatigue party. An investigation showed only two men had taken active steps and could be considered ringleaders in this matter, Corporal Knowles of "F" Troop and Constable Dunbar of "C" Troop. The remainder had not considered the work to be necessary so had not responded when the trumpeter sounded the "Fall-In." Knowles told a Staff Sergeant that he was not going to fall in and was asking others if they were going to do so when he was placed under arrest by Sergeant Clyde. Macleod spoke to the men, room by room, explained the seriousness of their offence and offered all of them, except Knowles and Dunbar, the choice of expressing regret or accepting punishment. All took advantage of the offer and expressed regret. Macleod reduced Knowles to the rank of constable.[9]

By Christmas the buildings at Fort Macleod were reasonably comfortable, there were supplies from Fort Benton and on Christmas Day there was a feast of buffalo, venison and antelope. The chiefs who had been invited for the day were treated to a military display which included the firing of a field gun. The celebration ended with a dance.

Tragedy struck as the year ended. Two constables from the detachment at Fort Kipp, Baxter and Wilson, were on leave at Fort Macleod. They left for Fort Kipp one morning and later the same day Inspector Denny started for Fort Whoop-Up, via Fort Kipp, because he had heard that the I.G. Baker bull train had arrived there with supplies and mail. He ran into a blizzard but forged on and eventually his pony walked through

- *A Double Duty* -

the gate at Fort Kipp and stopped in the middle of the square. Denny found that Baxter and Wilson, who should have been ahead of him, had not arrived. Later, when two horses with empty saddles came in, a search found the two on the trail, Baxter already dead and Wilson beyond help.

As the year 1875 arrived the force was spread across the west at Fort Macleod, Fort Kipp, Wood Mountain Post, Fort Edmonton, Fort Ellice, Swan River Barracks, Winnipeg and Fort Dufferin. Communication was tenuous and life was not easy. The members there felt forgotten by Ottawa since they had received no pay, were low on provisions and had received no supplies of clothing and equipment.

Fort Macleod, built quickly in a race against approaching winter, was not always comfortable. One member described it as log buildings with mud floors and mud roofs which were far from waterproof. It was not only the buildings that were in poor condition, the few horses not sent south to Sun River were also suffering and food supplies for the men were also running low. These conditions caused a great deal of dissatisfaction with some of the men, who had not received any pay since leaving Fort Dufferin nine months before, and now owed large amounts of money to the traders for clothing and tobacco. When the traders regaled them with stories of high pay for gold mining in Montana, eighteen of the men deserted and fled across the border. They were pursued by a party which returned to Fort Macleod twenty-four hours later without catching them. Assistant Commissioner Macleod sent a telegram to the Department of Justice and Commissioner French reporting that supplies would run out at the end of April, clothing was required at once, there was great dissatisfaction among the men at not being paid and eighteen had deserted.[10]

Ottawa eventually told Assistant Commissioner Macleod that money to pay the men was available in a bank in Helena, Montana, 300 miles away and that he should collect it. With a party which included Jerry Potts, Sub-Inspector Denny and Sergeants David Cochrane and Charles Ryan, he left Fort Macleod on March 12, 1875 in good weather. They camped near Fort Whoop-Up and when they were about to leave in the morning, Dave Akers, the old Civil War veteran who was still in Fort Whoop-Up growing cabbages, warned them that sun dogs suggested that there would be a blizzard within 24 hours.

The party moved steadily south in cold but clear weather with large herds of buffalo in sight. By noon the sun had disappeared and by the time they reached the Milk River the temperature was falling and a gale blew out of the North so hard that even the buffalo huddled together in the river valley. The men dug a snow cave but had no fuel for a fire and, as the storm grew worse, all of them were frostbitten and Sub-Inspector Denny's foot was frozen. They remained in their snow cave for two days and two nights while the storm raged around them. On the third day the snow stopped but the wind increased and, with their food running out, Jerry Potts suggested that they try to reach Rocky Springs, 30 miles south, where some crude huts would provide shelter.

The party moved through blowing snow with poor visibility, unable to see where they were going, and everyone except Jerry Potts lost all sense of direction. At one point, realizing that Sergeant Ryan was missing, they retraced their steps and found him sitting in the snow, unable to move. They picked him up, put him back on his horse, and continued on their way, still unable to see. Suddenly, as it grew dark, Jerry Potts stopped. His uncanny senses told him that they had arrived at Rocky Springs.

The weather had cleared up the next morning and, by noon, the party reached the Marias River where there was a United States Army detachment and also a trading post. The soldiers, thinking the party was whiskey smugglers, rode out to capture them. Once their identity was made known they were given a warm welcome. Captain Williams, the officer in charge, provided hot food, beds, fresh horses and a sleigh for their baggage and sent them, with an escort to Fort Shaw. Sub-Inspector Denny remained at Fort Shaw to regain his eyesight and to have a frozen toe amputated. On leaving Fort Shaw the rest of the party went to Helena.[11]

While Assistant Commissioner Macleod was enroute to Helena, desertion continued to be a problem. On March 13, 1875, three more men deserted but Inspector Allen captured and returned them the next day. While in Helena Macleod encountered most of the men who had recently deserted. As Sub-Inspector Denny described it,

- A Double Duty -

"after great hardships they had arrived in Helena, only to find their dreams of wealth easily acquired not up to expectations. The majority of them called shamefacedly on Colonel Macleod and begged to be taken back in the force. A few of the best were re-engaged."[12] The Deputy Minister of Justice authorized Macleod to take back the men, but he had apparently not consulted with, or even informed, Commissioner French of this decision. Macleod informed French that he had taken back deserters with the approval of the Minister of Justice. Assistant Commissioner Macleod explained to Hewitt Bernard, the Deputy Minister Minister of Justice, that the men's departure had been unexpected and "up to the time of the desertions I was quite unaware of there being any dissatisfaction amongst the men. I had often been asked as to when their pay would arrive and told them that I expected some arrangement would be made by which they could have it paid to their credit in Canada."[13]

Supt J.M. Walsh   GAI NA-1771-1

Although Ottawa had been told that the whiskey trade was eliminated, rumours were prevalent that it continued in the Cypress Hills. When three Indians from the area visited Lieutenant Governor Morris and told him that the traders had returned, rebuilt their fort on the site where the massacre had taken place, and were selling more liquor than ever, Ottawa directed that a fort be established in the Cypress Hills to control the area.[14]

The Cypress Hills rise from the prairie to form a plateau, 20 miles wide by 200 miles long, nearly 5.000 feet above sea level. When Inspector Walsh returned to Fort Macleod, with the horses that had wintered at Sun River, he was sent with his troop to the Cypress Hills to establish the new fort. With him were Sub-Inspectors Vernon Welch and Edwin Allen and the guide, Louis Léveillé, recently returned from

- *Establishing Law And Order In The West* -

Fort Dufferin. The troop, guided by Jerry Potts, left Fort Macleod on the evening of May 13, went via Fort Kipp to Fort Whoop-Up then crossed the St. Mary's River and camped, waiting for further orders and provisions from the I.G. Baker train. When they reached the Cypress Hills a location was selected on the floor of the broad valley of Battle Creek about a mile from the massacre site, and work started on construction of the fort. The new post was called Fort Walsh.

The precise selection of the site was apparently influenced by the presence of Edward McKay and his family who were squatters in the hills. Mr. McKay's grandson later recalled that when "B" Troop arrived and were looking for a location for the new fort, one member, Sub-Constable Oldham, the troop cook, rode into the hills and found the log cabins and barns of the McKay family. He reported his discovery to Inspector Walsh and the following day returned with some of the officers.[15] Mr. McKay had several attractive daughters so "B" Troop could see no need for further scouting and established their fort on this spot. The Troop Sergeant Major, J.H.G. Bray, later married one of Mr. McKay's daughters. The men cut 2,500 logs and 4,000 roofing poles from the surrounding hills and hauled them to the site. The outer walls were sunk three feet in trenches and stood twelve feet above the ground.

Two days after the troop arrived in the Cypress Hills, a tense situation arose when a band of Lakota appeared, apparently pushed across the boundary by the United States Army. The Sioux were relatively friendly until they noticed that two of Walsh's men were wearing cast off items of United States Army uniforms purchased from traders. The Sioux insisted that the policemen were "Long Knives," as they called American soldiers, but just as things were getting critical a large band of Cree appeared and the outnumbered Sioux departed.

Using a new trail from Fort Benton, 275 miles south, I.G. Baker & Co. provided Fort Walsh with hardware, furniture and food. There was soon quite a settlement around the fort, with trading posts of I.G. Baker & Co. and T.C. Power, both based in Fort Benton. I.G. Baker & Co. received large contracts to provide food and forage at

- *A Double Duty* -

Fort Walsh and acted as bankers for the Mounted Police members stationed there. There is an irony in this, since Isaac Gilbert Baker was the uncle of Alfred Hamilton who built Fort Hamilton, later known as Fort Whoop-Up, and I.G. Baker was said to have financed the endeavour. To watch the frontier crossing on the new trail, Inspector Walsh established a detachment at Kennedy's Crossing on the international boundary, where the trail from Fort Benton crossed the Milk River.

It was apparent, soon after the establishment of Fort Walsh, that there was a need for a post somewhere between Fort Macleod and Fort Edmonton. Assistant Commissioner Macleod assigned the task to Inspector Ephraim Brisebois, an officer who had considerable personal experience in the problems of leadership. The fifty men of "F" Troop travelled from Fort Macleod to the site selected for the new fort at the junction of the Bow and Elbow Rivers, now the location of the City of Calgary. The ubiquitous entrepreneurs, I.G. Baker & Co., cut and rafted timber down the river and contracted to build the fort. When construction started, the usual collection of missionaries and traders appeared and a village sprang up around the walls of the fort.

To the north, Inspector Jarvis and his 21 men spent a quiet winter at Fort Edmonton in quarters provided free by the Hudson's Bay Company. Early in 1875 Commissioner French instructed Jarvis to select a site on the south bank of the river between Fort Edmonton and Sturgeon Creek, build a fort, fence the land and plant crops. Jarvis selected a site at Sturgeon Creek, twenty miles downstream from Fort Edmonton. Richard Hardisty, Chief Factor for the Hudson's Bay Company at Fort Edmonton, thought the post should be built on the site now occupied by the University of Alberta. Hardisty and Jarvis reportedly argued about the site and Jarvis is alleged to have chosen the site downstream to spite Hardisty.[16] The local citizens at Fort Edmonton were not happy with the decision so they sent a petition to the Lieutenant Governor, enclosing the minutes of a settlers meeting. The settlers' Committee also spoke to Jarvis who told them they were too late, the contracts were let and there was no other suitable place nearer to Fort Edmonton.[17]

- Establishing Law And Order In The West -

In April 1875 Inspector Jarvis wrote to Commissioner French to say that he had selected a site some 16 miles downstream from Fort Edmonton and enclosed copies of the tenders for the timbers he had procured.[18] On May 13 French wrote to Jarvis to tell him that the order to establish a fort on the south side of the river was cancelled and "A" Troop was now under the command of the Assistant Commissioner at Fort Macleod who would give him instructions. Commissioner French followed this up with another letter expressing astonishment at Jarvis "assuming the responsibility of letting contracts for the barracks, a matter which I certainly would never think of doing without orders from Ottawa." He said his previous letter had been prepared in haste when he found a Hudson's Bay Company official was going to Fort Edmonton and "reference to Ottawa was impossible, believing that you could with *your own men* put up buildings (as the Assistant Commissioner did) and therefore that in any case no expenditure would accrue to the public." He noted that since "A" Troop now came under Assistant Commissioner Macleod, he trusted "that officer may approve both of the location and the contracts entered into by you, as otherwise you will be responsible for incurring an expense for which you had no proper authority."[19]

Rather than clearing up any misunderstanding resulting from his instructions, Commissioner French attempted to absolve himself of any responsibility and left it to Inspector Jarvis to fend for himself. To ensure that he would not be implicated, he wrote to the Deputy Minister of Justice, "you will observe that that officer has on very insufficient grounds made contracts and undertaken expenditures for which he had no proper authority." He enclosed copies of his correspondence with Jarvis, saying "I regret that in writing the expression 'procure timbers for building quarters' should be capable of being twisted into authority for contracting therefore with outside individuals."[20] Despite French's protests it seems clear that his meaning could very easily have been construed as obtaining timber from outside sources without any "twisting" of his words.

As the force established itself in Fort Macleod, Fort Walsh, Fort Edmonton, Swan River Barracks and the new fort on the Bow River, a priority task was the

- A Double Duty -

development of harmonious relations with the Indians. When the force first moved west, the Mounted Police inherited the goodwill with the Indians established by the Hudson's Bay Company over many years. The American traders with their illicit liquor had subsequently damaged the Indians' impression of the white man and it was now up to the police to restore the trust and confidence of the aboriginal people. The main responsibility for establishing goodwill with the Indians fell on Macleod. At the first meeting with the chiefs, he explained that justice would be the same for Indians and whites alike. As they found this to be true, the Indians began to place more trust in the Mounted Police. In the early years Macleod was almost solely responsible for Indian policy and the admiration and understanding of the aboriginals helped him to implement peaceful relations and prepare for the treaties which were to come. He was probably the most universally admired officer to have served in the North West Mounted Police.

The Mounted Police could exercise jurisdiction over the widespread territory because of their broad powers to arrest, try and sentence offenders. Initially, they were much harder on white men who ran afoul of the law. The Indians were given a period in which to become familiar with the new laws. In contrast, to the south, the United States Army, faced with divided jurisdiction and locally elected law officers who favoured white settlers, could often do little except resort to force.

In the area of Fort Macleod the chiefs were pleased to see the improvements in clothing, lodges and horses once the liquor trade was under control. By the summer of 1875, however, they grew concerned about other changes that were taking place. The Blackfoot could no longer control entry and activities in what they regarded as their own country and were appalled at Crees and Métis entering their traditional hunting grounds with impunity. While they were prepared to accept the Mounted Police posts, they were disturbed by the Métis settlements which sprang up around them.

The chiefs called a Council and a French Canadian living with the Blackfoot, Jean L'Hereux, prepared a petition to the Lieutenant Governor of the Northwest

- Establishing Law And Order In The West -

Territories based on their discussions. The petition reminded the government that Assistant Commissioner Macleod had promised them that "the White Men will not take the Indian lands without a Council of Her Majesty's Indian Commissioner and the respective Indian chiefs."[21] The Blackfoot wanted an early meeting, not to negotiate a treaty but to stop the invasion of their hunting grounds by whites, Métis and Indians of other tribes until a treaty was negotiated.

At this time the Canadian government made two incorrect and critical assumptions. The first was that the Blackfoot wanted a treaty when they only wanted to sit down with government officials to seek some way to control the unwanted influx of Crees, Métis and settlers. The second erroneous assumption was that a single chief could be dealt with as a ruler who could exercise complete control over the Blackfoot and bind them to an agreement.

The Blackfoot were not the only tribes who had concerns. There was also hostility among the Cree, Ojibwa and Assiniboines who had been at the treaty negotiations at Fort Qu'Appelle in 1874. They objected to surveyors who had started working around Hudson's Bay Company posts in Cree territory and the Boundary Commission workers who were moving toward their tribes' hunting grounds, all without consultation. They were also indignant that the large sum paid by Canada for Rupert's Land had gone to the Hudson's Bay Company and believed, not illogically, that the money should have come to them. Due to possible problems, Inspector L.N.F. Crozier and a detachment of 12 men were stationed at the Hudson's Bay Company post at Fort Carlton. They were to distribute good-will presents to the Indians, to be given on the understanding that they refrain from interfering with surveys or construction of the telegraph line.

Following the Fort Qu'Appelle Treaty the Indians had expected that treaties would be negotiated in 1875 with the bands along the Saskatchewan, but the government delayed discussions, increasing the hostility and apprehension. Had Canada proceeded with treaty negotiations in a quick and efficient manner in 1870, after the takeover of Rupert's Land, many problems would probably have been

- A Double Duty -

prevented. In the summer of 1875, when men and machinery clearing the right of way for the telegraph line approached Fort Pitt, they were stopped by several Cree who objected to their being there without consultation. The government belatedly realized that they had to make some kind of concilliatory gesture so they asked two messengers, the Reverend George McDougall and Inspector L.N.F. Crozier to deliver presents and a message that treaty negotiations would be held in the summer of 1876.

When the Reverend McDougall visited the camp of Big Bear and the Plains Cree they told him "we want none of the Queen's presents! When we set a fox trap we scatter pieces of meat all around but when the fox gets into the trap we knock him on the head. We want no baits! Let your chiefs come like men and talk to us."[22] On completing his mission, the Reverend McDougall reported to Lieutenant Governor Morris that although the Cree, "deplored the necessity of resorting to extreme measures, yet they were unanimous in their determination to oppose the running of lines, or the making of roads through their country, until a settlement between the Government and them had been effected."[23]

When Inspector Crozier set out he found that Reverend McDougall had already distributed presents and informed the Indians of the proposed treaty. Commissioner French told him not to go out on the plains but to distribute the presents to any Indians who might be about Carlton. When the wagon loads of presents arrived, Crozier received instructions from the Indian Commissioner, W. Provencher, to distribute the presents on the plains. Faced with contradictory orders Crozier obeyed the latest, and attempted to find the tribes on the plains but this proved impossible. When he met Big Bear he asked him to bring the other tribes together to hear the message. Big Bear, quite correctly, told him that it would be impossible to do so at that time of the year, when many were out hunting.[24] For some unknown reason Crozier became deranged and was found wandering on the plains. Assistant Commissioner Macleod was informed and had him brought back to Fort Macleod where he quickly recovered and returned to full duty. Crozier then had to explain to Commissioner French why he had disobeyed his order not to go out on the plains.

- 10 -

- Problems Of Command -

Commissioner French returned from the west with a great deal of pride in the force and what it had accomplished and he was obviously wounded by criticism appearing in the press and voiced in the House of Commons. In correspondence and official reports, he tended to over-react to any perceived or actual suggestions of problems in the force.

When Commissioner French arrived in Fort Benton from the Sweet Grass Hills, he received a telegram from Ottawa instructing him to return to a new headquarters near Fort Pelly rather than Fort Ellice. He immediately sent off an intemperate response expressing "extreme regret" at the choice of location. He noted that "the half-breeds who have been there could scarcely believe that a portion of the country thickly wooded and full of lakes and marshes should have been selected as the Field of Operations for a large portion of a Mounted Force and in fact laughed outright when I asked opinions as to its suitability." His telegram did nothing but infuriate his political masters in Ottawa and he was told that "the Premier was extremely annoyed to think that Colonel French had discussed the policy of the government with Half-Breeds."[1] He was asked to extract such remarks from his official despatch.

Commissioner French had always favoured returning to Winnipeg or Fort Dufferin and had previously argued against having two troops spend the winter at Fort Ellice. He was now adamant that the new location near Fort Pelly was equally unsuitable. This predisposition against what became known as Swan River Barracks may well have influenced his decision to call the Board of Officers which concluded that the unfinished buildings could not accommodate "E" and "F" Troops and the headquarters that winter. Finding Swan River Barracks unsuitable for his men and the forage insufficient for his animals, French continued to Winnipeg with most of his men, despite having received specific instructions that he was not to winter any of his force in Manitoba. On arrival in Winnipeg, he immediately became embroiled in a disagreement with Ottawa over both the location and the inadequacy of construction of the new headquarters.

Commissioner French complained about the waste of public funds on the incomplete and inadequate buildings at Swan River Barracks. His public complaints about the expenditure did not endear him to the politicians in Ottawa. This confrontation contributed largely to his eventual downfall. There was no doubt that he had deliberately disobeyed a direct order by returning to Manitoba. French would argue there was no other logical choice while his detractors would counter that he had intended to return to Winnipeg from the start, having rented a house, moved his family there and made tentative arrangements for accommodation for the force.

Due to a change in government and public criticism of the formation and deployment of the Mounted Police, Commissioner French was already on thin ice with the Minister of Justice. This could not have been helped by the obviously biased accounts given by officers such as Young and Richer who had been summarily dismissed by the Commissioner, or by many deserters who gave their highly coloured versions of events to the press. Now, having left "E" Troop in the unfinished Swan River Barracks under Inspector Carvell, he obtained housing and stables for the remainder at Winnipeg for six months at a cost of $250 per month. This brought down even more wrath from the Department of Justice in Ottawa, which accused French of making unauthorized expenditures and ordered him to move his force to Fort Dufferin for the winter.[2] There was some difficulty complying with this order since the Boundary Commission was not prepared to hand over the necessary amount of space and as late as December, 1874 French reported to the Minister that he and his men were still in Winnipeg due to the accommodation problem.[3] Commissioner French eventually complied with the order and moved the men but for some time remained in Winnipeg himself, along with his Adjutant, Paymaster and a small staff.

A note in the personnel file of Commissioner French suggests the level of dissatisfaction of the government regarding his bringing part of the force back to Manitoba. It states that "Colonel French only advised the Government of his action in this respect on arrival of that portion of the Force with him at Winnipeg and here again he was most unfortunate in the expression of his reasons for not remaining at Swan River." French's reluctance to go to Fort Dufferin is summarized in the same documents in terms that clearly show the deterioration in his relationship with the Minister of Justice: "The Government told the Force to go to Fort Dufferin for the winter. Colonel French made objection after objection to moving the Force to this place and time ran on without his complying with orders until finally the Minister of Justice informed him that unless the whole of the Force with him had removed to Dufferin by a given time he would be compelled to recommend his removal from Canadian service. The result was immediate compliance with orders but the actions of Colonel French from the first intimation of the decision as to Head Quarters to the removal to Dufferin appeared to be in defiance of the wishes of the government."[4]

Perhaps even more telling was the additional observation that "the contrast between the Commissioner and one Division with quarters etc. found for him and the Assistant Commissioner who was left with three Divisions but without quarters in the vicinity of the Rocky Mountains was most striking, the former making trouble, the latter meeting it cheerfully."[5] French had now been labelled a troublemaker in the mind of the Minister of Justice and every move he made would be carefully scrutinized. His situation was on the way to becoming untenable and intolerable and Ottawa would find many ways to increase his discomfort.

Commissioner French's case was not helped by Hugh Sutherland, the supervisor of the construction for Swan River Barracks. He reported that French told him in Winnipeg that he had received instructions "to go back to Pelly but would not go, nor yet would he ask the men to go - he did not think they would go if he asked them." He said French had also received instructions to go to Dufferin, "but had not then quite made up his mind what he would do."[6] Prime Minister Mackenzie told the House of Commons that French "only left a portion of the force at Fort Pelly when they should have left them all there. It was not in consequence of the unfitness of the buildings that the men were not left there. They came away I think very improperly."[7] The Prime

- *A Double Duty* -

Minister wrote to Lieutenant Governor Morris that the government had trouble with French, his general management seemed bad and "our attempt to have a semi-military force must be considered unsuccessful so far."[8]

While dealing with the backlog of administrative matters that had accrued in his absence in the west, Commissioner French wielded his pen to combat those he perceived as having wronged him or the force, including, *inter alia*, the Department of Justice, the press, the Hudson's Bay Company, and "ill conducted men and those who disobey orders by entirely passing by those placed in authority over them."[9] In the next few months French dealt with many matters varying from the trivial to the serious, always in an aggressive and somewhat confrontational manner which was not likely to win friends, either for him or for the Mounted Police. In his correspondence there is an edge of bitterness and, as control of the force was slowly taken from him, he tended to place the responsibility for problems on the Department of Justice, his subordinates and those who he came to perceive as being part of an "organized conspiracy" against him and the force.

The previous August, while the force was plodding across the plains, a problem arose in the small detachment left behind at Fort Ellice. To the discomfort of the fledgling force, the ubiquitous Sub-Constable Todd, who had suffered a self-inflicted pistol wound on the beach in Collingwood the previous autumn, had a warrant of commitment issued against him for stealing beaver furs from an Indian. Mr. McDonald of the Hudson's Bay Company, who was also a Justice of the Peace, caught Todd with the furs. Todd was taken to Winnipeg where the Court of Queen's Bench tried and convicted him and sentenced him to fourteen days in prison, since he had already been in custody for a considerable time.[10] The charge of larceny by a policeman raised some interest in political circles. Both the Honourable David Laird, Minister of the Interior, and Alexander Morris, the Lieutenant Governor, believed that in a case where a policeman had been guilty of theft from an Indian it would have a bad effect upon the Indians if such an offence was overlooked.[11]

- *Problems Of Command* -

Later in the year accounts totalling $475 were received covering the costs of bringing Todd to Winnipeg for trial and bringing witnesses from Fort Ellice. This brought the matter to the attention of the Deputy Minister of Justice who then asked why no report on the incident had been sent to the Minister.[12] Commissioner French responded to the Minister complaining that the expense had been unnecessary since the charge could have been dealt with by Mr. McDonald and Sub-Inspector Shurtliff at Fort Ellice or could have waited until French was in Fort Ellice, when he could have dealt with it as a Stipendiary Magistrate.[13] The Mounted Police also entered into correspondence disputing accounts submitted by the Department of Militia and Defence for rations and other support provided to the force at Fort Garry. These accounts included the cost of socks, drawers, undershirts, mitts and moccasins issued to Sub-Constable Todd while in the military hospital.[14]

Desertion had been a problem from the time the first men arrived in Manitoba. When the force moved west, a rear party was left in Fort Dufferin, with Paymaster E. Dalrymple Clark in charge. There was a legal problem about the arrest of deserters and Clark, writing to Colonel Bernard, the Deputy Minister of Justice, noted that "at present any of the men now under my charge may desert and even if I meet them on the streets of this city, I have no power to arrest them. This is hardly I should imagine what the Department intended."[15] The *Free Press* reported that a married member of the force by the name of Stone deserted at Fort Dufferin and went to Fort Garry, apparently because his wife was ill. He was arrested by the Mounted Police and put in jail in Winnipeg. A local barrister by the name of Thibaudeau had him released on the grounds that he could not legally be incarcerated. The barrister remarked that "the difficulty seems to have originated in some of the Mounted Police authorities having considered themselves a military force which they are not."[16]

Dalrymple Clark also prepared a list of deserters, including the name Richie [sic], identified as the brother of Inspector Richer who had been summarily removed from his post one day out of Fort Dufferin on the trek west. Clark had pursued "Richie" across the international boundary to Pembina, where he was drinking in a tavern with

- A Double Duty -

some companions, but they evaded capture by running off into the bush. Clark recovered some equipment in the tavern. Had he been successful in apprehending his man, there would have been grave doubts about the validity of his doing so in the United States and, in any case, the only punishment that would have resulted was a fine. Presumably this was the sub-constable who is said to have deserted by running across the boundary enroute west and then hurled epithets at the Commissioner from his sanctuary in the United States.

In 1873-74 the powers of punishment in the Mounted Police were far less than Commissioner French had been accustomed to in the Army. Even desertion was only subject to a fine at that time. By comparison soldiers were subject to much harsher discipline. For example, on November 22, 1873 at Fort Garry, Private George Legie and Private Richard Forsyth were both found guilty of desertion and sentenced to 336 days imprisonment with hard labour and deprived of their Land Grant.[17]

North West Mounted Police Officers 1874   GAI NA-2826-1

- Problems Of Command -

Descriptions of the internal discipline of the force at this time indicate that justice was often considered to be arbitrary, autocratic and unjust, sentiments which still echoed in the Mounted Police and the military a century later. This was a reflection of the military justice system of the time, which Commissioner French attempted to institute unchanged in the Mounted Police. Considering the conditions under which the men lived and worked there were some astonishingly trivial offences recorded. The Defaulters Sheet for Swan River Barracks in January, 1876 shows that three Sub-Constables - McLeod, Brooks and Sullivan, were charged and admonished "for using profane language in the barrack room."[18]

The lack of legal authority to impose military law on members of the force was a source of considerable frustration to their leaders. In the early days of the force, fines were the only legal punishment for members and they were levied in very large numbers, often for seemingly trivial offences, but "unofficial" and corporal punishments were common. The men had a belief that, once charged, an alleged offender would automatically be found guilty when they appeared before the Commissioner or another officer on summary trial. Sub-Constable Carscadden, who probably had first hand knowledge of the system, offered advice to the new recruit: "Foolish young fellow - make your mind up, for guilty or not you will be no more exempt than the worst character in the Force. Then when you are brought up, you will be fined; whether guilty or not, for the very fact of your appearance before our noble Commissioner as a prisoner constitutes a crime and you will suffer accordingly."[19]

At Swan River Barracks, Sub-Constable Carscadden complained that there were no rules or regulations for guidance on how to act and behave. He said, "our laws and lawgiver are all included in the one word; French. The Commissioner say so and so that is law. We do something or anything not consistent with the Commissioner's ideas of right and we are brought up to the Orderly Room and fined."[20] Venting his opposition to the system of fines, he asks "was it intended by the Minister of Justice (I say him because he is our head and to him alone can we look for Justice) that men would be harassed with fines continually from $5 to a month's pay even for the most

- A Double Duty -

trivial circumstances and often were men fined without the shadow of a charge being substantiated against them."[21]

This problem of powers of arrest and punishment was of concern to Commissioner French who complained that his powers of punishment only allowed fines. He cited the case of Sub-Constable Mooney, who had said he would do no more work and defied authority and could not be punished other than by a fine. The Commissioner noted that when he imposed a fine the other men frequently took up a subscription to pay it so that there was no real punishment to the offender.[22] He considered that "fining does well enough for trivial offences and neglect of duty, but for serious offences against discipline, such as desertion (of which the civil law does not ordinarily take cognizance) the system of fining must I think be little better than useless."[23]

Members writing directly to politicians or the press annoyed Commissioner French, who considered it a serious breach of discipline. Reacting to a letter sent to the Department of Justice by Sub-Constable Ste. Marie, he responded, "I beg to point out that if the members of this Force are encouraged to communicate with the Department directly thereby ignoring all those supposed to be placed in authority over them it will be very difficult to maintain anything like proper discipline in the Force." When asked by the Department of Justice to respond to a letter that had appeared in the press he observed that "the habit of writing to newspapers (often about trivial matters) is most objectionable . . . and entirely contrary to regulations. I very much fear, however, that if the Department will take notice of such communications this will increase instead of decrease."[24]

As 1875 came in, Commissioner French, who continued to be in difficulty with Ottawa, was separated from a large part of his command and had tenuous communication with them. Increasingly, the part of the force at Fort Macleod was receiving direction directly from Ottawa and he found that he was often unaware of what was going on in the force. Control of the Mounted Police was being taken out of his hands.

- *Problems Of Command* -

Still annoyed at the presence of the Mounted Police in Manitoba, the Minister of Justice demanded that Commissioner French explain why he had disobeyed the order that the portion of the force that returned with him should be stationed at Fort Pelly.[25] The accusation of disobedience of an order was very serious to a professional soldier, especially someone with the pride of French. After maintaining a silence for some time he responded to these accusations saying "while an officer in H.M. Regular Service, I have allowed myself to remain for these months under the stigma of having wilfully disobeyed orders. I had hoped that as the Department became fully alive to the state of affairs at Swan River, by the receipt of full reports thereon, my actions would have been endorsed." Showing some of the bitterness he must have felt at the treatment he had received, he added that "I regret very much the attitude which the Department has apparently taken towards me. I have slaved night, noon and morning in the public interest, and I feel that I have deserved a little more consideration than I have as yet experienced."[26]

For some unknown reason the Hudson's Bay Company also displeased Commissioner French and relations between the two dominant organizations in the west were not good. The animosity may have started with the use of Lower Fort Garry by the first contingent in 1873. An opinion was expressed that, "although the company was delighted to see that the NWMP was actually on the march west, that body's behaviour when it rented Lower Fort Garry during the winter of 1873-74 and the government's dilatoriness in paying the rent and other accounts had dampened various Hudson's Bay Company officers' ardor for the new body. Nevertheless, orders were sent out that everyone was to help these military strangers in every possible way - but to make sure that the company was reimbursed for every expense incurred."[27] French also warned Superintendent Jarvis in Fort Edmonton, to "bear in mind that you are to incur no expense at the H.B. Cos post at Edmonton that can possibly be avoided and where bills are inevitably incurred to mark off next to every item the reason for its being required."[28]

- A Double Duty -

In January 1875 Commissioner French wrote to Hewitt Bernard complaining that Hudson's Bay Company officials had, for the most part, shown "the greatest possible hostility to this Force, since they have found it being organized perfectly independent of them." He had a disagreement over a high bill for hay provided by the Hudson's Bay Company so he went over the heads of the local officials and referred it to the Chief Commissioner of the Hudson's Bay Company who, French reported, "was so ashamed of the charge that he offered to withdraw it altogether."[29] This would not have endeared him to local officials of the company. He may also have believed the Hudson's Bay Company was consistently overcharging the Mounted Police, which would explain his instruction to Inspector Jarvis to purchase as little as possible from them at Fort Edmonton.

Commissioner French told the Minister of Justice that "the mischievous and alarming reports offered concerning the Force last summer were circulated mainly by Hudson's Bay Company officers and notably by Mr. McDonald at Fort Ellice and Mr. Clarke at Carlton." French was particularly incensed at reported statements that a Hudson's Bay Company official had boasted that the Mounted Police could not get across the west without the help of the Hudson's Bay Company. Such a boast, whether true or not, did not appear to justify the indignant reaction in Commissioner French's letters and, in the case of "A" Troop enroute to Fort Edmonton, seemed to hold some truth. In a surprising statement French described Mr. McDonald as "the gentleman who arrested one of our men, who being intoxicated from the effects of liquor procured in the H.B. Co's premises at Fort Ellice, took from an Indian some furs of a trifling value."[30] This seems to indicate a belief that the arrest and conviction of Sub-Constable John Todd on a charge of larceny was, in some way, motivated by jealousy and was the fault of the Hudson's Bay Company rather than Todd.

Although his Annual Report for 1874 credited Captain D.R. Cameron, R.A., Commissioner of Her Majesty's North American Boundary Commission, with having provided valuable assistance, there is considerable evidence that this relationship was not entirely amicable. Commissioner French complained that the Boundary

- Problems Of Command -

Commission had failed to provide the agreed upon quantity of oats at White Mud River, causing severe inconvenience and, he believed, "loss in horse flesh to the Force under his command."[31] French also complained to Captain Cameron that the amount charged for the oats was greater than the cost which, he said, was not a normal practice between government agencies.[32]

Controversy with the Boundary Commission continued as Thomas Nixon, the Agent for the Department of Justice in Winnipeg, attempted to negotiate the purchase of the Boundary Commission buildings at Fort Dufferin. Captain Cameron said that the buildings were now worth much more than when they were built and the matter had to be adjudicated by a third party.[33] The frustration of Mr. Nixon was evident when he wrote to Colonel Bernard that he had not replied to a letter from the newly promoted Cameron "as from what I already know of the Major it will only end in a long and useless correspondence."[34]

Some matters that Commissioner French had to deal with, appear in retrospect, to have been trivial. The original Orders-in-Council appointing the commissioned officers of the Mounted Police had given them honourary military ranks and, in addition, many of them already held military ranks, although these were not necessarily the equivalent of their police ranks. In October 1874 Hewitt Bernard wrote to Thomas Nixon directing him to remember that there were no "Majors," "Captains" or any other military titles authorized by law in the Mounted Police and that "any assumption of a military title is objectionable and it is unauthorized."[35] On his return from the west Commissioner French took issue with this, noting that "there are officers in the Force under my command, well known not only in society but to many of the men of the Force, by their Militia rank, and it is quite impossible to exercise control over the style by which private persons may choose to address their friends, or even over that which men of the Force may use in ordinary conversation."[36] The Department of Justice apparently had second thoughts and Major Walsh and Colonel Jarvis, among others, continued to be referred to by military rank as, presumably, did Colonel Bernard.

- A Double Duty -

Commissioner French attempted to exercise command of his widely dispersed men. He wrote to Assistant Commissioner Macleod and Inspector Jarvis demanding details of matters in their reports. In a report in January 1875 he described Macleod as "a most valuable officer" who "has demonstrated his fitness in a manner that must be highly satisfactory to the Department." He described Jarvis as "a good duty officer who gets on well with his men though lax in reports and returns."[37]

The men sent to Fort Dufferin for the winter took over quantities of supplies, equipment and transport, including 40 teams of horses and a yoke of oxen, from the Boundary Commission, which had finished its work. In March 1875, when the men had to cut their own hay fifteen miles out on the prairie in bitterly cold weather, a petition was drawn up and presented to Sub-Inspector Walker asking that they not have to bring in their own hay. Two days later, on parade, Sub-Inspector Walker told them the petition was mutiny and tore it up in front of them.[38]

The Reverend John McDougall expressed concern that relations between the police and Indians were too close and this provoked an angry reaction from Commissioner French, who said, "I am of the opinion that it is preferable for this Force to act as friends of the Indians than to imitate the American soldiers and think they should be avoided as deadly enemies." He had instructed that all ranks should cultivate the most friendly relations with the Indians and "to let them understand that our mission is to fight *for them* instead of *against them*." He agreed, however, that "from a missionary point of view I can readily see how objectionable free intercourse between our men and the Indians would appear."

Dealing at the same time with complaints of "laxity of discipline at every post" in the west, French pointed out that for all practical purposes this portion of the force had been taken out of his hands. He said that if it was true, as alleged by the Reverend McDougall, that there was a "general impression" that the force in the west was "demoralized" there should be "an inquiry into how it became so, and the taking of immediate steps to remedy such an unfortunate state of affairs."[39]

- Problems Of Command -

Commissioner French considered conditions at Swan River Barracks and Fort Dufferin to be so bad that he informed the Minister of Justice that, "I beg in conclusion to place on record my opinion that under the circumstances at present existing at Swan River and Dufferin it would not be fair to hold the officers wholly responsible at these posts for either the drill or discipline of the men there."[40] He did not elaborate on his reasons for reaching this pessimistic conclusion but, given that he was still in command of the members in both locations, he should have been taking action to correct the "circumstances" rather than absolving the officers of their responsibilities.

With a rearrangement of the reporting structure for the force, "A" Division at Fort Saskatchewan was placed under the Assistant Commissioner at Fort Macleod. Commissioner French now found himself more frequently bypassed and not kept informed of what was going on. Ottawa seemed determined to make life difficult and frequently struck at his most vulnerable point, his pride, which must have often left him feeling humiliated. He received a reprimand from the Minister of Justice for authorizing gratuities from the Fine Fund, a common and authorized practice in the military at that time and something he had done routinely as Commandant of the School of Artillery. Unfortunately, the Police Act did not authorize the Commissioner to make such payments and he submitted an apology to the Minister of Justice. In writing to the Minister, he pointed out that the Minister's letter appeared to have been drafted by Constable Fortescue, a member of the Mounted Police who was working in Ottawa at the time. He requested that in future, confidential letters finding fault with his actions should, if possible, "be written by a clerk of the Department of Justice rather than by a subordinate member of the Corps in which I am supposed to maintain discipline."[41]

By now Commissioner French could feel control of the force slipping from his grasp. When the Minister of Justice instructed Assistant Commissioner Macleod to send telegrams in duplicate, one to the Commissioner and one to Ottawa, he ordered Macleod to "keep me at all times fully informed on the state of your Force and of any information likely to be useful and a copy of your official Journal, monthly if possible."[42] Obviously annoyed, French wrote to Macleod reprimanding him because

- A Double Duty -

he did not keep him "at all times fully informed on the state of the Force. Learned of the death of men frozen last year from the press. Learned of the desertions from a Sub-Constable."[43] He followed this up with a sharp letter about the desertions, saying, "it appears unaccountable to me that men who's main grievance (as you believe) was want of pay, should desert and leave nine month's pay behind. The pursuit of these deserters has apparently been carried out in a very half hearted manner."[44]

What Commissioner French does not deal with is why the men had not been paid. The problem was not new. The Army had, for many years, used a pay allotment system to make payments to wives and families of absent members. The Department of Justice had not implemented such a system despite the urging of Commissioner French.[45] He was in command, and the paymaster was a member of his headquarters staff, so the responsibility for ensuring that the men were paid was clearly his. He should also have arranged to have necessary supplies, such as replacement uniforms, sent to Fort Macleod. In a letter to the Minister of Justice he said that when instruction was given for Assistant Commissioner Macleod to send telegrams in duplicate he "refrained from sending instructions, except matters of mere detail, because he feared they would clash with instructions sent by the Minister of Justice."[46] This appears to have been an abdication of his responsibility as a leader.

- 11 -

Swan River Barracks

While "D" Troop and part of "E" Troop wintered uncomfortably at Fort Dufferin, the larger part of "E" Troop spent the winter of 1874-75 at Swan River Barracks under appalling conditions, attempting to survive in the partially completed buildings. Swan River Barracks had been built in great haste because the work crew did not arrive on site until September 10, 1874 and Mr. Hugh Sutherland, who was in charge, reported that he was "very much afraid of the weather setting in wet and cold before we get any of the buildings enclosed as I am informed that last year snow fell about the 20th of September."[1] This late start, coupled with Commissioner French and his force returning from the west earlier than expected, meant that the barracks were not sufficiently completed to accommodate all the men, although a large part of "E" Troop was left to winter there.

When "E" Troop first arrived there was a priority on gathering as much hay as possible for the winter and building stables for the horses. Since most of the upland hay had been burned in prairie fires, the men cut as much grass as possible in nearby swamps, some covered by snow. Sub-Constable Carscadden said this haying was not so hard when there was dry land to stand on, "but when we had to stand in water over our ankels [sic] with pieces of boots on our feet, then our suffering really begun. The weather was freezing cold but not cold enough to make ice in one night able to bear us so here we are breaking thro' the ice and splashing thro' the water making hay for our horses."[2] The winter was very severe. Snow entered the buildings through gaps in the walls and roofs, making life miserable for the men. During the winter nearly all their horses and cattle died due to the stress of the previous summer and the lack of feed.[3]

These conditions were not conducive to what is known as "good order and military discipline" and problems began to manifest themselves very soon after the men's arrival. As Fred Bagley described it; "to add a little variety to an otherwise drab existence the boys managed to stage a couple of mutinies, either one of which might

139

- A Double Duty -

have had serious consequences but for the firmness and tact of Sergt-Major (now Colonel) J.B. Mitchell." On November 23, 1874 the men had worked all day stocktaking and after supper, when Inspector Carvell ordered them to continue the work that night, the men refused. Inspector Carvell consulted Sergeant Major Mitchell, then told the men that he did not intend to order that they work all night, but that if they did so, he would issue extra rations and give them a holiday the next day. This was satisfactory and the men continued to work and, after midnight, received a supper of rice, bread and tea.[4]

Disciplinary problems arose again in February 1875. Three Indians brought in a woman for medical treatment. When they asked for something to eat, Sub-Inspector Shurtliff decided to send them to the barracks for supper and to replace the rations the following day. He sent Sub-Constable Banbury to warn Sub-Constable McCarthy, the cook. Banbury returned to say that McCarthy refused, so Shurtliff asked Sergeant Major Mitchell to see if it was possible to feed them. When McCarthy objected, Mitchell told him to give them bread, tea and syrup, which he did. The next morning Shurtliff ordered McCarthy arrested for not obeying the order to provide a meal.

Inspector Carvell investigated the incident, found all charges fully sustained, and fined McCarthy $10.00 for the offence. On being awarded this punishment McCarthy became so "extremely rude and insolent" that Carvell ordered him placed under close arrest in the guard tent.[5] Fred Bagley, who was present, says that a group of McCarthy's comrades released him and were subsequently placed under arrest themselves by Inspector Carvell. They were all found guilty of insubordination and the noncommissioned officers involved were reduced to the ranks and all of the participants were fined 30 days pay. To add insult to injury, Bagley says that Carvell ordered the release, without punishment, of McCarthy.[6]

Eventually, when spring came to Swan River Barracks there was no food remaining, other than bread and what the men called Rattlesnake pork. The name came from its nauseating appearance, with streaks of yellow, red and green among the fat. The alternative was "wet and dry" or tea and toast only. Rattlesnake pork was their

- Swan River Barracks -

staple diet until June when the remaining stock was ruled unfit for human consumption by a Board of Enquiry.[7]

With the coming of spring, the extensive dens of garter snakes on which Swan River Barracks had been built came to life. There were snakes everywhere, indoors and out, even in the beds. At the celebration of Queen Victoria's Birthday on May 24, 1875, one event was a contest to see how many snakes a team of men could kill in half an hour. Two teams of seven men killed a total of 1,110 snakes.[8]

On May 20, 1875 most of "D" Troop left Fort Dufferin for Swan River Barracks. The column camped at Winnipeg where there was a considerable delay loading baggage and provisions since several women and children were to accompany them. They also took on many new recruits, largely enlisted from time expired soldiers of the Fort Garry garrison. The column finally got away from Winnipeg on June 16, having waited for the trails to dry following heavy rains.

On leaving Winnipeg, an event took place which was to cause much adverse publicity for the Mounted Police when reported in the press. On the trail Sub-Constable Daley, who was riding in a wagon, started to cause trouble. Sub-Inspector Walker ordered that his wrists be tied together and strapped to the stirrup of a rider. Daley first pretended that he could not walk. Then, as soon as he had a chance, he ran away into the woods. When he was apprehended and tied to the stirrup once more, he struck the horse several times until it threw its rider. When the horse ran away Daley was injured, breaking his collar bone.[9]

The incident was reported in the *Free Press* and some time later a letter to the editor of the same paper, entitled "The Mounted Police Outrage", signed by "A Sufferer From Swan River" thanked the *Free Press* "for public mention of the outrage perpetrated by Captain John French on a man named Daley." Obviously not a supporter of the Commissioner or his brother, the writer concluded that "if it was not for the public press, we might very likely be worse treated than we are, not by men who have served Canada and know the people, but by blusterers like this Captain French. I think

- A Double Duty -

if the present government had been in power when Colonel French got command of this body, we should have been spared two tyrants."[10]

When this first appeared in the press it seemed the Department of Justice was completely unaware of the incident and Commissioner French had to provide an explanation several months after the event. This gave the appearance that there had been an attempt to cover up the occurence. French acknowledged that the incident had take place and explained that he had not reported it since he "considered it trivial and Daley did not complain."[11] He did not hold an investigation and Daley was not punished for his misconduct.

While this type of unofficial punishment was common in the military at the time, Commissioner French's description of the incident contains some questionable statements. He says that this was the only method that could be used in the absence of wheeled transport. In this case, they obviously had wheeled transport since Daley had been taken out of a wagon and one would think that he could have been tied up, handcuffed or otherwise restrained and simply tossed back into the wagon from whence he came. He also says that Daley was injured "in the slight manner shown in Dr. Kittson's statement." Dr. Kittson had to set a broken collar bone and in a later report recommended that, "although the strapping of a refractory man's wrists to the Stirrup of a Rider is authorized by military practice and precedence, I would respectfully suggest that as far as it concerns the Mounted Police Force such practice should not be allowed."[12] Given Ottawa's obvious annoyance with Commissioner French over several matters, particularly his attitude on Swan River Barracks and the unauthorized return of part of the force to Manitoba, it was unwise of him to have given the Minister of Justice further cause for displeasure by neglecting to properly investigate and report this incident. The fact that his brother was one of the officers involved compounded the error.

Enroute to Swan River Barracks, Commissioner French established a post at Shoal Lake, with mail carrying posts at Palestine, now Gladstone, Manitoba, Tanner's Crossing, now Minnedosa, Manitoba, Shoal Lake and Shell River. These posts were

- Swan River Barracks -

also to watch for liquor traffic. The Commissioner transfered the detachment at Fort Ellice to Shoal Lake where there was a significant amount of cart traffic.

Commissioner French and the train reached Swan River Barracks on July 7 and he was still not favourably impressed by the barracks. The men of "E" Troop had experienced a long, miserable winter, many had been ill and large numbers of cattle and horses had died. The men had only remnants of uniform but, despite this, they held a general parade on the arrival of Commissioner French. "Uniform consisted largely of deer skin jackets and trousers, all profusely befringed, large fox fur caps with the tails hanging down the backs of the men wearing them, with here and there throughout the ranks a remnant of a scarlet tunic showing. Colonel French rides to the parade ground and accosts one who appears to be the chief bandit, and indicating the "E" Troop ragamuffins, enquires: 'What is this Captain Carvell?' and is answered with 'My Troop, Sir, paraded for inspection by you as per orders.' One fierce look, and a hasty 'Good God' from the Colonel, and then, whirling about and spurring his thoroughbred mare, he is off like a shot. The parade is immediately dismissed."[13]

Commissioner French had a great deal of work ahead of him to bring Swan River Barracks up to an acceptable standard and the terrain on which it was built made this formidable task even more difficult. Sam Steele recalled that "before enough space could be cleared to enable the men to form properly on parade we had to build large fires over the rocks and adopt the primitive method of causing them to split when heated by pouring water on them."[14]

Before the newly arrived Commissioner French had time to settle in and tackle the problems at Swan River Barracks, he had to cope with an inspection visit by Major General E. Selby-Smyth, the Commanding General of the Canadian Militia. There had been a considerable amount of negative comment in the press about the management of the Mounted Police and the opposition in Parliament, under Sir John A. Macdonald, added to the criticism. *The Mail* in Toronto had described the organization of the force as defective and stated ". . . there was an indifference in detail, and a laxity of management that was apparent to an experienced eye even before the Force left

- A Double Duty -

Toronto." Most of the officers were described as "completely ignorant of their duties."[15] It was alleged that the trek west had been a failure and suggested that the Mounted Police should be merged into the Militia. To stem this criticism, Prime Minister Mackenzie asked Major General Selby-Smyth to go west to inspect police forts and report on the organization, equipment, distribution and general efficiency of the force. The General arrived at Winnipeg and set off with an escort from Shoal Lake under Sub-Inspector Walker.

General Selby-Smyth arrived at Swan River Barracks with news of a disturbance. While the general and his party were enroute from Winnipeg, events which had occured to the north-west were being blown up into a crisis. Métis communities traditionally elected leaders for the annual buffalo hunt in which the whole settlement participated as a group. The buffalo hunt was highly organized, with a strict but informal system of discipline. In December 1873 Gabriel Dumont had called together the people of St. Laurent on the South Saskatchewan River to discuss forming a local governing body which would, among other matters, regulate the hunt. Dumont was elected President of a Council, with eight councillors, which formally passed some of their traditional rules into the "Laws of St. Laurent." One of the main points in the section governing the buffalo hunt was a provision that no hunter could leave before the time authorized for departure. This provision was included to prevent small parties scaring away the buffalo herds before the main party arrived, thus denying the whole community its main source of food on which their lives depended. Provision was made for fines or other punishments for breaches of these rules.[16]

In the early summer of 1875 some Métis, led by a Hudson's Bay Company employee, Peter Ballendine, left surreptitiously for the hunt ahead of the main party. They were stopped by Dumont and his followers who levied a fine. When Ballendine refused to accept the validity of the rules and would not pay the fine, payment was exacted by confiscating an appropriate amount of equipment. Ballendine then went to the Hudson's Bay Company post at Fort Carlton and reported the matter to his employer, Chief Factor Lawrence Clarke, who was also a Justice of the Peace. Clarke,

- *Swan River Barracks* -

who was apparently well aware of the organization and rules of the hunt, wrote an alarmist letter to Lieutenant Governor Morris reporting that the Métis "assumed to themselves the right to enact laws, rules and regulations for the government of the colony and surrounding country, of a most tyrannical nature." He asked that a protective force be stationed at or near Carlton.[17]

By the time Clarke's letter arrived in Winnipeg, Major General Selby-Smyth was on his way to Swan River Barracks. Lieutenant Governor Morris sent Lieutenant Cotton, an artillery officer in the Fort Garry garrison, to take a message to Selby-Smyth advising him of the situation. Cotton, who later became an officer in the North West Mounted Police, delivered the message to the general on the trail before his arrival at Swan River Barracks. In his letter, Morris said that he hoped the Métis "had only designs to form a prairie hunt organization" but he was still concerned.

Arriving at Swan River Barracks, Major General Selby-Smyth showed Commissioner French the letter he had received on the trail earlier that morning, warning him of a possible insusrrection at St Laurent. French and an escort of 50 men left Swan River Barracks with the general's party and reached Fort Carlton eight days later. French found that the trouble had been greatly exaggerated and reported to the Minister of Justice that "as I expected, there is no reason for alarm with reference to the affair of Gabriel Dumont."[18] A small detachment of the Mounted Police under Inspector Lief Crozier was left at Fort Carlton as a precaution. Later, in his final report, French implicated both Lawrence Clarke and James Grahame of the Hudson's Bay Company as having provided Ballendine with goods and secretly sending him out ahead of the main body of hunters from the community. French enclosed a report from Constable Le Veiller at Shoal Lake which stated that the trouble did not amount to anything and was caused by the actions of the Hudson's Bay Company.[19] Clarke was certainly already known to Commissioner French, who had earlier complained about his spreading untrue rumours concerning the Mounted Police.

The government in Ottawa was not pleased with the false alarm at Fort Carlton and a memorandum by the Minister of Justice said that "there does not appear to have

145

- A Double Duty -

been the slightest foundation for the alarm expressed by Mr. Clarke JP, confirmed by Mr. Grahame, or the least justification for the pressing communication which resulted in the hurried expedition to Carlton." Ottawa asked the Lieutenant Governor to call upon Mr. Clarke, "for any explanation he may have to offer of his conduct."[20] Clarke, however, achieved at least one of his objectives by causing a Mounted Police detachment to be stationed at Fort Carlton. Later, the Earl of Carnarvon, writing to the Governor General, the Earl of Dufferin, put the matter neatly into perspective, "I have read W. Blake's full and able report with much interest and trust it may lead to provision being made at an early date for the administration of justice in this part of the Dominion under a legitimate system of law and government in the absence of which it would be difficult to take strong exception to the acts of a community which appears to have honestly endeavoured to maintain order by the best means in its power."[21]

In addition to his official inspection, the visit of Selby-Smyth to Swan River Barracks provided a fringe benefit to members of "D" and "E" Troops. As in other posts, the prohibition on taking liquor into the Northwest Territories was not popular with many members of the force who had been required to spend a long, cold and dry winter at Swan River Barracks. When the General and his party arrived, an enterprising man by the name of Doudoin, correctly surmising that they would not travel without "refreshments", searched their wagons. He found a keg which he took to the barracks and the two troops started a memorable party.[22]

Commissioner French returned to Swan River Barracks and Major General Selby-Smyth continued his trip to the west with a police escort. Assistant Commissioner Macleod and his men were at Tail Creek Crossing, all polished up and ready to meet the General, when they were told that he would cross at a point 90 miles away without trails to get them there. By a tremendous effort, the Mounted Police escort arrived, tattered and torn, and after a short parade, both parties moved south. They met Crowfoot and a large band near the Bow River. The Indians travelled along with them and joined them in camp that evening. At a Council around the campfire Crowfoot praised the Mounted Police to the general then questioned Selby-Smyth about treaties. The general promised to pass Crowfoot's views and questions on to Ottawa. Following this Major General Selby-Smyth went on to Fort Macleod and left via the United States.

In the report on his trip Major General Selby-Smyth was very positive about the police and about Commissioner French. He refuted any suggestion that French had shown a lack of foresight in the provision and transportation of oats on the march west. He was very generous in this regard and, lacking any documentary evidence, one can only speculate on how sympathetic he would have been to a brother Anglo-Irish officer of the British Army, seconded to a colonial force and under fire from politicians. Selby-Smyth recommended that the force establish a training depot which, in addition to drill and discipline, should provide instruction in the law and legal procedures since he was "inclined to the belief that at present there are not twenty men in the Force who would know how to execute a warrant or subpoena."[23]

When Commissioner French said farewell to Major General Selby-Smyth at Fort Carlton, he returned to the partially completed Swan River Barracks. He believed there was only a remote possibility of the Board of Works completing the outstanding work, so he put all the available men to work building a fence on two sides of the barracks.[24] Another interruption occurred almost immediately when Commissioner French received a despatch from Lieutenant Governor Morris directing that he send as strong a force as possible to Fort Qu'Appelle, via Fort Ellice, which doubled the distance. The police were to provide an escort for the Commissioners for Treaty 4 (The Qu'Appelle Treaty) who were going to Fort Ellice and Fort Qu'Appelle to sign on additional Indians who had not been present at the 1874 negotiations. Sub-Inspector McIllree went via Shell River, Shoal Lake and Fort Ellice to pick up every available man. Sub-Inspector Frechette left the portion of the force returning from Carlton at the Touchwood Hills and took as many men and horses as possible directly to Fort Qu'Appelle.

The government had heard there was to be a very large gathering of Indians and Lieutenant Governor Morris had been informed that some of them "were disposed to be turbulent."[25] W.J. Christie, who was to proceed to Fort Qu'Appelle to pay the

- A Double Duty -

Indians, noted that he was "afraid we shall have some trouble there, as those who were not present last year, think that the Treaty is only now to be made by them. I am to have a guard of Mounted Police of about 25 men with an officer, but I am afraid that will be too small a force and I intend to apply for more, say 50 men, but I am afraid they will not have that number to spare as there are a number off to Carlton with Colonel French and General Smyth."[26] The concerns proved to be unfounded and, as a result, there were eventually two officers, 34 men and 41 horses assembled at Fort Qu'Appelle while Swan River Barracks was left with no men or horses to do anything.

These long, often unnecessary, marches were hard on men and horses. Commissioner French expressed his concern about the condition of horses involved in long marches, stating that, "this failure of horses for want of oats is, *and must be a necessary consequence as long as this Force is left unprovided with means of transport for supplies.*" He noted that "of 27 horses that have died since August 1, 1875, debility and injury to the system produced by want of feed may be considered to be proximate cause of 17 deaths."[27]

Most of the men were soon able to return to Swan River Barracks and were quickly caught up labouring to correct its many deficiencies. The hospital was incomplete, without toilet or cooking facilities or a washroom. The contractor had not completed shops for the blacksmiths, carpenters or saddlers, and no latrines had been provided. The officers' married quarters were not finished and there was no guard room. The buildings needed plastering to make them habitable in the cold weather so during September, October and November every available man and horse worked at sawing lath and drawing sand for plastering. While plastering was being done, the men lived in tents which were decidedly uncomfortable as winter approached. They were also felling and hauling timber, threshing and gathering hay.

Commissioner French sent a litany of complaints about the barracks to Ottawa, citing the adverse conditions under which his men had to live. The Department of Public Works reacted to the complaints with disdain and contempt for men who had done so much. Thomas Scott, the architect in charge, responded to a complaint of unplaned floors and no officers' married quarters by suggesting that the planing of unplaned floors would be "a good punishment for soldiers" and excused the lack of officers' married quarters with the comment that, "married officers are not supposed to exist on a frontier."[28]

Whether Mr. Scott approved or not, there were married officers in the Northwest Territories and the daughter of Paymaster Griffiths, who was a child in 1875, has left a description of the trip from Winnipeg to Swan River Barracks and the condition of the barracks. During the trip from Winnipeg she recalled, "part of our baggage was a safe containing the pay of the troops for a considerable time to come and this cumbersome piece of impedimenta was a source of considerable trouble to us as over the rough trails it had a habit now and then of lurching roadwards and time and again it would have to be recovered."[29] After all the problems on the trail, the key to the paymaster's safe got lost and it had to be broken open. Paymaster Griffiths then kept the money in a large valise and when Commissioner French questioned how secure this arrangement was, Griffiths assured him that he always kept the valise under his head at night.[30]

Young Beatrice Griffiths was obviously not impressed with the barracks observing that "at Swan River Barracks we found a desolate outlook as while the barracks had been built close to the junction of Snake Creek with the Saskatchewan River, the river could not be seen. We could say we had a roof over our heads but the buildings were all in the rough and quite unfinished. A rough wood fence enclosed the buildings with a little guard house at one end and the stables at the other."[31] To bring some degree of civilization a minister was sent to Swan River Barracks but he did not adapt well and was not popular with the police. After about three months he became discouraged and departed.[32]

Liquor was a perpetual problem for the Commissioner, both in his role of enforcement of the liquor laws and the prevention of misuse by members of the force. Spirits could only be legally brought into the Northwest Territories with a permit from the Lieutenant Governor. Many of the officers had permits but they were not numbered and there was no record as to who had them. The Commissioner ordered all members to file their permits in the Orderly Room in an attempt to exercise some control. When he found Sub-Inspector Dickens receiving brandy in the mail without a permit he immediately had the bottle smashed. When the Surgeon gave a sub-constable what he described as a "small amount" of liquor and the man became unfit for duty, Commissioner French reported that, while the motive was generosity, he considered the Surgeon's conduct "reprehensible."[33] While deploring the illegal importation of spirits, French indignantly reported that some of the officers with permits who ordered brandy received "rot gut". They suspected that it had been watered down enroute by the wagon master.[34]

While building was a priority at Swan River Barracks, the post at Shoal Lake had also been busy. Conditions were far from comfortable at Shoal Lake where a member, writing home, said, "I am endeavouring to write to you at last under considerable difficulties, such as a young hailstorm of mosquitoes, black flies and another interesting insect - about the size of a tame bee . . . termed a bull dog from their playful habit of never losing their hold till the piece comes out - add to this a shower of black prairie dust that covers everything, penetrating everywhere and blackens everybody."[35] Between July 1 and September 9, 1875, the men at Shoal Lake searched over 1,000 carts but found liquor in only one.[36] William Parker relates that a sergeant used a fencing foil as a probe to expedite the searching of carts. Once, when searching a train of over 50 carts, he used the foil several times without finding any liquor. About two months later, the Hudson's Bay Company complained that a dozen felt hats had been pierced by a foil and ruined.[37] Lieutenant Governor Morris wrote to Commissioner French saying that he was "creditably informed that your men at Shoal Lake are searching for liquor by passing a sharp instrument through bags of flour and packages of dry goods. If this practice be really adopted it will lead to great irritation and some other mode of search can easily be resorted to."[38]

While attempting to get the buildings finished at Swan River Barracks, Commissioner French continued to frequently feel marginalized and left out of decisions affecting the force. The Department of Justice made decisions and took actions without consulting him and his requests often went unheeded. He had to ask the Minister of Justice to obtain from the Imperial Government copies of the surveys and reconnaissances in the vicinity of the Boundary Line prepared by the Boundary Commission. He reported that "Major Cameron, the Commissioner, frequently promised to supply one with copies of these surveys but I have not as yet received any."[39] French also complained to the Deputy Minister of Justice that he had sent instructions to Assistant Commissioner Macleod in July, 1875 to send him some buffalo robes, "but like too many orders sent to this same direction this was neither obeyed or acknowledged."[40]

Inspector Carvell, the old cavalry veteran, went off on leave never to return. He sent in his resignation from Boulder, Colorado. Commissioner French informed Hewitt Bernard of the fact and recommended the promotion of Sub-Inspector Walker to Inspector and commissioning Staff Sergeant Frank Norman in his place.[41] Bernard then sought the opinion of Assistant Commissioner Macleod who replied recommending the promotion of Sub-Inspector Jackson and the commissioning of Sergeant Antrobus.[42] When French saw the recommendation from Macleod he immediately wrote to Bernard saying, "I beg to express my surprise at one of my subordinates having been also called upon to nominate persons for promotion in the Corps which I am supposed to command, and will await with some impatience to see whether the recommendation of the Commanding Officer or the recommendation of a subordinate (who was virtually removed from the Force previous to the date of your letter) are acted upon."[43] The remark "virtually removed" is an indication of the change in French's attitude toward the Assistant Commissioner, described a year previously as "a most valuable officer" who "since left at Fort Macleod . . . has demonstrated his fitness in a manner that must be highly satisfactory to the Department."[44] The only response he got from his indignant letter was a communication from the Minister of Justice telling him that he had reason to believe that French had told Sub-Inspector Walker that he had been recommended for promotion. He instructed French not to do so again.[45]

- A Double Duty -

Commissioner French was apparently neither consulted nor informed of the appointment of James Macleod as a Stipendiary Magistrate and his departure from the post of Assistant Commissioner of the Mounted Police. He wrote to the Minister of Justice that he had read of the appointment in the 'Globe' of November 26, 1875, which quoted a telegram from Ottawa that said, "Colonel Macleod, at present commanding the Mounted Police at Belly River is to be appointed Stipendiary Magistrate for the North West and Major A.G. Irvine will succeed him in his command." French said "having received no official communication on the subject I would respectfully beg to be informed if any such alterations or promotions had taken place in the Force under my command."[46] This treatment of French was inexcusable. If the government wanted to relieve him of his command that was their option but to leave him in the appointment and make it impossible for him to properly execute his responsibilities was totally unfair. The Department of Justice had given up all pretence of dealing with French as head of the force and his position was becoming increasingly untenable, but he continued his attempts to try to exercise some control over his force following the appointment of A.G. Irvine as Assistant Commissioner.

On confirmation of Irvine's appointment, French wrote instructing him to "look up all General Orders and letters received, you will find a number of these have been unattended to, and see and attend to them at once, particularly in setting right the number of horses which were duplicated last Spring in a manner, which it is difficult to account for, unless done in the absence of the Assistant Commissioner. I have no returns of "A" Division since January 1875. The greatest laxity has prevailed in forwarding of returns and I think it advisable to tell you in time, that I am determined to put a stop to such a discreditable state of affairs."[47]

Commissioner French continued to try to fulfil his duties as Commanding Officer of the Mounted Police but it was a very difficult task when the portion of the force under the Assistant Commissioner at Fort Macleod reported directly to the Department of Justice in Ottawa. In December, still attempting to get details of the desertions that had taken place at Fort Macleod the previous March, he wrote to the Minister of Justice complaining that "owing to the imperfect and irregular manner in which returns have been forwarded from the Divisions under the command of the Assistant Commissioner, I am without the full information on this matter that I should be in possession of and I now beg to request that I may be supplied with the names of the men, and under what terms they were taken back, whether any charge, either of desertion or absence without leave, was ever brought against these men, or even any entry made on the defaulters sheet. From Despatch No. 71 signed by the Assistant Commissioner and addressed to Lieutenant Colonel Richardson it would appear that the Department are in possession of the facts that should be recorded in my Orderly Room."[48]

In March, Commissioner French sought permission to go to Ottawa to see the Minister of Justice in an attempt to straighten out the rapidly deteriorating relationship, but he was too late. In response he was told that the Minister was unable to arrange for his coming to Ottawa and asked for a report on what matters he considered required a personal meeting. Commissioner French submitted a very detailed list of topics requiring discussion and judged the matter to be sufficiently important that he offered to pay part of the cost of the trip. On April 26 he was told that the Minister was not disposed to authorizing his coming to Ottawa.[49]

Commissioner French now had a falling out with Paymaster Griffiths, who had been on his headquarters staff since the second contingent trained in Toronto in early 1874. Griffiths, who had been on the Red River Expedition in 1870, had apparently been helping Commissioner French with the heavy administrative burden surrounding the organization and training of the new force. He could not continue to volunteer his services and asked French to take him into the force since he was down to his last $20.[50] French recommended his acceptance and he became the Adjutant, a post he filled during the march west. Griffiths apparently performed his duties satisfactorily and the Commissioner recommended his promotion. Shortly after that Griffiths and Dalrymple Clark changed positions - Clark became Adjutant and Griffiths became Paymaster.[51]

A letter in the *Free Press* on November 20, 1875 questioned whether the Commissioner had the power to "warn settlers off the ground within a mile and a half

- A Double Duty -

on every side of police barracks at Swan River." The writer complained that this had been done in the case of someone named Mahoney who was a "respectable trader." The letter noted that this was a very different policy than practiced at Fort Macleod where Assistant Commissioner Macleod encouraged settlement. The writer stated, "there would be very little chance of the North West getting settled if all officers were like this sour despot who is not only hated by his own force but by others also, with whose personal freedom he constantly interferes." The letter was signed with the initials J.T.S. Commissioner French reported that he had good reason to believe that the signature J.T.S. and certain expressions used in the letter were "only *blinds* meant to mislead in arriving at the position of the real writer."[52]

At this point Commissioner French was convinced that there was an organized conspiracy against the officers of the force. He appears to have linked this in some way to Paymaster Griffiths and letters appearing in the press. Looking at the complaint in the *Free Press*, he somehow concluded that the only person affected was the wife of Paymaster Griffiths. French had objected to her making a squatter's claim on land likely to be used for the residence of the Governor of the Northwest Territories and believed the decision might have been considered high-handed and autocratic.

Commissioner French advised the Deputy Minister of Justice in March 1876 that he was "at the present time, in receipt of reliable information which discloses an organized conspiracy for vilifying officers of this Force, mainly carried on by scurrilous letters in disreputable newspapers, these statements being backed up regardless of truth, by private letters to subordinate officials at Ottawa, with the design that the contents should be mentioned to higher authority. I have the best reasons for believing that, at least in one instance, a private letter from a very subordinate officer of the Force finding fault with my methods of conducting the affairs of the Force, was successfully brought to the notice of one if not two ministers of the government. I expect ere long to be able to bring charges home to the individuals concerned but, in the meantime, I beg to request that this letter may not be allowed to fall into other hands but your own."[53]

- *Swan River Barracks* -

Commissioner French's perception that the Paymaster was somehow involved in an organized conspiracy caused a rapid deterioration in their relationship. In his Annual Report for 1875 French wrote that Paymaster Griffiths had arrived at Swan River Barracks from Winnipeg with eight men, seven wagons and fourteen horses. He was annoyed because he expected some stores in the wagons but said, to his astonishment, they mostly carried Griffiths' baggage, which could have come by ox train. French reported that because of loading the young horses on this trip "scarcely any of them were fit to accompany the General [Selby-Smyth] and Party."[54]

The Minister of Justice read this report and had his Deputy ask Commissioner French whether he had taken any action in this case and why he had not informed the Minister at the time about Griffiths' actions.[55] French replied that he found the Paymaster's conduct reprehensible, especially since he had not brought articles that were urgently required, such as light helmets.[56] Since there were seven wagons, with a probable capacity of 2,000 lbs. each, the inference of overloading seems far-fetched. Obviously Paymaster Griffiths was still not in Commissioner French's good books and the matter would only get worse.

The next confrontation came quickly when there were inexplicable delays in the delivery of stores from Winnipeg to Swan River Barracks by wagon train. It was alleged that Wagon Master O'Donnell was "supplied with liquor at, or enroute to, Swan River and was sufficiently under the influence for several days and unable to look after his wagon train which was delayed."[57] After a preliminary investigation Commissioner French reported that nobody at Swan River Barracks had given O'Donnell sufficient liquor to make anyone intoxicated. Shortly thereafter, Thomas Nixon informed Bernard that Sub-Inspector John French had given liquor to the wagon master.[58]

Evidence at the Inquiry showed that John French had gone to Fort Pelly with O'Donnell to meet his wagon train and on the return journey, a distance of about ten miles, O'Donnell removed a box from one of his wagons and placed it in the sleigh in which he and French were riding. The box, from Bannatyne Grocers, was addressed to Master Claude Griffiths, son of the Paymaster, and contained spirits. Since this

- A Double Duty -

liquor was being imported into the Northwest Territories without a permit, French should technically have confiscated and spilled it, and his failure to do so was considered dereliction of duty.

Paymaster Griffiths was in more serious trouble since he did not have a permit and had not reported receiving the liquor. Commissioner French considered this "disgraceful conduct" and Griffiths was suspended for having "infringed liquor laws and his services . . . dispensed with."[59] French wrote to the Minister of Justice "this officer's case is a most lamentable one; although old enough to have and hold his own opinion, he was driven on by a very diabolical influence under which his sense of right and wrong as well as honour and gratitude appears to have been smothered."[60]

Commissioner French could now hardly make a move without it being reported to Ottawa, with a subsequent request from the Department of Justice that he provide an explanation of his actions. Some of the problems may have stemmed from his relations with Thomas Nixon, the agent for the Department of Justice in Winnipeg, who had reported difficulties with French as early as February 1875 and had kept Ottawa pretty well informed ever since.[61] An example occurred in May 1876 when two Sub-Constables, Scouten and Lund, were sent from Swan River Barracks to Winnipeg with two wagons and four horses to pick up Staff Sergeant Price and some men who had come down the Assiniboine River with a party of invalids. Nixon informed Hugh Richardson in the Department of the Secretary of State in Ottawa, that he did not know the purpose of the two men being in Winnipeg.

Commissioner French was asked to provide an explanation to the Minister. He, quite rightly, was highly annoyed at this micro-management of the Mounted Police by Ottawa and replied that he "did not think it necessary to inform the Department of this matter of ordinary routine, and I consider that the person who did furnish such information to the Department must have known perfectly well the business on which the party was sent. As he must have telegraphed the information to Ottawa, and thereby caused expense and the further expense of the present telegram to me, I beg respectfully to suggest that he be charged the expense of both telegrams as a warning against further needless officiousness."[62]

Commissioner French's days were now numbered. On July 22, 1876 Cabinet was informed that, "it appears the condition of the Force and particularly of those two Divisions more immediately under the command of Colonel French is very unsatisfactory and the Committee believe that it will be absolutely necessary in order to maintain discipline and introduce the necessary reforms in management of the Force that a change must be made in the command. It was therefore recommend that Colonel French be informed that his services will be no longer required and Lieutenant Colonel James Farquharson Macleod C.M.G., formerly Assistant Commissioner, be appointed in the room of Colonel French."[63]

This put Colonel French in a very difficult position and was a tremendous blow to his pride, dignity and professional reputation. He now had to resort to damage control and wrote to the Secretary of State in order to mitigate the situation. The Secretary of State then advised Cabinet that he had received a communication from Lieutenant Colonel French, "from which it appears certain letters addressed to him from the Office of the Secretary of State in the month of June were not received, and appear to have been abstracted from the mails between Winnipeg and Palestine. The letters required Colonel French to report anew on a variety of subjects that had for some time antecedent been the subject of discussion with that officer, his former reports not having been considered satisfactory. Colonel French alleged that for some time previously he had it in contemplation to tender his resignation, and that, had the missing letters been received by him, he would no longer have hesitated in resigning command of the Force."[64]

Lieutenant Colonel French's resignation was accepted and the Privy Council Order dispensing with his services was cancelled in part, making his departure a resignation rather than a dismissal. If, in fact, letters addressed to Commissioner French were "abstracted from the mails" between Winnipeg and Swan River Barracks this might support his belief that there was an "organized conspiracy." The mail from

- A Double Duty -

Winnipeg to Palestine, and on to Swan River Barracks was controlled by the Mounted Police.

There was irony in the Government of Canada firing French since, on a previous occasion, while serving with the Royal Artillery, he had been in bad repute with his superiors in the British Army for being overly pro-Canadian during discussions of the transfer of responsibility for the defence of Canada. The War Office had been prepared to take him back to Britain but the Cabinet in Ottawa intervened and he remained here.[65]

The departure of Commissioner French ended a chapter in the history of the Mounted Police and the force was very much the product of his views on discipline and organization. There were mixed feelings about him in the force, as there are with any commanding officer. With the notable exception of the two officers dismissed at Fort Dufferin, he appears to have had the support of most of his commissioned officers. The men were divided. Many of those who had served with him in the Artillery at Kingston, or had known him elsewhere, supported him. These included strong supporters such as Colonel J.B. Mitchell, who later wrote that without Commissioner French the North West Mounted Police would never have come into being. Among his detractors were a number of articulate sub-constables such as Carscadden, Finlayson and D'Artigue, who have left written records of their opinion of the Commissioner.

The stampede at Fort Dufferin in 1874 seems to have marked a watershed in Commissioner French's command of the Mounted Police. It seems that nothing was the same after that, although his troubles were probably increased by the defeat of the Macdonald government. In a letter to Colonel G.E. Saunders, Commissioner French's son wrote that the thunderstorm at Fort Dufferin was a bad start for the march, coupled with unsuitable political appointees and interference from Ottawa. He said that no one would ever know what his father had to go through in the early days of the Force, especially since he was a personal friend of Sir John A. Macdonald.[66]

Commissioner French was given a dignified sendoff at Swan River Barracks. Before he departed, the non-commissioned officers of the force presented him with a

- *Swan River Barracks* -

watch and the men presented Mrs. French a silver tea service. Then on Monday August 28, 1876, those members of the Mounted Police in Winnipeg and the "gunners" of the garrison, went to the dock to bid farewell to Colonel and Mrs French as they embarked on the steamer *Minnesota*. Sergeant Major Francis and Sergeant DesForges made an address. The assembled men cheered Commissioner and Mrs. French as the steamer departed.[67] The *Free Press* extended a thoughtful and dignified tribute on the end of Colonel French's appointment as Commissioner, noting that "the duty of organizing a force like the Mounted Police in an immense tract of country to a great extent almost a *terra incognita* was a task necessarily arduous and difficult and the part taken by Col. French in the establishment of law and order in the North-West will permanently identify him with its history."[68]

On his return to duty with the Royal Artillery in Britain, French was made a Companion of the Order of St. Michael and St. George for his service in Canada. In a sad epilogue to his service in the force, Major French in 1878 wrote to Sir John A. Macdonald, who was now back in power, explaining that when he resigned the Minister of the Interior refused to pay his passage and that of his family back to Britain on the grounds that he had been in Canada when he accepted the appointment. Given that at the time of his acceptance, he was holding a seconded appointment for which his return fare would have been paid, this seems to set a new low in bureaucratic pettiness and served only to rub salt in his wounds.[69]

On July 20, 1876 James Farquharson Macleod C.M.G., who had left the force as Assistant Commissioner just over six months previously, was appointed to succeed Lieutenant Colonel French. Macleod was very popular and widely trusted as a man with a reputation for keeping his word.

- 12 -

Changes On The Plains

As command of the force changed, conditions on the western plains were also changing. In the west, 1876 came in with bitterly cold weather. While there were still large numbers of buffalo allowing the Indians to continue their nomadic way of life, these herds were disappearing rapidly and a crisis was not far off. With the arrival of the Mounted Police, the liquor traffic was largely curtailed and white men who had exploited aboriginal peoples were dealt with firmly. As the perception of danger waned, the Métis settlements at Wood Mountain, Batoche and Fort Qu'Appelle became more permanent and the Métis hunters ventured into Blackfoot hunting grounds they would previously have been afraid to enter. There was almost no crime among the Indians, other than horse stealing. This had been a culturally acceptable activity until now, bringing honour to young warriors. Early in 1876 some attempts were made to start raising cattle herds on the open ranges with herds brought north from Montana, but when the cattle were turned loose they quickly merged with the buffalo and were never seen again.

Life was still hard for the policemen. William Parker relates how, in January 1876, he took six constables, 18 horses and sleds from Swan River Barracks to Shoal Lake, a round trip of 280 miles, because stocks of oats were running low at Swan River Barracks. The trip down took six days in bitterly cold weather and one horse died on the way. They brought back 9,000 pounds of oats and 1,000 pounds of freight, as well as a large amount of hay for the horses. With the temperature at a constant -40°F and the snow so deep they had trouble getting through it, there was some concern about whether they would make it back. The whole party suffered from frostbite and on their return to Swan River Barracks all the constables were hospitalized with snow blindness.[1]

To the west, at Bow River, Inspector Brisebois had started to refer to the post in official correspondence as Fort Brisebois, possibly because Fort Macleod and Fort

- Changes On The Plains -

Walsh had been named after the officers commanding the men who built the forts. The fort at Bow River had been built by a contractor and the idea of it being called Fort Brisebois was not popular with the members stationed there. Brisebois had a series of clashes with his men, just as he had done in every previous appointment since joining the force. At Bow River he appeared to favour the Métis and in December 1875, he ordered some men to build log cabins for his interpreters, Piscan Munroe and E. Berard. The men refused and the other members of the garrison would not take them into custody. The troops then mutinied and prepared a list of complaints against Brisebois, which was signed by nearly all the sub-constables. W. Leslie Wood, a fur trader, wrote to Richard Hardisty at Edmonton House telling him that the Mounted Police force at the Elbow "are in revolt. . . . the whole are now their own Bosses, waiting for Col. Macleod's arrival to set things straight. The men here sent a list of Charges against the Captain to Col. McLeod [sic], some of them Crushing Ones. I believe the Captain thinks his position is not worth much."[2]

The men also complained that Brisebois had taken a Métis woman from a nearby camp into his quarters but the straw that broke the camel's back was when he "took the only iron stove which the men had been using for cooking."[3] Word of this reached Fort Macleod and Commissioner Macleod and Assistant Commissioner Irvine came to investigate. Macleod assembled the men and explained the impropriety of signing the document and not making their complaint in the proper way. One man was punished for insubordination. Somewhat surprisingly, Macleod noted that there was nothing to warrant suspension of Brisebois.[4]

In reporting this incident, Assistant Commissioner Irvine informed the Minister of Justice that Inspector Brisebois had acted without consulting his superiors when he ordered documents to be headed Fort Brisebois. Irvine cancelled the order since it was unauthorized and went against the wishes of the people there. Commissioner Macleod decided that the fort should be named after an old castle on the Isle of Mull, said to have once belonged to the Clan Macleod; it became Fort Calgary. Ottawa was told that Calgary meant "clear running water" in Gaelic.

- A Double Duty -

While there was relatively little crime by Indians, serious offences were not entirely unknown and sometimes involved a challenge to the authority of the police to test whether they were serious about their determination to enforce the law. One such case was that of Pox, wanted for beating his wife to death a year previously. Pox returned from Montana where he had been hiding and was in a camp some 30 miles from Fort Walsh where he boasted to the Crees how he had outwitted the police who, he said "were long on thought but short on deeds and possessed poor memories." He said he would soon return to Fort Macleod where "he was satisfied no harm would befall him." [5] When the chief in the Cree camp, Little Black Bear, informed the Mounted Police in Fort Macleod of the presence of Pox, Sub-Inspector Vernon Welch went, with four men, to apprehend him. Pox was not at the camp when they arrived but the chief expected him to return shortly and promised to send word when he was back. When Little Black Bear later informed the police that Pox was back in camp, Welch was able to arrest him.

Lieutenant Governor Morris received information during the summer that Sitting Bull had sent a gift of tobacco to the Blackfoot, with an invitation to join them in a war against the whites.[6] This was confirmed when Sub-Inspector Denny intercepted several hundred Blackfoot in the Red Deer Valley while arresting a suspect named Nataya, alleged to have committed a murder near the forks of the Red Deer and South Saskatchewan Rivers. The Blackfoot later held a Council with Denny present and told him of the Sioux in Montana sending them tobacco which they wanted them to smoke and then join in a war against the United States Army. In return, the Sioux promised to give the Blackfoot captured United States Army mules and horses, as well as white women prisoners. Their messenger said that when they had defeated their American foes they would come to Canada and join the Blackfoot in exterminating the whites. When the Blackfoot refused to smoke the tobacco the Sioux threatened that they would come to Canada and fight the Blackfoot when they had finished killing off the American soldiers.

- *Changes On The Plains* -

Crowfoot asked Sub-Inspector Denny if the police would come to the aid of the Blackfoot if they were attacked and was assured that they would. Crowfoot's words reflected the ever increasing concern of the Blackfoot about incursions into their hunting territory. Denny reported that the chief told him "we all see that the day is coming when the buffalo will all be killed and we shall have nothing more to live on, and then you will come into our camp and see the poor Blackfoot starving." "I know," he said, "that the heart of the White soldier will be sorry for us and they will tell the great mother who will not let her children starve." He said, "we are getting shut in, the Crees are coming in to our country from the north, and the White man from the south and east, and they are all destroying our means of living; but still, although we plainly see these days coming we will not join the Sioux against the Whites, but will depend upon you to help us."[7] Denny's report on this meeting eventually reached Britain and a copy was sent to Queen Victoria who directed that the Blackfoot be told that Her Majesty ". . . has been much gratified by the evidence of their loyalty and attachment."[8]

The activities of the Sioux were ominous, given the possibility they could cross the boundary. There was considerable interest in westward expansion in the United States at this time and the government was under great pressure to abrogate treaties made with the Indians. The Fort Laramie Treaty of 1868 had recognized a huge reservation for the Sioux and other northern tribes, covering most of what is now South Dakota, west of the Missouri, and also granted hunting rights in what was called unceded territory. According to the treaty the Black Hills were clearly included in the Great Sioux Reservation.

Just as the Mounted Police were starting west from Fort Dufferin, the *Free Press* of July 11, 1874 told of an Indian woman bringing a gold nugget the size of an egg into Fort Laramie, claiming it had been found in the Black Hills.[9] These stories of gold in the Black Hills increased the pressure on the government and in 1874, in violation of their treaty with the Sioux, they reluctantly sent a geological expedition into the area with the intention of establishing once and for all whether there was gold in the Black Hills. A force of 1,200 soldiers led by Lieutenant Colonel George Armstrong Custer

- A Double Duty -

accompanied the small geological party. There was no opposition to the expedition since Sitting Bull and Crazy Horse were both in the west with their warriors hunting buffalo. Lieutenant Colonel Custer issued a report confirming that there was gold and, in direct violation of the Fort Laramie Treaty, invited people to come and get it.

Custer's report precipitated a gold rush so that by the winter of 1875-76 there were about 15,000 prospectors in the Black Hills. The United States Government was unable to withstand the pressure to open the area and took no action against these intruders. When the Indians realized they would get no support they took matters into their own hands. Large numbers of Sioux roamed the countryside, stealing horses, killing cattle and burning houses. This prompted the government to order the Sioux to return to their reservations by the end of January 1876. Some returned, many others, including Sitting Bull, defied the order and prepared to fight.

In early 1876, the United States Army began hunting down Sioux and Cheyennes who had been declared "hostiles." Part of this force, the 7th Cavalry, was commanded by Lieutenant Colonel Custer, who had led the column into the Black Hills in 1874 and was remembered with considerable enmity by the Sioux. Lieutenant Colonel Custer was often called General Custer, a brevet or honourary rank he held because he had been a very young general in the Civil War. He was in bad repute with the President and his own superiors and was, therefore, anxious to do something to regain his past glory and stature. He was a flamboyant, impetuous and sometimes seemingly reckless officer whose bravery was beyond question. It is interesting that these characteristics of the American officer most closely associated with Sitting Bull were shared by Superintendent Walsh, the Canadian officer most often associated with Sitting Bull.

Lieutenant Governor Morris wrote to the Secretary of State warning that, if the Sioux found themselves unable to cope with the military force being deployed against them, they would cross into Canada, probably around the Turtle or Wood Mountains, and use this as a base for operations against the Americans. He further warned that "the influx of a large body of these warlike Sioux, driven hither by the hostile forces of the Americans, and pursuing for food the buffalo into the hunting grounds of the Half-

- Changes On The Plains -

breeds, the Cree and the Blackfeet Indians, would be an event of the gravest possible character."[10]

On June 25, 1876 Lieutenant Colonel Custer rode at the head of the 7th Cavalry. He led one of the three columns in a force under General Alfred H. Terry, riding to converge on a large number of Indians concentrating in the area of the Little Big Horn River in Montana. Moving forward, Custer came in contact with the Sioux before the other columns were in place. "He [Custer] departed from Terry's plan even though the circumstances on which it was premised turned out to be exactly as foreseen. He precipitated a battle a day early, with worn-out men and horses, and without knowing the strength and position of the enemy. He committed his regiment piecemeal, and at the critical time no component was in supporting range of the others."[11] As a result there were 225 dead Americans at Little Big Horn and the Sioux were being pursued by the United States Army, seeking revenge. Sitting Bull quickly realized that his actions would bring the wrath of the whole U.S. Army down on him and that, realistically, he had only two choices, to flee to Mexico or to Canada. The Sioux started to drift northward toward Canada.

While these events were unfolding on the western plains, Inspector James Walker was in eastern Canada on a recruiting trip. In Ottawa he received instructions to establish a post at "Battle Ford," at the forks of the North Saskatchewan and Battle Rivers. He was also ordered to provide an escort for the Commissioners of Treaty No. 6, who would be meeting with Crees, Saulteaux and Chippewayan in that area in long delayed treaty negotiations. On his return to Swan River Barracks, Walker and an escort of men from "E" Troop left for Fort Carlton to make preparations for the treaty negotiations. At Duck Lake, they bypassed Chief Beardy and several of his band who, it was rumoured, had no intention of taking part in treaty negotiations. When they completed preparations at Fort Carlton, the escort moved 100 miles west to Battleford where they selected a site for the new post. Leaving Sub-Inspector Frechette and a party to build the fort, Walker and the rest of the men returned to Fort Carlton, where a large number of Indians had assembled. Fort Carlton was a typical Hudson's Bay

- *A Double Duty* -

Company post with log walls, bastions and loopholes. The living quarters and stores were located inside the fort.

At Fort Carlton a rumour was circulating that Chief Beardy and his band at Duck Lake planned to halt the treaty commissioners on the trail and require them to negotiate a special treaty before they would be allowed to go on to Fort Carlton. Walker viewed this rumour seriously and took immediate action. "Early next morning I started with my troop to Batoche where I expected the Commissioners to cross the river. When about half way, we overtook the Duck Lake Indians, chief and warriors, on their way to Batoche. They were about the most surprised Indians I ever saw. It was the first time they had seen the mounted redcoats and apparently did not know we were in the country. The fact that we came from behind bewildered them."[12] Any idea of blocking the official party evaporated and when they came off the ferry at Dumont's Crossing they were welcomed profusely by Chief Beardy, although he would still not come to the treaty gathering at Fort Carlton because he wanted separate negotiations at Duck Lake.

On August 8, 1876, after Inspector Walker and "E" Troop had departed for Fort Carlton, the newly appointed Commissioner James Macleod arrived unexpectedly at Swan River Barracks. He was accompanied by Inspector Herchmer and Sub-Inspector Dalrymple Clark. They arrived during the night when a severe storm occured, with rain coming down in sheets and a wind so strong that it carried an outbuilding across the river.[13] The Commissioner had come to move the headquarters from Swan River Barracks to Fort Macleod due to the increased tension along the United States Boundary. There was a possibility that the Sioux might come into Canada and use it as a base for retaliatory forays across the border. Fort Macleod was being enlarged to take the increase in strength and four 7-pounder mountain guns and ammunition were purchased from the Militia at Fort Garry and sent to Fort Walsh.

Having also heard the rumours that the Indians intended to stop the Lieutenant Governor from crossing the South Saskatchewan River, Commissioner Macleod wanted to get on the trail without delay. The route to Fort Macleod was via Fort Carlton where the treaty negotiations were taking place. "D" Troop was ordered to parade in marching order. The men obviously knew that something was happening but not everyone knew that they were destined for Fort Macleod. Sub-Constable Frank Carruthers left the following description: "One night, or more correctly one morning, about two o'clock we received orders to be ready by morning to start for a three week trip only taking field kit with us which interpreted means that we were to take 1 blanket, 2 shirts, 2 pair socks, 1 tunic, 1 serge, 1 pair pants, 1 pair drawers, 1 overcoat, 1 undershirt, all of which we carry on our saddle. We marched first to Fort Carlton 280 miles, which we thought was the end of our journey. Here we formed a guard of honour to the Governor who was treating with the Indians, but we were obliged to accompany him to Pitt where he held another treaty, and here, to our surprise, we got orders to proceed to McLeod [sic], via Battle River and Cyprus [sic] Hills."[14]

Swan River Barracks, sometimes referred to as Livingstone, was never suitable as the headquarters for the North West Mounted Police and the seat of government of the Northwest Territories. Many westerners considered it an expensive mistake foisted on them by politicians in Ottawa who knew nothing of the west. The Mounted Police were never to return to Swan River Barracks in large numbers and the buildings burned to the ground a few years later so "Livingstone, like a mule, without pride of ancestry or hope of posterity, had a working life of three years before it was abandoned to the oblivion into which its Ottawa creators should have followed it."[15]

The Commissioner and "D" Troop joined Inspector Walker and "E" Troop at Fort Carlton on August 18 and provided an escort for the Treaty Commissioners there and later at Fort Pitt. The treaty negotiations were a spectacle, with aboriginal peoples singing, dancing, beating drums and putting on amazing displays of horseback riding. The chiefs passed a pipe to the Lieutenant Governor, who was resplendent in cocked hat, gold braid and lace. He explained that the time had come for the aboriginal peoples to "make permanent homes for themselves, to till the soil and to prepare for the time when the buffalo and other game would be no more."[16]

At the Council tent, the Lieutenant Governor made a long speech to the Indians, saying that the Great White Mother had sent him to make a treaty with them. He also

- A Double Duty -

said he knew that the Indians had spoken of stopping him from crossing the South Saskatchewan River. He said they might as well try to stop the running waters of the river, as the Queen's soldiers were as thick as the grass on the prairies. Reporting on the treaty, Alexander Morris wrote that had his suggestions for measures such as regulations for the preservation of the buffalo been adopted, the Indians trained to farm and the Métis persuaded to settle down, the major social questions in the Northwest Territories would have been solved.

Chief Beardy sent a message asking for provisions but was told that if he wanted food he should come to Fort Carlton. He sent a second messenger asking about the terms of the treaty and was told that if he wanted to know, he should come to Fort Carlton. Governor Morris explained to those who were at Fort Carlton that every family would get their own home on chosen land with one square mile of land for every family of five, schools would be provided as would equipment for farming, oxen, cows and seeds for potatoes, oats, barley and wheat. The government promised the chiefs uniforms and silver medals. Ammunition and twine would be provided and every man, woman and child would receive $12.00, each chief $25.00 and each headman $15.00 with the money paid annually after that. The Indians asked for time to consider and, after their own deliberations, signed the treaty.

When the treaty was signed Governor Morris invited the Duck Lake Indians to meet him at Commissioner James McKay's camp a few miles from Fort Carlton. At that meeting, three more chiefs signed the treaty. The commissioners then moved on to Fort Pitt and repeated the process with the Crees there. The treaty negotiations and the annual payments of treaty money acted as a magnet to entrepreneurial traders so "from far and near trader after trader had come to make certain that, if he could help it, no treaty money should be left idle in the Indians' hands."[17]

With the large number of people gathering for the treaty negotiations, a herd of about 200 cattle had been driven up from Montana to provide rations. A group of police recruits was left to herd them. They allowed the cattle to graze on the plains during the day and moved them into a draw at night, where they were checked every

- Changes On The Plains -

half hour or so. One morning there were few cattle in sight and when the herders rounded up those that remained, 137 were missing. A search party went out to look for them but the cattle had merged with a buffalo herd and were never seen again.

Following the signing of the treaty at Fort Carlton and Fort Pitt, the Mounted Police returned to Battleford, then turned south across the plains toward Fort Walsh. Sub-Constable Carruthers recorded that "two days from Battle River we came to a long steep hill and when we got past the top of it we lost sight of land, that is we entered the great plains." He described the monotony as "nothing in sight for weeks but blue sky and brown earth, for the green luxuriant prairie grass is a myth, at least north of the boundary line."

An encounter with a prairie fire can be an awe inspiring experience. As the column moved across the plains, Sub-Constable Carruthers explained that "one day . . . I was riding in the advance guard, a few officers about half a mile ahead, when suddenly we saw a little column of smoke rise between us and the officers. We got the order to gallop at once but before we got up to it - about 600 yards of the prairie was in a blaze and spreading in great strides and leaps before a strong wind which was blowing it right towards the baggage train; provisions train I ought to say for we had no baggage train, worst luck. Well we dismounted, linked horses, took our coats and commenced fighting the fire while the waggons galloped up and barely managed to get to windward of the fire in time. Half an hour afterwards the plain was black behind us as far as we could see." The prairie fire had swept a huge area and for three days the column crossed the burnt prairie, causing Carruthers to wonder "how the horses lived for those three days I don't know, but live they did and travelled from daylight to dark too" until they reached the South Saskatchewan near its junction with the Red Deer River.[18]

It is sometimes hard for those who have not confronted the problem to imagine how much of an obstacle a river such as the South Saskatchewan presented to a column with 30 heavily loaded wagons, 12 yoke of oxen, 80 horses and 100 men when there was no bridge, no ford, and no boats. The river was 150 to 200 yards wide, deep and with a strong current. Before anything else could be done, the men had to do a great deal of heavy physical labour to cut the banks sufficiently to make a safe descent for the horses. Following this the actual river crossing could get under way.

The men unloaded the wagons and lashed them in pairs with wagon reaches at each end and tarpaulins underneath and along the sides. They also cut trees along the river bank to make a raft. The accounts left by the men suggest that despite the hard work there was considerable enjoyment from the venture. Frank Carruthers said, "we kept this up for three days never resting, never dry. Sometimes we made safe journeys, sometimes we sank, sometimes we had to put back to the side we started from but at last we were all across."[19] Later in the afternoon they constructed a raft. It was loaded with the heavy cargo such as oats, wagon wheels and ammunition. On its maiden voyage, with a huge load piled on it, there were several men with heavy oars working as hard as they could but the grossly overloaded raft was sinking fast. It sank a short distance from shore, in shallow water.

There was a major problem with the horses and oxen not even willing to enter the water, much less swim across to the other side. When the guides could do nothing with them, Sergeant Major J.B. Mitchell and Sub-Constable Charles Daly stripped and went to work. Mitchell started to cross but his horse immediately turned and came back so he got a stick and tried again. On this attempt he slipped off in deep water but grasped the horse's neck and struck with the stick every time it tried to go back, and finally made it across. Daly's horse rolled over and he went under but came up with a good hold on the horse's tail and they followed the Sergeant Major's horse across. When the rest of the horses saw them on the far bank, they swam across to join them. Sub-Constable Sanderson recorded that after the crossing the cold, wet men received hospital comforts from Dr. Kittson, "the first and last I ever saw publicly served out."[20] The column then marched on to Fort Walsh where "E" Troop remained and, after two weeks, the Commissioner and "D" Troop went on to Fort Macleod.

When the Blackfoot heard of the treaty negotiations at Fort Pitt and Fort Carlton they complained that the Cree were getting preferential treatment. The Blackfoot were

- Changes On The Plains -

anxious to meet a Commissioner or representative of the Queen to discuss the problems they had outlined in the petition they had submitted, but there had been no response. Given the tense situation in the west and events at the Little Big Horn, the government now realized that action had to be taken to secure the Blackfoot lands.

As soon as word reached Ottawa about the battle at Little Big Horn, a telegram was immediately sent to Inspector Walsh. He was on leave with his wife and daughter at Hot Springs, Arkansas. The telegram informed him of what had happened and the possibility that the Sioux would seek refuge in Canada. He left immediately for Ottawa then travelled on to Fort Walsh. When he arrived the whole garrison turned out to greet him at the entrance to the fort which was decorated with evergreens, flags and banners. His men gave him three cheers as he arrived.[21] At this time the Sioux were still south of the border but were said to be drifting slowly north, so he immediately sent scouts to shadow them and report on their activities. Early in October, hearing that a large number of Sioux had assembled, he took a small patrol 90 miles south-east to Rocky Creek but found that the Sioux were still on the other side of the boundary, hunting buffalo between the Missouri River and the border.

Word reached Fort Walsh in November 1876 that a large band of Sioux had crossed the boundary and made camp near Wood Mountain, a Métis community centred on the trading post of Jean Louis Légaré. Sub-Inspector Frechette immediately went to investigate and report on the situation. When Frechette and his men had not returned in three weeks, Inspector Walsh became concerned for their safety and set out to check on them. Two days out on the trail they met Sub-Inspector Frechette's party, weary and worn since they had been delayed by cold weather but in good spirits.[22] Frechette reported that an additional 52 lodges had crossed, bringing the total to 109 lodges.

After four days of travelling in extreme cold, Inspector Walsh and his men reached the Sioux camp. They remained for two days, holding Council with Black Moon, a hereditary chief of the Lakotas, who had crossed the boundary with 500 men, 1,000 women, 1,400 children, 3,500 horses and 30 United States Army mules. Inspector Walsh told Black Moon and his followers that they would have to obey the

- A Double Duty -

laws of the Great Mother. The Sioux said that they were tired of being hunted and only sought somewhere where they could live in peace. They were camping at Wood Mountain next to the lodges of White Eagle's band of Sisseton Sioux who crossed the border into Canada after the Minnesota Massacre of 1862 and had been peaceful and law-abiding. The newly arrived Sioux said that they wished to live in the same manner. They claimed to be "Sagonash" or British Indians who had supported the British in both the Revolutionary War and the War of 1812. They proudly displayed medals given to their grandfathers by King George III. Since their people were hungry they pleaded with Inspector Walsh to allow them sufficient ammunition with which to hunt buffalo and he gave Jean Légaré permission to sell them a small quantity.

The return journey from Wood Mountain to Fort Walsh took nine days in intense cold, deep snow and continuous storms with rations growing short, so that "a band of buffalo we fortunately came across on our seventh day saved us from being forced to eat horse flesh."[23] Five of their horses died before they got back to Fort Walsh. Inspector Walsh recommended establishing small subposts at the foot, or east end, of the Cypress Hills and reopening the post at Wood Mountain. Later, the first post was imaginatively called East End. The person placed in charge at Wood Mountain was Constable A.R. Macdonell, who was to have a very distinguished career in the North West Mounted Police and the military.

The year 1876 saw the end of the three-year enlistment term of the '73 Originals, many of whom had taken up the option of leaving with a land grant of 160 acres to start ranching and be among the first white settlers. Replacements were recruited in Eastern Canada then sent west via steamer to Duluth, rail to Bismarck, North Dakota and then by river boat to Fort Benton. From Fort Benton the trip to Fort Macleod or Fort Walsh was by horse or ox team if they were lucky, or on their own two feet in many cases. Except for the concern caused by the Sioux, life in Fort Walsh and Fort Macleod was relatively quiet. There was some excitement when the first horse thief convicted by the force, one James Brooks, a fugitive from Montana, was sentenced to five years in

- *Changes On The Plains* -

prison. He had to be escorted 1,300 km. to his new home in Stony Mountain Penitentiary just outside Winnipeg.

As 1876 drew to a close, the Sioux who had crossed the boundary settled in quietly at Wood Mountain where, fortunately, buffalo were still to be found in good numbers. The presence of these Sioux and the possibility of more following close behind them created a dangerous situation. The Sioux could upset the balance in the west, where the territory between Wood Mountain and the Rockies was considered Blackfoot hunting grounds. The Blackfoot were already upset at the influx of Métis, other Canadian Indians and white settlers, and would not welcome their traditional enemies, the Sioux. If the police could not keep the Sioux in check, the Blackfoot were fully prepared to do so. So, as Christmas festivities and feasts took place at Fort Macleod and Fort Walsh, the presence of the Sioux was continually in the back of the minds of everyone there.

- 13 -

Sitting Bull And The Sioux

As the year 1877 dawned, the Canadian Government watched the events unfolding in the Cypress Hills and Wood Mountain with great concern. By this time, Canadian Indians were supposed to have chosen reserves and taken up new ways of life, although the necessary surveys were not completed and there were problems and delays in providing supplies and equipment. The aboriginal people were in no hurry to settle down on reserves. As long as there were buffalo to hunt, the tribes would continue to hunt them, but they were not happy to share the diminishing herds with the Sioux. The Canadian Government could not afford to have trouble with either the Sioux, their own Indians or any combination of the two. They took the matter up with the United States government, hoping that some way could be found to induce the Sioux to return south of the border. The Lakota showed no inclination to move, looking instead for the same treatment accorded the Sioux who had come to Canada in the aftermath of the Minnesota Massacre.

In March, word reached Fort Walsh that Sitting Bull, with a large number of his followers, had crossed the Missouri River and was moving north in the direction of Wood Mountain. In April, when scouts reported that Sitting Bull was moving up Rock Creek, Inspector Walsh set out for Wood Mountain and established a camp between Pinto Horse Butte and the western end of Wood Mountain. When he found no sign of Indians in the area, he took three scouts, Daniels, a policeman; Léveillé, a Cree Métis; and Morin, a Sioux Métis, and travelled south until they came to the Mud House on the White Mud River. Here the group divided into two to scout in a circle and return to the camp for the night. About six or seven miles out, Walsh found a fresh trail showing a large number of Indians moving north, so he and Morin followed them. Léveillé and Daniels eventually came across the same trail and seeing the signs of police horses, knew Walsh and Morin were ahead of them and hurried to catch up.

- *Sitting Bull And The Sioux* -

When Indians were seen on the hilltops watching them, the policemen knew they were now inside the outer perimeter and close to the main camp which was located just north of the international boundary. They came upon the main body of the band on the other bank of the stream, setting up their camp. The sudden appearance of Walsh's party startled the Indians who had not been warned by their own scouts and thought they were the advance party of an American force pursuing them from Montana. Women and children were screaming, tearing down partly erected lodges and running for the hills. The Indians at the ford barred Inspector Walsh and his men from crossing the stream which was no more than fifty yards wide at this point. The two groups were at a stand-off, close enough to easily talk to each other. The Indians accused Walsh's group of being the vanguard of an American force and, while the policemen and scouts were trying to convince them of their error, Léveillé and Daniels galloped up, giving the Sioux additional cause for alarm.

The Sioux were so touchy that when Walsh's men attempted to cross the ford, the Indians drew their guns. After lengthy discussion, the Indians allowed the policemen to cross and enter the camp where they asked for the chief and found they were in the camp of Four Horns. The chief told them the band were "followers of my adopted son, Sitting Bull, who is yet south of the Missouri, but looking this way."[1] Inspector Walsh asked Four Horns for the opportunity to speak to his sub-chiefs and warriors. While waiting for the Council, the chief invited the policemen to enter an extremely large lodge, made of new skins. They found the lodge "clean and neat and beautifully arranged . . . with wicker back rests and laid out into sections running around the wall. Some of the sections were curtained with bright-colored cloth and nicely looped up at the bottom, rugs and mats covering the bottom of the sections." It was "the grandest establishment any of them had ever seen on the prairie."

Inspector Walsh, given a section of the lodge, stretched himself out, went to sleep and was wakened by Daniels when Four Horns and his band were assembled. He addressed them, going into detail about British law and telling them that they were not to kill, steal, lie, do injury to any person or property and not disturb or remove anything without permission. When he had finished his explanation he concluded by saying "if you obey these laws, you and your families can sleep sound here; you are as safe as if walled around by ten thousand warriors, but if you think you cannot conform to these laws, return from whence you came, for you cannot live upon British soil no more than fish can live without water." Four Horns then shook hands with Walsh and responded; "we are tired men, women and children and hoping for rest; we want peace; we only ask to be allowed to hunt the buffalo - your words we take into our breasts; we will obey them."

At this point a courier arrived from the United States and entered the Council. He sat down opposite Inspector Walsh and, in an aggressive manner, said that the first time he had seen Walsh was at Fort Buford on the Missouri and the last time had been in the camp of General Miles, the arch enemy of the Sioux. He said, "you tell these people you are a Red coat, you are a long knife American." There was consternation throughout the Council. Walsh denied the accusation and agreed to stay in the Sioux camp that night if Four Horns would allow two or three young men of his band to carry a message south to the camp of Medicine Bear and Black Horn, who knew Walsh well and would vouch for him. The next day Medicine Bear and Black Horn arrived to denounce Walsh's accuser, who escaped in the confusion. Medicine Bear told the Council that Inspector Walsh was a British Chief and, "to live in the country north of the line, they must obey the law as it was laid down by him." Black Horn told them to "listen to his words. His tongue is not crooked."

Concerned at the arrival of such large numbers of Sioux, Commissioner Macleod wrote to the Secretary of State that "no time should be lost in dealing with the Sioux who have crossed into our Territory, as if they are allowed time to recuperate I fear they may cause some trouble and will not be so easily dealt with as they would be in their present enfeebled condition."[2] The Lieutenant Governor recommended to Ottawa that the Indians be told as soon as possible of the government's intentions. He also expressed concern that the large influx would put pressure on the buffalo and increase tension with the Canadian Indians.

- Sitting Bull And The Sioux -

In May Four Horns moved north and two weeks later Sitting Bull was reported to be approaching the boundary line. Inspector Walsh took a party of policemen and scouts to Pinto Horse Buttes to await the arrival of Sitting Bull, but when they reached the area they found the trail of a large number of Indians who had recently moved north. Sitting Bull had already arrived. Walsh and his men followed the trail and the next morning, after three hours on the march, found Indians on the hilltops watching their approach. They kept moving forward through larger and larger crowds of Indians until they found themselves in the middle of the Sioux camp. The policemen set up their own camp while the scouts, Léveillé and Solomon, who spoke Lakota, explained the purpose of their visit. Spotted Eagle of the Sans Arcs greeted them and told them they were in the camp of Sitting Bull. That evening Inspector Walsh was given a seat in the centre of the circle at a Council with Sitting Bull. He explained to Sitting Bull and his band, in the same way he had done with Four Horns, the basic tenets of British justice. The police party stayed overnight and as they prepared to leave in the morning three Indians rode into camp leading five horses. The scout, Solomon, recognized one of the men as White Dog, an Assiniboine with an unsavoury reputation and both Solomon and Léveillé recognized the horses as belonging to Father Jules Decorby, a priest with the Métis in the Cypress Hills. Walsh then instructed Sergeant McCutcheon to arrest White Dog and his colleagues, who were now surrounded by about 50 warriors listening to White Dog boast about his trip across the plains.

White Dog grew indignant when accused of stealing the horses. He claimed that the horses were his and he would not give them up and would not be arrested. As excitement spread through the camp, Inspector Walsh placed him under arrest and had one of his men bring up some leg irons. He ordered White Dog to tell him where he got

Sitting Bull   GAI NA-659-15

the horses and what he intended to do with them or he would put the leg irons on him and take him back to Fort Walsh.

White Dog told Walsh that he had found the horses wandering on the plains east of the Cypress Hills and said that he had taken them according to local custom and was unaware that it was against the law. The policemen knew that he was not telling the truth but believed that the Sioux had learned a lesson from the public humiliation of White Dog and they released him. As he turned to go, White Dog said "I shall meet you again" and Walsh, though he had heard him, asked the interpreter to have him repeat the words just to be sure. White Dog refused to do so. Walsh then ordered him to withdraw the remark or he would take him to Fort Walsh. White Dog then said that he had not intended the words to be threatening. Inspector Walsh accepted this; he had won a moral victory when White Dog showed his fear of Canadian law in the presence of the Sioux.

The Sioux settled in several camps, under different chiefs, spread over many miles north and west of Wood Mountain. Their presence created a dilemma for the government in Ottawa. If the Mounted Police alienated the Sioux they would jeopardize the fragile peace on the frontier but, at the same time, if they helped the Sioux it would cause trouble with the Canadian tribes, especially the Blackfoot. They chose a good Canadian compromise. The Sioux were allowed to stay, provided they were peaceful, but they would be given no assistance. General Miles appeared, for the moment, to be quite satisfied with the outcome. Writing to his wife Mary from "Camp on the trail immediately south of the Boundary" on July 25, 1877, he told her "we have followed the trail of Sitting Bull and a large body of Indians to the Canadian line and cleared the country again of hostile Indians."[3]

The Sioux camps were adjacent to the hunting grounds of their traditional enemies, the Blackfoot and Crees. When the buffalo herds moved into the Wood Mountain area, the Canadian Indians could not pursue them without challenging the Sioux, although "already the edible resources on their own lands were becoming scarce."[4] The situation settled into an uneasy peace but the Blackfoot were growing more and more concerned. They had not signed a treaty and the continued incursions by whites, Métis and other Canadian Indians worried them. Now the coming of the Sioux threatened the fragile balance of power on the plains. The Sioux realized, on the other hand, that "the Mounted Police and the Canadian government were their only protection against American soldiers who might follow them across the border. Their own fears would mandate cooperation with the Canadian authorities."[5]

While the main focus of attention was on the Sioux, the force was involved in several other activities. Part of the workload of the Mounted Police was suppressing the liquor trade and illegal gambling. There were a surprising number of ex-policemen arrested for bringing whisky into the territory and many serving members among their customers. In April, when the Mounted Police broke up an elusive liquor ring operating near Fort Macleod, they initially arrested two men and seized 106 gallons of whisky. The next day, two others were caught and a few days later a 45-gallon barrel of whisky was found on the prairies. "A fifth man, who was met on the prairie by a constable of the police force, cut loose a keg of whisky which was attached to his saddle and by the fleetness of his horse succeeded in making his escape." The four who had been apprehended were fined $200 each or six months in prison.[6] The *Free Press* reported that the men had attempted to elude the police by riding down a precipitous bank to the St. Mary's River and jettisoning casks of alcohol while fording the river. The casks were later raised and the contents poured out.[7]

Up until 1877 gambling was not illegal although the drinking which frequently accompanied it was an offence unless there was a permit for the liquor. The police were quite tolerant about friendly games but, from time to time, took action against blatant offenders. On one occasion, a roundup of gamblers netted some seven suspects, including Father Scollen the Roman Catholic priest. Six of the men were fined $250 each but Father Scollen, deemed to have only been "looking on," was freed.[8]

In the spring of 1877, with the ominous presence of Sitting Bull weighing on them heavily, the Canadian Government grew concerned about the low stocks of ammunition held by the Mounted Police. There was insufficient ammunition to sustain

- A Double Duty -

full scale fighting so the government decided to send an additional supply to Fort Walsh and needed a reliable person who would ensure that it got there. Sergeant Major J.B. Mitchell, well known for his even-handed handling of the Swan River Barracks mutiny and swimming the horses across the South Saskatchewan River, was at his home in Gananoque, Ontario, having just taken his discharge on completion of his three-year term. He was asked to return to the force for a short period to accompany the ammunition shipment. He agreed to take it as far as Fort Benton and turn it over to I.G. Baker & Co. for furtherance by bull train to Fort Walsh. The United States agreed to allow the ammunition to pass customs in specially marked boxes. Seven carloads were shipped by rail from Sarnia, Ontario to Bismarck, North Dakota, with one car from Winnipeg being added at Brainerd, Minnesota. The shipment was then to move up the Missouri by river steamer from Bismarck to Fort Benton, Montana.

As soon as Mitchell left Sarnia a comedy of errors ensued. At Brainerd he found the carload of ammunition had already gone westward to Bismarck. At Bismarck he found that the river steamer waiting for the ammunition, having received the carload from Winnipeg, had sailed for Fort Benton. After several days of frantic activity another steamboat was obtained, the remainder of the ammunition loaded and the trip up the river started. Sixty miles short of Fort Benton the boat had to stop at Cow Island because the river was too shallow to go any further. The ammunition was unloaded onto the river bank where, fortunately, the United States Army provided soldiers from Fort Benton to guard the shipment. The I.G. Baker & Co. representative turned up, Mitchell got his receipt and returned to Ganonoque to continue his private plans.

In addition to the tension caused by the presence of the Sioux, the police had to deal with several incidents which required the courage, determination and quick decision making for which the force was known in the west. In May, 1877 a Saulteaux Chief, Little Child, camped with a small band about 15 miles from Fort Walsh, had a problem when about 250 lodges of South Assiniboines, under Crow's Dance, came from the United States and camped nearby. Crow's Dance claimed authority over the entire Cypress Hills. When Little Child refused to accept his authority, Crow's Dance's

- Sitting Bull And The Sioux -

warriors attacked his camp, wrecking lodges, shooting dogs and threatening women and children. Crow's Dance had boasted that if a Redcoat came to his camp he would cut his heart out and eat it. An hour after hearing of this, Inspector Walsh, with Surgeon Kittson, Inspector Edwin Allen, the guide Louis Léveillé and 14 men headed for the Assiniboine camp. After locating the camp, Walsh decided to make a surprise arrest. Leaving Kittson and three men at a small butte to build a breastwork of stones, in case a fight broke out, Walsh and his men trotted into the Indian camp in the night. They located Crow's Dance's lodge and surrounded it. Walsh entered the lodge and quickly reappeared with the chief in tow. The party then took Crow's Dance, another chief called Crooked Arm, and several of their henchmen and moved back to "Kittson's Butte."

There was a confrontation which ended with Inspector Walsh telling the remaining leaders of the Assiniboines that he would take the chief and twelve others to Fort Walsh for trial. The police made a careful withdrawal, followed by a large number of angry Assiniboines, but got back safely to Fort Walsh with the prisoners. At the trial, which started the day after their return, eleven of the younger Indians were released by Walsh with a severe caution. The following day Crow's Dance and Crooked Arm were tried by Assistant Commissioner Irvine. Crow's Dance got six months hard labour and Crooked Arm received two months. Assistant Commissioner Irvine, in a report to The Honourable R.W. Scott, Secretary of State, wrote that: "I cannot too highly write of Inspector Walsh's prompt conduct in this matter and it must be a matter of congratulations to feel that fifteen of our men can ride into an enormous camp of Indians and take out as prisoners, thirteen of the head men." The Secretary of State asked that Irvine "convey to Inspector Walsh his appreciation of the courage and determination shown by him and the men under his command in carrying out the arrest."[9]

A short time later, Assistant Commissioner Irvine and Inspector Walsh were preparing to visit with a large band of Blackfoot who had moved east to hunt buffalo and were in danger of clashing with the Sioux. Just before they left, they received word

- A Double Duty -

from Sitting Bull that he was holding three Americans in his camp and wanted to know what to do with them. The party left next day for Pinto Horse Butte and spent a night, enroute, in a large Assiniboine encampment. The Assiniboines complained about Crow's Dance and Crooked Arm being in jail. They had picked the wrong person. Rather than being sympathetic, Irvine, who had tried and sentenced the pair, gave the band a lecture about keeping the law.

The party moved on to the Sioux camp, rode through it and pitched their tents on the far side. A man beckoned Assistant Commissioner Irvine to follow him and led him to a group, including Sitting Bull, who stepped forward and shook hands. Sitting Bull held a large Council, a pipe was passed and speeches made. Sitting Bull repeated how badly the Americans had treated the Sioux and said that they "hoped the White Mother would protect them and prevent the Long Knives from following. With bitterness they referred to the three Americans who had come to their camp."[10] In a rash move, the United States government had sent the Reverend Martin Marty to speak with Sitting Bull and persuade him to return to the United States. Marty, accompanied by John Howard, General Miles' chief scout, and an interpreter, had been in the Sioux camp for eight days. Turner wrote that "had it not been for the pledge between Superintendent Walsh and the Sioux chieftain, there would have been slim hope of escape for Father Marty and assuredly none for the other two."[11]

There was a second Council that afternoon, with the three white interlopers present. Sitting Bull turned on the priest and asked "why did you wait till half my people were killed before you came?" Turning to Assistant Commissioner Irvine, Sitting Bull asked "will the White Mother protect us while we remain?" On being assured of this, he turned again to the priest and said "why should I return only to give up my arms and horses?"[12] Late that night Sitting Bull came to Irvine's tent and they had a long conversation through an interpreter. When he left the tent, Sitting Bull shook Irvine's hand and presented him with his beaded moccasins as a souvenir. In his report on this incident Irvine noted: "If Inspector Walsh, in his interview with Sitting Bull, had not told him to send to him if any one came into his camp, there is but little doubt but that the scout and interpreter would have been shot. Sitting Bull said as much. The Priest, of course, would have been safe."[13] It is doubtful that anyone would have taken a bet on it.

The next "persuader" to sit in Sitting Bull's lodge was Father Jean-Baptiste Genin. Originally from Ottawa, and highly respected by the Indians, he was well known to the Sioux who called him Black Gown. He arrived on a crusade to persuade Sitting Bull and his followers to return to the United States. Out of respect, the Sioux received him hospitably and listened to him politely but they would not consider moving. Father Genin was disappointed and blamed the Mounted Police who, he believed, had been overgenerous in their treatment of the Sioux.

Meanwhile, in the United States, another unjust war was being waged, this one against the Nez Perce Indians. The United States Government had attempted to evict them from their homes in the Valley of the Wallowa in Oregon Territory and move them onto reservations. The Nez Perce, under Chief Joseph, refused to go. When the United States Army attempted to force them onto reservations, a conflict broke out. After initial victories, the Nez Perce, badly outnumbered, moved across Montana in a series of running battles. They managed to evade General Miles until his troops finally encircled them at the Bear Paw Mountains in Montana, about 100 miles south of Fort Walsh. As one historian noted: The Nez Perces "outmarched, outwilled and outfought all the U.S. Army could throw against them."[14]

Sitting Bull and the Sioux were fully aware of what was happening since scouts and messengers passed freely between the Bear Paw Mountains and Wood Mountain. The Sioux hated General Miles and there was strong support for riding south to rescue the Nez Perce. Many young warriors and at least one chief, Rain-in-the-Face, were prepared for war. There were old scores to settle.

Inspector Walsh was at Fort Walsh when he heard that the Nez Perce had been attacked by General Miles just below the border. He hurried back to Wood Mountain where drums were beating in the Sioux camp and hundreds of chanting young warriors had stripped and painted their faces and bodies. The Council was meeting in a session

- A Double Duty -

that lasted all day and through the night and there appeared to be unanimous support for going to the aid of the Nez Perce. Inspector Walsh, using all the persuasive power he could muster, cautioned Sitting Bull against actively helping the Nez Perce. He warned him that any such activity would mean loss of the sanctuary they had found in Canada. He told the chiefs, "the man who crosses the boundary line from this camp is, from the moment he puts foot on United States soil, our enemy. Hence forth we shall be to him, if he returns, what he says United States soldiers are to him today - wolves seeking his blood."[15] With support from chiefs such as Spotted Eagle and Broad Tail, Walsh convinced the Council not to intervene and the warriors were told that there would be no fight. If this account is accurate there has rarely been an event in Canadian history so dependent on the persuasive power of one man. There are those who consider that Inspector Walsh saved General Miles from destruction at the Bear Paw Mountains.[16]

The Sioux heard that a Nez Perce war chief, White Bird, had broken out of General Miles' siege and they moved toward the international boundary to help the survivors cross the line. When asked by Spotted Eagle how the refugees would be received, Walsh assured him they would be safe in Canada. When scouts reported a large number of whites approaching from the boundary, the Sioux camp was in an uproar, believing that the Americans were on the way to attack them. Walsh, followed by about 200 warriors, rode out to investigate. He found the new arrivals were White Bird with 98 men, 50 women, a similar number of children and 300 horses. He and his men escorted them back to Wood Mountain where the Sioux cared for them. Canada now had the refugee Nez Perce added to their problem while the Indian wars continued just south of the border.

Nobody was certain that the United States troops would respect the border and "as Sherman knew, the hostile Indians were in Canada. To allow the ambitious Miles anywhere near the border with a strong force seemed like a prescription for an international incident."[17] Miles wanted to pursue the Sioux into Canada just as General Mackenzie had pursued the Apaches into Mexico in 1872, but General Sherman cautioned that "... because as you explained Generals Sheridan and Mackenzie once consented to act unlawfully and violently in defiance of my authority in a certain political contingency, is no reason why I should imitate so bad an example."[18] General Miles reluctantly stayed south of the boundary.

Since their arrival the Mounted Police had been successful in severely reducing the sale of liquor to the great benefit of the aboriginal people. Father Constantine Scollen, a Roman Catholic priest, wrote the Lieutenant Governor about the change, recalling that "in the summer of 1874, I was travelling amongst the Blackfoot. It was painful to me to see the state of poverty to which they had been reduced. Formerly they had been the most opulent Indians in the country, and now they were clothed in rags, without horses and without guns. But this was the year of their salvation; that very summer the Mounted Police were struggling against the difficulties of a long journey across the barren plains in order to bring them help. This noble corps reached their destination that same fall, and with magic effect put an entire stop to the abominable traffic of whiskey with the Indians. Since that time, the Blackfoot Indians are becoming more and more prosperous. They are now well clothed and well furnished with horses and guns. During the last two years I have calculated that they have bought two thousand horses to replace those they had given for whiskey."[19]

The 1876 Treaties signed by the Crees, Assiniboine and Saulteaux, left only a small part of the territory between the international boundary and the 54th parallel where aboriginal title had not been extinguished by treaty. The chiefs of the Blood, Peigan and Blackfoot bands became concerned when these other treaties were signed. Their lands were being increasingly encroached upon by white settlers, Métis hunters, and Indians of other tribes, leaving the Blackfoot uncertain what the future would bring. After long delays, Lieutenant Governor Morris decided to negotiate a treaty in 1877.

This treaty was to be signed at a central location where the Blackfoot were in the habit of assembling. The tribes of the Blackfoot Nation greeted the proposal with different attitudes. Some, such as the Bloods, did not really want to negotiate a treaty. They wanted to sit down with a representative of the Queen to discuss their grievances

- A Double Duty -

and work out a solution to the encroachment on their lands. They had asked for this type of discussion many times. Other leaders, looking back on their unfortunate experience with the American treaty in 1855, considered such treaties worthless. By this time a few cattle had been introduced, Cree and Métis were encroaching farther and farther into Blackfoot lands and, in the east, pressure for a transcontinental railway was increasing. Crowfoot, who was more hopeful than many of his colleagues, believed that they would gain all the protection they required through a treaty.

The government proceeded with its plans and in August 1877 appointed Lieutenant Governor David Laird and Commissioner Macleod to negotiate a treaty with the Blackfoot and other tribes in the area. The presence of a large number of Sioux in the Wood Mountain area introduced a sense of urgency so the government was anxious to formalize its relationship with the Blackfoot. Commissioner Macleod sent a message to the Blackfoot, Bloods, North Peigans, Sarcee and Stonies, informing them that the treaty negotiations would start on September 17, 1877 at Fort Macleod. This was apparently done without consulting these tribes, despite their being the parties most directly concerned. There was an immediate negative reaction and Crowfoot refused to attend negotiations at Fort Macleod. He insisted on a site in the north, in his own area. Reluctantly, the Treaty Commissioners changed the location to Blackfoot Crossing. While this change of venue may have pleased Crowfoot, it had the opposite effect on the chiefs of the Bloods and Peigans. The Mounted Police had to be very persuasive, faced with this dissension, but they eventually persuaded the other chiefs to agree to attend at Blackfoot Crossing. This was critical since all the chiefs had to agree to the treaty before it could be ratified.

There was nothing unusual in Crowfoot being able to influence the government's decision on the location of the treaty negotiations. The Mounted Police had carefully cultivated his friendship since their first days at Fort Macleod and conferred special status on him. Because they did not fully understand the manner in which chiefs worked, the police "thought every group of people had a titular political head, a social structure with some ultimate, responsible person to lead and coerce. They did not perceive that Blackfoot leadership consisted, not of one head-chief, but of a fluctuating number of chiefs of small autonomous bands."[20] They considered Crowfoot to be such a supreme chief for the Blackfoot Nation, including the Bloods and Peigans. This created problems when they unknowingly ignored other important chiefs.

In September 1877 the treaty negotiations took place at Blackfoot Crossing on the Bow River, near the present site of Gleichen, about sixty miles from Calgary. The tribes present included the Blackfoot, Bloods, Peigans and Mountain Assiniboines or Stonies. "F" Troop of the Mounted Police, under Inspector Crozier, came from Calgary to prepare the site. Lieutenant Governor Laird travelled from Battleford with a Mounted Police escort under Assistant Commissioner Irvine, while Commissioner Macleod came from Fort Macleod with "C" and "D" Troops, the artillery and the baggage trains. "The police contingent, including those from Calgary, consisted of 108 officers and men, 119 horses and the two 9-pounder guns which had been brought westward on the march of 1874."[21] By the middle of September, large numbers of Blackfoot were assembled at the treaty site with tents and lodges spread out for miles and thousands of ponies grazing nearby. By September 16, a Sunday, the site was alive with scarlet tunics, aboriginal costumes and the garb of traders and missionaries. That also, was the day that the government treaty party arrived to find, to their dismay, that there were only small numbers of Peigans and almost no Bloods among the aboriginal peoples assembled there.

On September 17, a ceremonial blast from a 9-pounder field gun opened the ceremony. The commissioners still hoped the Bloods would arrive so Lieutenant Governor Laird decided that he would not hasten matters. Following a short meeting, there was a two-day adjournment. An announcement was made that if anyone needed food they should contact the police who would provide beef, flour, tea, sugar and tobacco. Crowfoot would not accept rations before hearing the terms of the proposed treaty.

When the parties met again on September 19, the major chiefs of the Bloods had not arrived so there were Blackfoot, North Peigans, a few Bloods and the Stonies and

- A Double Duty -

Sarcee. Lieutenant Governor Laird started proceedings by outlining, to those present, the terms of the treaty. He pointed out that the buffalo would be gone in a few short years so the Queen wanted to assist the Indians to raise cattle and grow grain along with the white settlers. They were also told they would be given a sum of money each year to use as they wished. The money would be useful but given that some buffalo remained on the plains, the Blackfoot were unlikely to be interested in breeding stock or agricultural implements.

The Indians went into Council to consider this proposal. Some were for signing and some against and they looked to Crowfoot for guidance. Crowfoot was in a quandary. As Lieutenant Governor Laird had said, the buffalo were disappearing and would soon be gone, leaving the Blackfoot destitute and dependent on the white man. At the same time, Crowfoot could not see his people starting to farm if there were still buffalo on the plains to be hunted. On balance he believed the treaty to be favourable to his people but he was not ready to commit himself until the Blood chiefs arrived and were involved in making the decision.

September 20 was not a good day for the treaty commissioners. Crowfoot and Old Sun both said they would wait until the following day to speak. The only chief who spoke was Medicine Calf, also known as Button Chief, who gave credit to the Mounted Police. He said that the Great Mother had sent the Mounted Police to stop the whisky trade and he could now sleep safely. He said that before the arrival of the Mounted Police he was frightened by every sound in the night and his sleep was broken but he could now sleep soundly and was not afraid. He went on to deplore the lack of compensation for timber used by the Mounted Police and by white settlers in the Indian's hunting grounds. Lieutenant Governor Laird subjected Medicine Calf's speech to ridicule, saying that the Indians should pay the government for getting rid of the whisky traders and bringing security to the area, rather than the whites having to compensate them for timber. At the end of the day Bearpaw, a Stoney chief, was the only one to openly favour the treaty. The Blackfoot did not speak and the few Bloods present were opposed.

- *Sitting Bull And The Sioux* -

On Friday night Red Crow and the main Blood tribe arrived, and to the relief of Crowfoot, the whole Blackfoot Nation was now assembled and a collective decision could be made. That night, Crowfoot and Red Crow held a Council and in the morning Red Crow met with his chiefs to outline the proposals. Despite some opposition, he obtained approval of his Council to sign the treaty if Crowfoot and his band decided to sign. The final decision rested with Crowfoot.

Crowfoot, like the other chiefs, still had doubts about the treaty. He did not want white settlers to come in and occupy the land but the Mounted Police had saved his tribe from the whisky traders and he trusted Commissioner Macleod. When the negotiations resumed, he rose and said he had been given good advice by Macleod. He pointed out that if the Mounted Police had not arrived, few Indians would have survived since bad men and whisky were killing them so quickly. He said that he trusted the police and would sign the treaty.

Red Crow also praised Commissioner Macleod and the Mounted Police. He said that in the three years since they met Macleod had made many promises to him and had kept them all. He said that he trusted Macleod and would leave matters to him. He agreed to sign. The Indians then signed the treaty, sometimes known as Treaty No. 7 or The Great Blackfoot Treaty. Lieutenant Governor Laird praised the police for their part in the negotiations.

The aboriginals gathered for the Treaty 7 negotiations represented a cultural and linguistic diversity, which created difficulties. There is evidence that there were serious problems with translators during the discussions. In some cases the translators were incompetent while, in others, no translator could be found. There are now claims that the terms of Treaty 7 were never fully explained to the tribes, especially the idea that they would surrender their land. This is based on the premise that surrendering the land was alien to them and they thought they were only agreeing to share the land.

Following the formal signing, some 4,392 Indians were paid treaty money by Inspector Winder, Sub-Inspector Denny and Sub-Inspector Antrobus with currency obtained from I.G. Baker & Co. in Fort Benton. The money was in Canadian and

- A Double Duty -

Treaty No. 7: Crowfoot Speaking　　　　　　　　　　　　　　　　GAI NA-40-1

United States banknotes in denominations from $1.00 to $20.00. Money was new to many Indians so traders often took advantage of them. The Indians got the police to count their change after a transaction since unscrupulous traders frequently gave them labels from fruit jars or cans as money.[22] The policemen also had to work hard to decide the correct numbers in each family when making payment since some would return to say they had counted incorrectly, had additional wives or other relatives and sometimes more children, even those that were expected.

The signing of Treaty No. 7 was a significant event in Canadian history. The way was clear for construction of the railroad and settlement of the plains. This was done in a peaceful way without widespread bloodshed, largely due to the fair, firm and friendly approach by the Mounted Police on one hand, and the cooperation of the aboriginals on the other. The Canadian government had secured its western frontier.

While the Sioux were causing no actual trouble at this time, their presence continued to worry the Canadian government. The Chargé d'Affairs at the British Legation in Washington, D.C. made a formal request that the United States government induce the Sioux to return south of the border. The United States made a counter complaint that American Blackfoot Indians were buying weapons in Canada and asked that they be stopped.[23] Prime Minister Mackenzie was so worried by the idea of either having to maintain and feed the Sioux at enormous cost or, alternatively, to fight them, he even considered allowing American troops into Canada to expel them.[24]

In theory Great Britain still handled foreign affairs for Canada but when nothing came of British efforts in Washington, the government in Ottawa decided to bypass normal diplomatic channels. David Mills, the Minister of the Interior, went to Washington to present the Canadian view. He eventually met with the Secretary and Under Secretary of the Interior, the Secretary of War and President Hayes himself. After considerable discussion the United States agreed to send a commission to speak to the Sioux and offer them conditions under which they could return to their reservations below the border. Much to the surprise of the Mounted Police, the commissioners appointed were Brigadier General Alfred H. Terry and General Albert G. Lawrence. Terry had recently been fighting the Sioux and he was an unlikely choice as leader of a commission to persuade them to surrender. The Commissioners were authorized to offer a presidential pardon, a reservation and cattle, all contingent upon the Sioux surrendering their weapons and horses.

On August 15, 1877 the Secretary of State, the Honourable R.W. Scott, sent a message to Commissioner Macleod who was busy making arrangements for Treaty Number 7. The message instructed him to cooperate with the Terry Commission but not to unduly press the Indians. He was told, "our actions must be persuasive, not compulsory."[25] On September 28, Macleod and a group of men who had been at the ceremony for Treaty Number 7 left Blackfoot Crossing for the Cypress Hills 200 miles away. Enroute the party was engulfed in a blinding snowstorm and reached Fort Walsh after four days on the trail. Meanwhile, Inspector Walsh, who had gone to Wood Mountain with the Nez Perce refugees, had the daunting task of persuading Sitting Bull to come to Fort Walsh to meet the Americans. Sitting Bull refused. He was puzzled

- A Double Duty -

about why the United States wanted to persuade him to return while, at the same time, they were forcing the Nez Perce to leave.

Inspector Walsh used all his personal influence with Sitting Bull but failed to persuade him to come to Fort Walsh. He then enlisted the aid of his two interpreters, Louis Léveillé and Joseph Morin, both of them able to speak Lakota, but they too were unsuccessful. Father Genin, who had arrived independently ahead of General Terry, had two Métis, Antoine Ouillette and André Larivée, in his lodge. After much persuasion, these two got Sitting Bull to reluctantly agree to meet General Terry at Fort Walsh. Inspector Walsh left Pinto Horse Buttes with a party of Sioux including Sitting Bull and Spotted Eagle.

The United States Government asked that the meeting be held at Fort Walsh and requested a Mounted Police escort for the commissioners from the point where the Fort Benton-Fort Walsh Trail crosses the boundary. When Commissioner Macleod heard that the United States commissioners were delayed, he decided to go to Sitting Bull's camp. Inspector Walsh and Sitting Bull left Wood Mountain about the same time Macleod left Fort Walsh and they met halfway. As the combined party moved back toward Fort Walsh the Sioux were increasingly reluctant about the meeting and said "that no matter what happened they had not the slightest intention of surrendering to the United States Government" and returning across the border."[26]

While Sitting Bull settled in at Fort Walsh, Commissioner Macleod took an escort of twelve constables, carrying lances with red and white pennons, to meet General Terry and his commission at Kennedy's Crossing on the Milk River. The three companies of cavalry escorting the commission were ordered to camp and wait while the infantry company in charge of the wagon train was allowed to proceed with the commissioners to Fort Walsh.

The conference took place on October 17, 1877 in the Fort Walsh Officer's Mess. There were buffalo robes spread on the floor for the Sioux and small tables for the American commissioners, the press and the recorders. The police sat in a neutral position to the side. Sitting Bull came in first, settled himself on a buffalo robe and started to smoke his pipe. He was joined by the war chief, Spotted Eagle, who carried his three pronged tomahawk, "a stout staff several feet long, from which three long knife-blades projected at right angles near the end, to form a combined war hatchet and tomahawk."[27] When Commissioner Macleod and his officers entered, Sitting Bull jumped up and shook hands with them.

General Terry was the first to speak, telling the Sioux that the President wanted peace and had instructed him to say that if the Sioux returned to their country and refrained from hostilities a full pardon would be granted for all acts committed in the past and no attempt would be made to punish them. He added that they would be required to give up their horses and weapons. When General Terry finished speaking, "Sitting Bull rose slowly to his feet, threw back his blanket and strode forward." After a short silence, he made a sweeping gesture with his arm and started to speak: "For 64 years you have persecuted my people. I ask you what have we done that caused us to depart from our own country? I will tell you. We had no place to go, so we took refuge here. It was on this side of the boundary I first learned to shoot and be a man. For that reason I have come back. I was kept ever on the move until I was compelled to forsake my own lands and come here. I was raised close to, and today shake hands with, these people." He paused and strode toward Commissioner Macleod and Inspector Walsh, shook hands with both of them, and continued, "that is the way I came to know these people, and that is the way I propose to live. We did not give you our country; you took it from us. Look how I stand with these people. . . . Look at me. You think I am a fool, but you are a greater fool than I am. This house, the home of the English, is a medicine house (the abode of truth) and you come here to tell us lies. We do not want to hear them. Now I have said enough. You can go back. Say no more. Take your lies with you. I will stay with these people. The country we came from belonged to us, you took it from us; we will live here."[28]

The American officers were taken aback. Other speakers followed, then Sitting Bull introduced The-One-Who-Speaks-Once, the wife of The-Bear-That-Scatters. This was a premeditated insult since women were normally barred from participating

- *A Double Duty* -

Sitting Bull Council At Fort Walsh.   GAI NA-5091-1

in Sioux councils. She told the Americans to go back where they came from. General Terry asked if he was to tell the President that the Sioux refused the offers made to them. Sitting Bull replied, "I could tell you more, but I am through. If we told you more you would not believe us; that is all I have to say. This part of the country does not belong to your people. You belong on the other side; this side is ours. You can take it easy going home."[29] The conference was finished. Sitting Bull ignored the Americans, shook hands with the police officers and left.

Later, Commissioner Macleod met with Sitting Bull in his lodge to see if any hope of reaching an agreement remained. He emphasized that although the Sioux claimed to be British Indians the Queen's government regarded them as American Indians who had taken refuge in Canada. Their only hope for survival was the buffalo, a resource that would soon cease to exist, and they could then expect nothing from the government except protection, provided they behaved peaceably. Macleod pointed out that these decisions affected their children as well as themselves and warned that if they crossed the border with hostile intent they would have the Police and the British Government as enemies, as well as the Americans. The Sioux remained adamant in their commitment to the position given the Terry Commission.

- 14 -

Problems On The Plains

Canada's Indian policy was based on moving aboriginals onto reserves and teaching them how to farm so that they could become self-sufficient. This involved an initial financial outlay for seed, cattle, implements and farm instructors. Since the government was perpetually short of money, they did not expend these funds until it was considered absolutely necessary. The government believed the four tribes of the Blackfoot Confederacy, along with the Crees, Assiniboines and Saulteaux could subsist on the buffalo for some time while they were moving toward the desired self-sufficiency. Events combined to defeat the government's careful calculations. The Sioux and Nez Perce who had moved into Canada consumed an immense amount of buffalo meat at a time when the herds were declining rapidly.

The early part of the winter in 1878 was mild and the light snow allowed the country around Fort Walsh to be burned off and tribes in Canada could not hunt on their usual hunting grounds. The Blackfoot moved eastward to find buffalo and came closer and closer to the Sioux while the other tribes and the Métis buffalo hunters pursued the same diminishing meat supply. The potential for conflict increased. At this time there was a series of prairie fires covering large sections of grazing land along the international boundary and many believed the fires had been deliberately set by Americans to retain the buffalo on their hunting grounds.

The chiefs who signed Treaty 7 were given a number of promises, including inter-tribal peace, treaty money, cattle and farm implements, freedom of movement, hunting and fishing rights and preservation of the buffalo. They relied on the government to help meet the rapid changes occuring around them. It now appeared the government had no intention of keeping its promises. Settlers were exerting more and more pressure on Indian lands and the government used treaties as its main tool for extinguishing Indian land title. When the Indians continued their nomadic hunting while the buffalo were quickly disappearing, the government found a new tool for

- Problems On The Plains -

coercion - food. Some officials considered hungry Indians would be compliant Indians, not realizing that hungry people can be dangerous people.

It was during this period, through neglect, parsimony, racist and paternalistic attitudes and outright incompetence that the officials charged with Indian affairs created the basis for most of the problems found today in relations between the federal and provincial governments and aboriginal peoples in Western Canada. Often those with primary responsibility were nowhere to be found when things got difficult and the police were usually left to sort things out. When insufficient food was provided and the police gave their supplies to the Indians, they were accused of encouraging them not to go to their reserves.

In 1878 Inspector Walsh went back to Ottawa to confer with the authorities and returned with a draft of new recruits. At this time rumours were rife about a confederation of tribes against whites. While travelling through the United States, Walsh gave a several press interviews rebutting these stories and emphasizing that the Sioux were not part of any such plan. On his return trip, when interviewed by a journalist from the *Chicago Times,* he said he believed the Sioux and Nez Perce could be induced to return to the United States but it would take time.

Walsh was very popular with the press because he usually provided colourful quotations, but this popularity with newspaper correspondents was ultimately to be held against him. Earlier in the year, annoyed at items in the press, Commissioner Macleod instructed Assistant Commissioner Irvine at Fort Walsh to, "make an official enquiry under oath as to how a correspondent of the *New York Herald* got copies of two letters written by Inspector Walsh to me." He noted that Inspector Walsh disclaimed all knowledge of the matter so the irregularity must have occurred in the Orderly Room.[1]

Throughout the west, horse stealing continued to be a problem. In April the Sioux reported the loss of several horses from their camp. Assistant Commissioner Irvine, Inspector McIllree and six men trailed the thieves for several days and recovered two of the horses from Indian camps they visited. A Saulteaux chief, Red Dog, told Irvine the rest of the horses were in a camp of South Assiniboines who came from

- A Double Duty -

across the border. The next day Irvine and McIllree continued the pursuit to a camp of 300 lodges and were shown into the chief's lodge where the councillors were assembled.

After smoking a pipe, Irvine explained why they were there and asked for the horses. The policemen were surrounded by hundreds of Indians who were in an ugly mood and did not believe they had to obey laws on this side of the boundary. The chief, in a display of bravado, said that he did not fear the Mounted Police. Red Dog, the Saulteaux chief, intervened and explained that those who came north had to obey the law. The Assiniboine chief then backed down and the following morning the Mounted Police recovered 27 of the Sioux horses. Irvine appropriated two or three of the band's horses to make up for those that were still missing and the horses were returned to the Sioux at Fort Walsh.

The main area of Mounted Police activity now centred on Fort Walsh so Commissioner Macleod redeployed his forces to provide the necessary strength The numbers at Wood Mountain Post and Fort Walsh were increased and headquarters moved from Fort Macleod to Fort Walsh, closer to the center of the action. Because of the tension in the area and the potential for inter-tribal clashes, the police had to be constantly alert so that they could deal with small incidents before they got out of hand.

The United States government heard the Nez Perce refugees in Canada wanted to return home so they sent three of their tribe members, captured in the Bear Paw Mountains, to speak to the refugees at their camp near Fort Walsh. They were accompanied as far as Fort Walsh by Lieutenant George W. Baird, who was to escort the Nez Perce back to the United States if they decided to return. Baird had a letter of introduction to Commissioner Macleod from Major General Nelson A. Miles. Macleod wrote back to Miles to tell him that he considered it "inadvisable that either Mr. Baird, or the interpreters, should proceed to the Indian camp, as both the Sioux, and White Bird the Nez Perces chief, have expressed their intense aversion to American officers and Scouts visiting their camps." Macleod advised Miles that he had sent Assistant

- *Problems On The Plains* -

Commissioner Irvine with a small escort to take the three Nez Perces to meet the refugees who "have expressed a desire to Col. Irvine to return."[2]

Early in 1879 there were persistent rumours about a confederation of Indians and Métis to eliminate all whites. Big Bear, a Cree who had refused to sign the treaty at Fort Pitt, was hanging around near Fort Walsh and he was suspected of causing some of the trouble so Inspector Crozier was sent to investigate. Crozier was warned that if he visited Big Bear's camp he would not come out alive. Despite these ominous warnings Crozier called on Big Bear who denied any intention of causing trouble.

Father Genin, the missionary who thought he could influence Sitting Bull, returned to try again. After his previous failure, he complained the Mounted Police were too protective of the Sioux and were spoiling Sitting Bull when they should have been forcing him to leave. This time, when Father Genin failed again, he told the press that Sitting Bull and his followers were unhappy in Canada and were not being treated well. He said there was a shortage of buffalo and other game so Sitting Bull was supposedly ready to move back to the United States. He also said that Sitting Bull intended to call a Council of all Indians on the Canadian side of the boundary to demand food and, if none was provided, to attack the Mounted Police. He intimated that Sitting Bull would return to the United States if he had a guarantee of safety. As a result of his outspoken comments, Father Genin got his knuckles rapped by the United States Army. Major Guido Ilges of the 7th Infantry at Fort Benton wrote to tell him, "I am instructed to say to you that you must hereafter abstain from meddling with any of our Indians . . . and that your offer to bring, through your own instrumentality, the hostile Indians into submission is respectfully declined."[3]

One activity which involved a large number of policemen was the annual payment of treaty money. A large Mounted Police contingent went to Sounding Lake, about 100 miles south-west of Battleford, both to supervise adhesions of Cree Indians to Treaty Number Six and to make annuity payments. Assistant Commissioner Irvine came from Fort Walsh with part of "F" Troop, while a small detachment under Inspector Walker escorted Lieutenant Governor Laird to Sounding Lake. Most of the

- A Double Duty -

Cree signed the treaty and accepted payment but some were still not willing to do so, particularly followers of Big Bear and Chief Beardy.

Big Bear had been labelled, somewhat unfairly, as a trouble maker. As the leader of the largest band of Crees on the plains, he had refused to sign Treaty Number Six in 1876 because "he saw that unless the people united in the face of white settlement they were lost. Refusing official gifts being distributed before Treaty Six negotiations, he said he did not want to be baited so that the government could put a rope around his neck.... Big Bear did not like the terms being offered for Treaty Six, in particular the provision that Canadian law would become the law of the land; as he perceived it, the treaty would forfeit his people's autonomy."[4] At Sounding Lake, Big Bear again refused to sign and, claiming to speak for all who had signed Treaty Number Six, he argued that the allowances were insufficient. Lieutenant Governor Laird told Big Bear he was unable to alter the terms of the treaty but would ensure that Big Bear's concerns were heard in Ottawa. Big Bear said he would return the following year to hear the response.

To offset the influence of Big Bear and his attempts to organize the Indians in order to obtain better treaty terms, Ottawa searched for other chiefs who were ready to negotiate and sign. Some of them held out for a few years but several capitulated. Another notable irritant to the treaty negotiators was Chief Beardy of the Cree, because "in common with other dissenting chiefs, he maintained that since the Europeans had caused the buffalo to disappear, it was now their responsibility to provide for Indians."[5] Beardy carried his objections to the point of threatening to seize the trading post at Duck Lake.

Although Chief Beardy and the Duck Lake Cree eventually signed the treaty they "claimed they had made a more favourable treaty than the others; they grumbled incessantly and demanded more money than was paid their brethren who had signed the treaty at Carlton, Pitt and Sounding Lake."[6] Due to the discontent stirred up by Big Bear and Beardy, Lieutenant Governor Laird went with Inspector Walker to Duck Lake to speak to the Crees. When he explained the terms of the treaty, an Indian stood up

- Problems On The Plains -

and said he did not believe him. Laird then indignantly left the meeting, leaving Walker to tell the Indians that they had insulted the chief of the Great White Mother. When he subsequently paid the treaty money and distributed food some accepted but Chief Beardy and his followers continued to refuse. The government supplies were then locked in the trading post of Stobart, Eden & Co. at Duck Lake and the police departed for Fort Carlton and Prince Albert.

Word soon reached Fort Carlton that some of Beardy's Indians had visited the trading post at Duck Lake demanding the supplies and threatening to help themselves if the trader did not hand over the food. At dawn, Inspector Walker, a sergeant and two men were on the trail back to Duck Lake where they went directly to Stobart's store. The Indians appeared, armed and in full war paint, riding in circles, uttering cries and firing into the air. They crowded into the little stockade and formed up in front of the store. Walker then appeared with his three men, armed with revolvers and carbines. Addressing Chief Beardy through an interpreter, Walker told him that he had made a grave mistake by opposing the White Mother's representative. He told the Indians that if they took the White Mother's supplies from the store his men would shoot the first person to attempt it. Chief Beardy then relented, the Mounted Police paid treaty money, distributed food and presents and advised the Indians to return to their lodges and behave themselves.

The shortage of buffalo forced many Indian and Métis hunters to hunt in the area near the forks of the South Saskatchewan and Red Deer Rivers. There was a considerable amount of discontent because of the poor hunting. A survey party in this area, led by A.P. Patrick, had a confrontation with a group of Crees and Assiniboines who told them to stop work. When the surveyors refused to cease work the Indians seized their horses and said that no one in Canada had the right to occupy their land. Big Bear then appeared and after further discussion, the surveyors suspended work while Patrick went to Fort Walsh to report the incident. He returned with Assistant Commissioner Irvine, Inspector Antrobus and 26 men, armed with newly issued Winchester carbines. On their way they met a band of Bloods led by Chief Blackfoot

- A Double Duty -

Old Woman. From the chief they learned that Big Bear's camp was not far off. The Bloods wanted to join the police against Big Bear but Irvine, thinking this unwise, took along only the chief and one other member.

When they reached Big Bear's camp it appeared to be on a war footing, with no women or children in sight. Assistant Commissioner Irvine and his men went straight past the Indian lodges and stopped at the surveyor's camp with a stream of Indians following them. Irvine told Big Bear that he would have him arrested and locked up if he interfered with the survey. Serendipitously, a Blackfoot messenger from Fort Walsh arrived at that moment with mail for the surveyors. Big Bear decided there was a conspiracy against him between the Bloods, Blackfoot, and the police. He turned conciliatory, allowed the surveyors to continue their work unmolested, and promised not to interfere in the future.

Superintendent Walsh, who had been in Ottawa, received instructions to keep a close eye on the Sioux and continue to try to persuade them to return to the United States. Shortly after his return to Fort Walsh in the fall of 1879, Walsh went to Wood Mountain where he heard that during his absence Louis Riel had visited a nearby Métis settlement and was now camped just south of the United States boundary. Riel had, in fact, been there, having made the trip from Pembina to Wood Mountain by ox cart. As Thomas Flanagan notes, "his presence in Canada was illegal and he would not have run the risk without some reason. His purpose was to establish contact with Sitting Bull."[7] Leaving Wood Mountain, Riel joined a community of buffalo hunters in Montana. Walsh, who employed scouts and other intelligence sources to keep abreast of Riel's activities, passed word that should Riel come north of the boundary he would be arrested.

Louis Riel was working on his vision of a native confederacy based on the Métis buffalo hunting community in Montana, whose members traded with or were related to all the Indian tribes in the region. If he could unite the Indians and Métis, "Riel's strategy was to use the horse-stealing that went on incessantly among all tribes as a pretext to attack the North West Mounted Police. Wood Mountain would be taken first,

- *Problems On The Plains* -

then Fort Walsh, Macleod and Battleford, the capital of the North-West. The objective was to declare a provisional government and sign a treaty with Ottawa. To prepare for a June invasion, all the tribes should congregate on the last day of May at the Tiger Hills on the Milk River."[8]

When Walsh heard that Riel had obtained a promise from the South Assiniboines to support a confederation to unite the Indians and Métis from Saskatchewan to the Missouri, he immediately went south to Montana where he visited an Assiniboine camp at Wolf Point, north of the Milk River. The chief, Red Stone, showed him the confederation agreement but would not give him a copy. Riel claimed the Indians and Métis were suffering injustices which would be corrected by the proposed federation. Walsh was able to persuade Red Stone to destroy his copy of the document which bound the Assiniboines to Riel's federation and to send a message to Riel to say the Assiniboines wished to withdraw from the agreement.

In October Riel announced that with the coming of spring he would be the dictator of the prairies and Crowfoot would be his first lieutenant. Riel coveted the assistance of the Sioux and claimed that if they joined him the Blackfoot would also join. He had some initial success, with nearly all the Teton Sioux slipping quietly across the Milk River to join him while many Métis gathered nearby. Walsh quietly ordered the sale of arms and ammunition stopped, then collected and secured all the traders' stocks. He obtained a promise from Red Dog that the Assiniboines would not join Riel and similar pledges from Sitting Bull, Long Dog, Broad Tail, Dull Knife, Stone Dog, Spotted Eagle, Black Bull and Black Horn.

Superintendent Walsh then attempted to disrupt Riel's camp and dislodge him from the Milk River, both to show that he did not have the sympathy of the Americans and to split his followers into small bands away from his influence. The Métis were camped at the Wolf Point and Fort Belknap Agencies and had to apply for permission to winter on the reservations. The agents were unhappy about their presence but had no means of forcing them to leave. Walsh suggested to the Indians on the reservations that they should complain about the Teton Sioux and Métis being there. The agents duly reported to the United States Department of the Interior, but there was no major effort by the United States Army to evict them that winter, although they were told they would have to leave in the spring.[9] Riel was not pleased with Walsh's activities. He wrote that "if efforts to pacify Tetons have not been successful it is due to the underworking influence of the Canadian Mounted Police."[10]

Meanwhile, the officers and men of the Mounted Police were keeping peace in the west in the face of the failure of the government's Indian policy. On October 16, 1878 Sir John A. Macdonald and the Conservatives defeated Alexander Mackenzie's Liberal government and returned to office. In addition to being Prime Minister, Sir John A. Macdonald was Minister of the Interior and the control and administration of the Mounted Police was transferred to that department from the Secretary of State. In keeping with his frugal and parsimonious nature, Macdonald's government rewarded the efforts of the police by slashing their pay so that veteran constables were only getting 50¢ a day. Many men ending their three-year engagement would not stay in the Force under these conditions. At this time there was also a change in officers' rank titles; Inspectors became Superintendents, while Sub-Inspectors became Inspectors.

January 1879 brought bitterly cold weather with deep snow. The buffalo had not returned in their usual numbers and all across the west Indians were on the verge of starvation. Canada now had two major and related problems in the west - the Sioux and the destitution of the Canadian Indian bands. This should have been a year for consolidating gains and moving forward since the way was now clear for the Canadian Pacific Railway to be completed and for settlers to move onto what had been Indian hunting grounds. Instead, the unexpectedly rapid demise of the buffalo herds caught the government unaware and the two major activities of the police were now watching the Sioux and providing humanitarian relief to starving aboriginals.

Famine threatened the Sioux in Canada just as it did the other tribes. Some of them decided to return to the United States and go onto their reservations and in March and April of 1879 about 200 lodges left Wood Mountain. Others fell back on their tradition of following the remaining buffalo. Sitting Bull established his main camp

Starvation And The Sioux

north of the boundary while his followers established a hunting camp south of the border on the Milk River.

When the Indian Agent at Fort Peck complained that the Sioux were encroaching on the game on his reservation, the United States Army ordered Sitting Bull's old enemy, General Miles, to take to the field and drive them back across the border. The advance elements of Miles' force had an unexpected encounter with a Sioux hunting party. The Sioux fell back slowly until their women and children were safely across the Milk River, then they counterattacked. Miles' scouts were hard pressed until Miles arrived with two rapid-fire Hotchkiss guns. These were highly effective 2-pounder mountain guns that fired accurately up to 4,000 yards. The Indians had nothing to match them.

Sitting Bull and his party crossed the boundary and General Miles and his troops reluctantly halted at Rocky Creek, just to the south. Sitting Bull, in position just north of the boundary, supposedly had General Miles badly outnumbered but refrained from attacking him. Miles, who was quite pleased with himself, saw things differently, relating in a letter to his wife that "we drove the Sitting Bull following out of the country, so badly frightened that they promise not to come back again."[11]

Superintendent Walsh was at Wood Mountain with Lieutenant Tillson of the United States Army who had come north to look for American deserters. When he heard of the skirmish between Miles and Sitting Bull, Tillson recognized that discretion was the better part of valour and asked for an escort back to the boundary. Walsh and a few men accompanied him and camped north of the line while Tillson crossed over and went to General Miles' camp. That evening Walsh was invited to visit Miles and he did so again the next day. Describing the visit, the anti-British, pro-Fenian newspaper correspondent, John Finerty, said, "he was a right pleasant man, with a strong love for Sitting Bull and his tribe. The Major did not inflict a red coat upon us, but was dressed in a very handsome buckskin suit."[12]

General Miles told Superintendent Walsh that he had orders to drive all hostile Indians back across the line. Miles believed that the Métis traders were providing the

- A Double Duty -

Sioux with food, ammunition and other supplies and the best way to disrupt this logistic support was to round them up. He said that any Métis found trading ammunition with United States Indians would have their property confiscated. Miles also informed Walsh that any Sioux who wished to come south of the boundary would have to give up their horses and weapons and go to an agency. Walsh agreed to pass the message to the Sioux.

Superintendent Walsh returned to Wood Mountain and shortly thereafter two Métis arrived to report that General Miles had made prisoners of about 300 families of Canadian Métis and asked Walsh to intercede on their behalf. He travelled back to see Miles and managed to have many of the Métis released. On his return, at the request of General Miles, he brought John Finerty, a correspondent for the *Chicago Times* to visit the Sioux camp. Finerty, who was either very brave or very foolish, appreciated being under the protection of Superintendent Walsh since this gave him an opportunity which, as he put it,"otherwise might never have fallen to my lot, or that could only be attained by the sacrifice of my hair and a scalp once taken, like a neck once broken, is beyond all human aid."[13]

When Walsh and his party returned to the Sioux camp on Mushroom Creek at Wood Mountain, the Indians became very excited. They had heard that Superintendent Walsh and the Sioux who had accompanied him were murdered in Miles' camp. They held a Council and Walsh gave them the messages from Miles. The Sioux initially looked on Finerty with displeasure and hostility but opened up a little as time went on. Finerty, who had always believed the estimates of the number of Sioux at Wood Mountain had been exaggerated, was surprised at the size of the camp. When he left, the police provided him with an escort of four men under Sergeant Major Francis and, on the trail, Finerty was fascinated by the tales of the veteran with his Crimean and Turkish campaign medals.

In October 1879 that perennial optimist, The Reverend Martin Marty, who had visited the Sioux shortly after their arrival at Wood Mountain, came again in another attempt to persuade them to return to the United States. He was escorted to the Sioux

- Problems On The Plains -

camp by Inspector Cotton and fifteen men. Sitting Bull refused to budge. On his way back the Reverend Marty came back to see Superintendent Walsh at Wood Mountain and Walsh personally escorted him to Wolf Point on his departure.

The disappearance of the buffalo and the friction between the Sioux and General Miles on the boundary were not the only things going on in the area. Sitting Bull organized a sun dance to raise the morale and spirits of his young warriors and succeeded almost too well. On their way back from trading at Wood Mountain, Sitting Bull and his band "liberated" several horses belonging to Pierre Poitras, a small rancher in the area. Poitras followed them and Sitting Bull told him he could have his horses back if he gave him ten of the best of them. Poitras complained to Superintendent Walsh who immediately set off to the Sioux camp where he told Sitting Bull that if he did not surrender the horses, he would ask the American military to help move him and his followers across the boundary. Sitting Bull was angry but had no choice, so he returned the horses.

A few weeks later, Sitting Bull and a large retinue, including Four Horns and Black Moon, turned up at Wood Mountain demanding provisions. Superintendent Walsh lost his temper and told Sitting Bull he should go to the trading post since he was an American. Sitting Bull cautioned him to be careful as he was talking to the head of the Sioux Nation. Walsh was not impressed and told Sitting Bull that if there was any more horse stealing he would put him in irons. When Sitting Bull pointed a finger at him, Walsh told him to behave or he would throw him out. Sitting Bull got angry and reached for his revolver. Before he could free it, Walsh seized him and threw him bodily out the door and, as he attempted to rise, kicked him from behind. Sitting Bull again attempted to draw his revolver but his colleagues restrained him. Walsh went to the barracks and told his men to expect trouble.

Superintendent Walsh had two poles from the hay corral laid across the trail to the fort, the local equivalent of drawing a line in the sand. As Sitting Bull and his people approached, Walsh had the interpreter tell them not to move past the poles. He stood with his men who had rifles ready. The Indians came to the poles and stopped.

- A Double Duty -

Walsh said he did not want them hanging around and gave them five minutes to leave. Thankfully, they did.

Meanwhile, Big Bear's band was still stirring things up on the Red Deer River. Some of his followers, led by Wandering Spirit, dispersed a hunting brigade of Métis "by seizing their ponies and abusing their women and children." Inspector Sam Steele, with Louis Léveillé as guide and interpreter, led a strong patrol to the Red Deer River and found the Indian camp. The policemen surrounded the lodges and apprehended the offenders. Assistant Commissioner Irvine tried them at Fort Walsh and sent them to prison.[14]

The police continued to spend an inordinate amount of time making treaty payments, often under ludicrous circumstances. There were instances where very substantial sums of money arrived in large boxes containing uncut sheets of $1.00 bills which had to somehow be separated, usually with scissors, before payments could be made. Sergeant Fitzpatrick wrote that he and Constable Moffat once went 117 miles to Fort Ellice to pick up treaty money and received $246,000 in $1.00 bills, packed in nine large wooden cases.[15] Once, when the time came for treaty payments to the Cree at Sounding Lake, the money did not arrive from Winnipeg on schedule. Indian Commissioner Dewdney had cheques printed by the press of the *Battleford Herald* in denominations of $50, $20, $10, $5 and $2. Payments started slowly since there was some reluctance to accept the cheques, but finished quite quickly when it was announced that buffalo were approaching from the south. Big Bear and his followers, true to form, intervened with many complaints.

In the autumn of 1879, tragedy came to Fort Walsh. For their first five years in the west, no policeman had lost his life by violence and no member of the force had shot anyone, with the possible exception of Sub-Constable Todd who shot himself in the arm. This tranquility ended with the murder of Constable Marmaduke Graburn. At Fort Walsh, all the horses were in need of rest and those with minor ailments grazed on nearby pastures in the summer and fall, often at "Horse Camp." On November 17, a scout named Jules Quesnelle was in charge, assisted by Constables Graburn and

- *Problems On The Plains* -

George Johnston who had joined the force in Ottawa a short time before. Graburn and Quesnelle, who had been out with the horses, stopped on their way back to pick some greens at a vegetable garden. On reaching camp, Graburn recalled that he had left a small axe and a lariat at the garden and went back for them. About this time the camp had received daily visits from a small band of Bloods, constantly begging for food and one, Star Child, was a persistent beggar. Once, having given Star Child all the food the camp could spare and still being pushed for more, Graburn shouted at Star Child to get out, calling him a "miserable dog." Star Child departed.

On the evening of November 17 it started to snow. It grew dark and late but Graburn failed to return. When his horse turned up with the saddle empty his absence was reported to Fort Walsh where Superintendent Crozier immediately ordered a search by Jerry Potts and Louis Léveillé, with his two sons. The searchers followed the trail of one shod horse and two Indian ponies. After persistent searching, Potts found Graburn's forage cap. Louis Léveillé then found Graburn's body at the bottom of a bush filled coulee with a bullet hole in the back of the neck. A search failed to locate Star Child who was an immediate suspect.

The following year the police arrested two young Bloods suspected of horse stealing. While in the guardroom they were identified as having been in the Blood camp near the scene of Constable Graburn's death. As was customary their wives were allowed to visit them. One afternoon while out for exercise the suspects broke away and raced toward a Blood camp on the hillside while their wives simultaneously rushed to meet them and hand them Winchester rifles and ammunition belts. Superintendent Crozier, Inspector Cotton and Surgeon Kennedy, who were playing tennis in front of the fort, took up the pursuit. Meanwhile, Inspector Steele directed several mounted men to join the chase. They overtook the two within half a mile, defied their raised rifles and soon had them back in cells.

That evening the prisoners asked for a secret midnight meeting with Superintendent Crozier in his quarters, requesting that the windows be covered so that nobody could spy on them. At the meeting with Crozier, the Indians gave a description

- A Double Duty -

of the murderer. Word was sent to Commissioner Macleod, who was in Fort Benton, telling him that Star Child was hiding in the Bear Paw Mountains and with the assistance of American authorities he could probably be apprehended. To the astonishment of the Commissioner, the local sheriff would not move to help them unless guaranteed a fee of $5,000 so, for the moment, Star Child remained free.

Starvation was widespread among the Indians that year. At every Mounted Police post there were starving people seeking assistance and "the bison, once 'countless' because there were so many, were rapidly becoming 'countless' because there were none left - so it was increasingly difficult for Amerindians and Métis to pursue their accustomed ways of life. While all who depended on bison were affected, the problem was particularly acute for Amerindians, not so much because of unwillingness to adapt to changing conditions. . . .but because of the suddenness with which it was occurring."[16]

Faced with this crisis, the Indians turned to the only white people whose word they trusted, the Mounted Police, who gave them all the assistance possible. At Battleford, increasing numbers of Indians of all tribes appeared in starving condition. The situation was the same all along the North Saskatchewan. To the south, hundreds of Indians flocked to Fort Macleod, where the demand for supplies became so heavy that, at one time, only six bags of flour remained in the storeroom. Crowfoot sent messages to Fort Macleod that his people were dying of starvation. At Fort Calgary the Blackfoot had become destitute since there were so few buffalo and they appealed to Inspector Denny for help. When he found that the Indians were starving and even resorting to eating grass, Denny took it upon himself to purchase and issue beef at the rate of 2,000 pounds a day. He fed Blackfoot, Stonies and some Métis.[17]

Commissioner Macleod was in Ottawa, being treated royally, unaware that his political masters had started to grease the skids to get rid of him. Sir John A. Macdonald, a personal friend of George French who left the position of Commissioner under the Mackenzie government, now turned a jaundiced eye on his successor, James Macleod. Macdonald fussed about details while Macleod preferred to be in the action.

- *Problems On The Plains* -

Finding an expense claim of $5.00 for a Toronto cab, the Prime Minister got extremely upset. He dashed off a letter to Macleod stating "I have had an opportunity of looking at the expense attendant on the Mounted Police Force and I must tell you in all candour that I am horrified at the expense, and until explained, at the *prima facia* evidence of want of economy."[18]

Commissioner Macleod, in a long reply, expressed surprise at the Prime Minister's letter, saying "I was quite unprepared to receive such a letter outlining charges of extravagance and want of economy in my administration of the affairs of the Force." He went on to recount, in great detail, how he had practiced every possible economy and ended by saying, "I am fully sensitive, Sir John, to how much I am indebted to you for placing me on the Force and I am deeply grateful for the kind interest you have in me. I sincerely trust I may be able to manage the affairs of the Force entrusted to me so as to meet with your approval."[19] This was a vain hope. Once Sir John A. Macdonald had a notion that someone should go, his days were numbered.

Commissioner Macleod returned from Eastern Canada with Edgar Dewdney, the Indian Commissioner and some recruits. On the way up the Missouri, their boat met thousands of buffalo swimming north across the river a few miles west of Fort Buford. This was the last great migration of buffalo to the north. The buffalo remained in a region from the Bear Paw Mountains, south of the Milk River, across the Missouri River to the Judith Basin. Hunters continued to slaughter the buffalo there and, "thousands of beasts were killed and left untouched by knives or merely shorn of tongues and choicest cuts."[20] Meanwhile, north of the boundary, thousands of Indians in Canada were starving.

Commissioner Macleod and Edgar Dewdney visited Blackfoot Crossing, where they found thirteen hundred destitute Indians, emaciated and weak. Most of them had traded their horses and firearms, eaten their dogs and were now searching for gophers and mice. The Commissioner made arrangements to provide one pound of beef and half a pound of flour per person daily. At Fort Walsh, the Mounted Police gave what help they could and rationed out their own meagre supplies. They were beset by non-treaty Indians who demanded supplies. "Chief of these were Big Bear with his conglomeration of non-treaty Indians and Piapot. . ... The latter and his Cree following of several hundred had wandered from the Qu'Appelle Valley in search of buffalo and hovered in the neighbourhood of the Cypress Hills, constantly showing up at Fort Walsh with insistent demands for provisions."[21]

Starvation was a real danger for the Sioux as well, having been evicted from their hunting camp south of the border during the summer. The Prime Minister, Sir John A. Macdonald, told the Indian Commissioner, Edgar Dewdney, that the Sioux would have to be clearly told that they could not become permanent residents of Canada and that they should "no longer delay in making overtures to the United States to be allowed to return and settle in their own country."[22]

While Superintendent Walsh was keeping a watch on the Sioux at Wood Mountain, possibly preventing serious clashes between them and the other tribes, the Métis or the United States Army, his political masters were increasingly unhappy about his activities. In November, Commissioner Macleod received a letter from the Minister of the Interior in Ottawa, forwarding a complaint from the United States Secretary of State that Canadian Indians and Sioux of Sitting Bull's band were repeatedly crossing the boundary into the United States. It was suggested that Canada might find a practical solution to the problem.

The basis of the complaint was a letter to Washington from the Indian Agent at Fort Buford on the Missouri, enclosing a letter from Superintendent Walsh written the previous month from Wood Mountain. In the letter, Walsh said that he believed that all the Métis on the Milk River were Canadian and entitled to take up lands on the Canadian side of the border. Walsh said the Canadian Government was anxious to have these people abandon the chase and commence agricultural pursuits and expressed the opinion that this could not be accomplished as long as they were allowed to hunt in the Milk River country. In actual fact, the government was quite happy to have them remain in the United States where they accrued no expense.

- Problems On The Plains -

Superintendent Walsh was now under increased scrutiny from Ottawa. The Minister reminded Macleod that the Superintendent had "entirely exceeded his duties and powers" and that the Minister considered such a proceeding as one "calling for grave censure." He pointed out that Walsh "should not have taken it upon himself to address an officer of the United States Government on a matter involving government policy without direct authority, and even then, without such communication being conducted through proper channels." Furthermore, he noted that Walsh's conduct was "calculated to obstruct the government policy in its relations with the United States regarding the right of Indians and half-breeds of the plains to follow the buffalo for the purpose of obtaining food, whether in the United States or Canadian territory."[23]

Superintendent Walsh told Commissioner Macleod that he had only intended to tell the Indian Agent at Fort Buford that the Canadian Government did not wish the Métis to trespass on the Indian Reservation under that agent's control and could not be held responsible for their actions. He also wished to persuade the Indian Agent to remove this camp of the Métis if possible, as it was rumoured that Louis Riel, with some followers, was about to take up residence nearby after requesting the Métis in the Northwest Territories to join him on the Milk River. Walsh also said that the large aggregation of Métis south of the boundary was intercepting the northward migration of the buffalo, to the injury of Indians north of the boundary.

Sir John A. Macdonald was now sure that Walsh was the villain in dealing with Sitting Bull. He told the Governor General, the Marquis of Lorne, that there "are grave suspicions that Major Walsh has not been behaving in a straight forward manner in his dealings with Sitting Bull."[24] He later told Lorne that he feared "Major Walsh is pulling the strings through Thompson the deserter from the Mounted Police to prevent 'Bull' from surrendering."[25] The Thompson referred to was an ex-mounted policemen reportedly living with Sitting Bull's band and dissuading them from surrendering. Sir John A. Macdonald gave Superintendent Walsh an additional two months leave to keep him in Ontario so he could not return west and influence Sitting Bull. He told Lorne, "I regret much being obliged to play with this man Walsh, as he deserves dismissal.

- A Double Duty -

But if he were cashiered he would (for he is a bold desperate fellow) at once go westward and from mere spite urge the Indians to hostile measures so as to cause an imbroglio."[26]

Horse theft continued to be a problem. In August 1879 a Cree named Jingling Bells arrived in Fort Macleod. When Constable Arnold McCauley's watch disappeared, Jingling Bells suddenly had an identical one. He received a 30-day sentence but learned to open leg irons and three days into his sentence he escaped. The following year he returned to a Blood camp in disguise, but his disguise was not too good because he was recaptured by Corporal Patterson. When he got out, he went back to horse stealing on a grander scale. He stole the entire herd of the Morley Indians and set off for the border. A sentry at Fort Macleod heard the horses passing in the night and sent out a patrol. Jingling Bells was arrested again and subsequently went back to jail for an additional three years.

When the remaining buffalo in Canada dwindled to numbers insufficient to feed the bands, some started to move south of the boundary where the last of the larger herds could still be found. In the fall of 1879 Crowfoot and the Blackfoot were also strongly encouraged by Indian Commissioner Dewdney to follow the buffalo to Montana. He later boasted that by persuading them to do so he had saved the Canadian government at least $100,000.[27] The Blackfoot moved south to the Milk River near the Bear Paw Mountains where the Métis had built a semi-permanent village. Here they joined the Bloods, Peigans, Sarcees and Assiniboines, all hunting for food. Without the Mounted Police to control them, whisky traders moved in and lawless activity resumed.

Louis Riel, the Métis leader from Red River, who was in the settlement, met with chiefs of the various tribes hunting in the area. He told Crowfoot the buffalo had left the Blackfoot hunting grounds because the Mounted Police were there, that the Canadian government would not meet its treaty obligations and would not look after the Blackfoot.[28] He invited Crowfoot to a large council of the Indians and Métis to be held at the Tiger Hills in Montana in the spring of 1880.

- *Problems On The Plains* -

Crowfoot, who had faith in the Mounted Police and believed his peoples' problems could be solved without an uprising, was unwilling to join with Riel. The fact that the Blackfoot had a long standing animosity with the Métis made the chance of an alliance even less likely. Crowfoot moved his band further south but Métis messengers continued to pressure the Blackfoot to join them. Later they were joined by Big Bear and his band and they spent the winter together in the area. The Métis also moved south so Crowfoot, Big Bear and Riel lived in close proximity throughout the winter. Riel also attempted to persuade Big Bear, who had less reason to have faith in Canada than Crowfoot, to join him. Despite Riel's persuasion, Big Bear was not interested in aiding Riel and persuaded some of his fellow chiefs to reject the proposed "grand alliance," but trouble was on the horizon.

Sioux Camp   NLC C62639

- 15 -

Tension Rising

In 1880, conditions on the plains continued to be bad with destitute Indians gathering in large numbers near police posts. As the buffalo disappeared, the government reluctantly undertook to feed the Indians. In areas such as Battleford, Fort Walsh and Fort Macleod this was done by contracts, usually with I.G. Baker & Co., on the same terms as the police contracts. Beef replaced whisky as the most lucrative commodity for the Fort Benton traders, with contracts escalating to close to half a million dollars by 1882-83. The profitable contracts let to American traders in Fort Benton were due, in part, to transportation advantages. Freight moved into Montana by river steamers could be delivered to Fort Macleod at significantly less cost than delivery from Manitoba. This advantage remained until the completion of the Canadian Pacific Railway.[1]

Despite their incredible destitution, there was little crime attributable to Indians. John Jennings notes that in 1879 sixteen Indians were arrested and only four convicted of a crime. During the same year, eighteen whites were charged. In 1880 only eight Indians were convicted of crimes, five of them for horse stealing. Other than horse stealing Indian crime was practically non-existent.[2]

White encroachment on the plains continued to increase and the federal government introduced a system of leasing vast areas of grazing land for one cent an acre annually for a minimum of twenty-one years. This encouraged the expansion of cattle ranching on the former Indian hunting grounds. At the same time, the contract for completion of the Canadian Pacific Railway was signed as tribes were slowly being moved onto reserves, opening the way for more and more white settlement.

By this time the buffalo had largely disappeared from the Canadian plains, although there were some to be found in diminishing numbers in Montana. In April 1880, there were about 150 lodges of Sioux in the Wood Mountain area, all in danger of starvation and many ill from lack of food or eating meat from diseased animals.

- Tension Rising -

Superintendent Walsh issued small amounts of food to save their lives and the policemen at Wood Mountain shared their own rations with them. The trader, Jean Louis Légaré, virtually emptied his trading post to sustain the Sioux. In May some buffalo were reported to be at Milk River and hunting parties started to return with fresh meat. When the Indians, who had been hunting in Montana, returned to Fort Walsh in the spring there were about 5,000 starving people around the fort. One innovative measure that reduced hunger and starvation was providing the Indians with tackle and nets and showing them how to use the equipment to fish.

Another local trader at Wood Mountain, by the name of Allen, was manager of the Kendall and Smith trading post. He was disliked by the Indians who threatened to get even with him for short-changing them. When a group of Sioux appeared one evening demanding to be let in to the store, Allen and his staff barricaded the door. When the post opened the next day, the Indians crowded in, accused Allen of cheating them and demanded compensation. They entered the Allen's living quarters, seized a small child and took it into the store where they threatened its life if Allen did not meet their demands. Allen held a rifle to a barrel of powder and threatened to fire if the child was harmed. There was an impasse.

One of the staff at the trading post got out and reported the situation to Superintendent Walsh who was sick in his quarters. Walsh sent Sergeant Henry Hamilton with three constables and an interpreter, "Cajou" Morin, to sort things out. They told the Indians that the whites were not to be harmed, Mrs. Allen and the baby were to be brought to Walsh unharmed and all Indians were to be out of the trading post within 15 minutes. One of the constables, by coincidence also named Allen, forced the Indian holding the baby to surrender it. When Mr. and Mrs. Allen were freed, they were escorted to see Superintendent Walsh who was sitting on a box outside his quarters. Walsh, who was not fond of Allen, told them to pack and leave Wood Mountain.

More tension and difficulty soon followed when a Sioux Indian was arrested for making himself obnoxious to Jean Louis Légaré. This put Sitting Bull in a difficult position. He had been losing influence among his rapidly diminishing subordinates and had to do something in order not to lose face. There was a stormy Council meeting and he announced that he would rescue the prisoner. When Sitting Bull and some warriors approached the post at Wood Mountain, they were faced by Superintendent Walsh and 20 policemen. After a short standoff the Indians left. Some time later Sitting Bull came to the post and apologized to Walsh for this incident.

Walsh was having some success persuading the Sioux to leave and eventually Sitting Bull gave up his opposition. He said, "the people of my camp who wish to return to agencies can do so, I will place no obstacle in their way." Sitting Bull had serious concerns about how he would be received personally in the United States but told Walsh that he would have to go "if the 'White Mother' is determined to drive me out of her country and force me into the hands of people I know are but awaiting, like hungry wolves, to take my life."[3]

In the summer of 1880 there was a general reassignment of North West Mounted Police officers. Superintendent Herchmer was moved from Shoal Lake to Battleford, Walker went to Fort Walsh, Jarvis to Fort Macleod, and Crozier replaced Walsh at Wood Mountain. Walsh, who was suspected by the politicians in Ottawa of being too friendly with Sitting Bull and of delaying the return of the Sioux to the United States, was sent to Fort Qu'Appelle.

Sitting Bull was unhappy about Walsh leaving. He said he would like to stay in Canada but, if this was impossible, he would like Walsh to intercede for him. Walsh recorded that "in 1880 just before my departure from Wood Mountain for the East Bull called on me requesting that I go to Washington and present his case to the President and ask if the conditions and treatment extended to the people who had returned from his Camp to the United States would be extended to him personally should he return, or was he to be singled out and made responsible for every depredation committed in the prairie in the last twenty years."[4] Superintendent Walsh told Sitting Bull that he would do so if the Canadian Government gave him permission. When he left, Sitting Bull presented Walsh with his war bonnet.

- Tension Rising -

While at home on sick leave, Superintendent Walsh wrote to support Sitting Bull being allowed to remain in Canada. If this was not possible, he asked to be allowed to go to Washington D.C. to see the President of the United States to seek assurances about the conditions under which Sitting Bull could return to that country. Sir John A. Macdonald told Walsh that he could not go to Washington and ordered Commissioner Irvine to "instruct Crozier to inform Sitting Bull that Superintendent Walsh will not return to Fort Walsh or Wood Mountain and that he has no authority to go to Washington."[5] Walsh was becoming an irritant to Sir John A. Macdonald and would suffer the consequences.

Walsh's replacement at Wood Mountain, Superintendent L.N.F. Crozier, now escalated the pressure to have Sitting Bull and the remaining Sioux return to the United States. The Sioux numbers had been reduced by many lodges returning to the United States and the remainder were starving. Sitting Bull's influence was at a low point and Crozier further alienated him by treating him with disdain, talking directly with sub-chiefs and applying psychological pressure on families by emphasizing the plight of their children. In July Crozier succeeded in persuading Spotted Eagle, a close supporter of Sitting Bull's, to leave with 65 lodges. Later in the year, Sitting Bull's friend Low Dog and his band left to move south. Sitting Bull travelled some distance with them then turned and came back to the campsites of the once mighty Sioux. What the white man could not do, starvation had done.

The United States Government made a final attempt to persuade Sitting Bull and his remaining followers to return to the United States, surrender their arms and horses, and take up life on the reservation. This time the messenger was Edwin H. Allison, a well known scout and Sioux interpreter sent from Fort Buford. Sitting Bull was in a desperate situation with food becoming scarcer and scarcer but he clung to the hope that his friend, Superintendent Walsh, might have been successful in making some arrangement for him. Allison succeeded in having a small number of lodges move, but the majority were discouraged by the continued presence of United States troops just south of the border in Montana.

- A Double Duty -

Up north on the Saskatchewan, Superintendent Herchmer was moving west with "D" Troop as part of the general redeployment in the summer of 1880. At Duck Lake they ran into problems with Chief Beardy, who had never been happy about the treaty process and, being reluctant to hand over his hunting grounds for a small annuity, was considered a trouble maker by the government. When the Indians moved onto the reserves, the government provided them with cattle and oxen to be used for farming purposes. In Beardy's opinion, immediate hunger took priority over future farming activity so he ordered three of the animals killed for a feast. The government did not share his priorities and a warrant was sworn out for his arrest. This warrant was to be executed by the only policeman at Duck Lake, Constable W.C. Ramsay, who wisely sought assistance from Sergeant H. Keenan at Prince Albert. Fortunately, as they were setting off to arrest Chief Beardy, Superintendent Herchmer and "D" Troop appeared.

Armed with a new warrant, Superintendent Herchmer, Inspector Antrobus and six policemen went to Duck Lake where Chief Beardy and some of his band were loitering around the Council House. When he saw the policemen, Chief Beardy called to his men to get their weapons but before they had time to do anything, Beardy, One Arrow and Cut Knife were taken into custody. The situation was tense. Some Indians fired into the air and Superintendent Herchmer had to warn them that if anyone was hurt, Beardy would be shot. The Indians who had surrounded the six policemen followed closely behind as the prisoners were taken to the trading post.

A preliminary hearing was held in the trading post with 200 Cree assembled in front of the building, ready to come to the aid of the chiefs. When Sergeant Parker and the remainder of "D" Troop suddenly appeared, the surprised Indians moved off toward the reserve. There was some concern that there would be an attempt to free the chiefs on the way to Battleford the next day. Superintendent Herchmer took them to Prince Albert, in the opposite direction, thwarting any plan for a rescue. The three chiefs were tried at Prince Albert where they were acquitted by a jury. Another Indian, Omenakaw, arrested later, was found guilty and had to pay for the cattle.

- Tension Rising -

At Fort Calgary, Inspector Denny learned of the murder of a Cree, some time previously, by a Blood or Blackfoot so he took six men and an interpreter and went to Blackfoot Crossing to investigate. About 1,000 Blackfoot and a large number of Crees were assembled about 3 miles apart on the high ground above the Bow River and the situation looked precarious. The Blackfoot told Denny that the killer had already gone. He then arranged a meeting of tribal leaders to settle the matter. As a result, the Crees agreed to move away and the Blackfoot agreed to provide compensation, in the form of horses, to the family of the dead man. This reduced the tension and probably prevented a clash between the two bands.

In November, a band of Sarcees arrived at Fort Calgary from Blackfoot Crossing, ostensibly on their way to a new reserve further west. They had been on a common reserve with the Blackfoot at Blackfoot Crossing and were very unhappy with this arrangement. At Fort Calgary they refused to move on and began to issue threats and make demands on the trading posts of the Hudson's Bay Company and I.G. Baker & Co. The Mounted Police detachment at Fort Calgary consisted of a sergeant and three constables who were hopelessly outnumbered. Word was sent to Fort Macleod and Inspector Denny, Sergeant Lauder and 30 men came to Fort Calgary and faced up to Chief Bull's Head and his band.

The Sarcees who refused to return to Blackfoot Crossing were told that rations would be provided at Fort Macleod if they went there for the winter. The Indians demanded that rations be provided for them at Fort Calgary and a standoff ensued. Since there was no food available at Fort Calgary the Sarcees eventually agreed to go to a camp on the Old Man's River. The Indian Agent, who had come from Fort Macleod, decamped to Morley, leaving the problem to the North West Mounted Police.

Inspector Denny now had to escort 500 disgruntled Sarcee to a camp 100 miles away but they refused to move! The situation did not look good. After three days, Bull's Head agreed to move the next day but said the band's ponies were in such poor condition they would require help to move their lodges and equipment. The Mounted Police provided carts but the Indians still refused to move. Inspector Denny, who had

- A Double Duty -

run out of patience by this time, had his men form up on the edge of the camp with loaded rifles while he and Sergeant Lauder pulled down the lodges. The Sarcee were angry and a shot was fired, passing close to the sergeant, but in the end the firmness of the police kept things in hand. By afternoon they were on the trail and after 11 days, with -35⁰F temperatures and driving snow, they reached the Old Man's River.

In his official report on this incident Assistant Commissioner Irvine quotes James F. Macleod as saying, "I think it a very fortunate thing that this display of force was made." In his usual critical fashion Irvine could not resist adding, "I regret to notice the want of knowledge shown by Inspector Denny as regards official correspondence, as in his letter he deals with various subjects in addition to his report on the trip to Calgary."[6] Given the amply demonstrated ability of those in Ottawa to find fault with virtually everything, there seemed to be no need to point this out.

While much quieter than the posts to the south, Edmonton was also having its share of excitement. December 1880 saw the culmination of a crime that started the previous year near Fort Saskatchewan. Swift Runner, a Cree Indian, had taken his family to new trapping grounds on Sturgeon Creek where he always seemed to have food. He returned from trapping but could not explain the whereabouts of his wife and children. His wife's family got suspicious and reported the matter to Superintendent Jarvis who turned the case over to Inspector Sévrère Gagnon. An exhaustive investigation revealed that Swift Runner was abnormally influenced by troubled dreams in which Ween-de-go, the Cannibal Spirit, urged him to indulge in cannibalism. He followed this urging and had murdered and eaten his family. He was sentenced to be hanged on December 20, 1880. Staff Sergeant Fred Bagley, who had come west with the police in 1874 as a fifteen year old trumpeter, was in charge of the arrangements.

In 1880 there were many changes and events which affected members of the North West Mounted Police. In April the term of service increased from three to five years and Bounty Land Warrants, which gave the right to 160 acres of land, were limited to members who had joined the force before July 1, 1879. In addition, by Departmental Order, there were significant reductions in pay. For those already in the

- Tension Rising -

force the pay of a constable, which had been 75¢ a day for each year of a three-year enlistment, would now be 50¢ a day for the first year and 75¢ a day for the remainder of the five-year enlistment. The pay of a constable engaged after April 1, 1880 was set at 40¢ a day for the first year and 50¢ a day for the next four years, subject to good behaviour.[7] Corporals promoted after April 1, 1880 would get 60¢ a day and sergeants 75¢ a day. Senior sergeants of each division got $1.00 and staff sergeants $1.50. Constables promoted after April 1, 1880 who were still getting 75¢ a day were to continue at that rate during their current term of service. Corporals promoted to sergeant after April 1, 1880, who had been getting 90¢ a day, would continue at that rate.

Applications to enter the force still exceeded vacancies so the government decided to take advantage of this and cut expenditures by shortchanging those who had served them so well. This was a short sighted move. Many valuable, experienced officers left the force when these new punitive rules were introduced. Sam Steele commented that "the consequence of this remarkable regulation was that none of the old hands would re-engage to get less pay than the recruits. No high-spirited man would submit to such treatment, and the result was that the force was given a blow from which it took some years to recover."[8]

Recruits from eastern Canada still came west in the summer by rail and boat to Fort Benton, Montana, then overland, often on foot, to Fort Walsh. One recruit, Frederick Shaw, who was a graduate dental surgeon, related how he and his comrades reached Fort Benton without any money. One of the men, a barber by trade, set up a chair on the sidewalk and began cutting hair. When Shaw saw his colleague making money, he set up two chairs and established a sidewalk dental practice. A third member, L.P. DeVeber, was about to open a physician and surgeon's office when they had to move on to Fort Walsh.[9]

In this year, the force lost the first commissioned officer to die in service when E. Dalrymple Clark, the Adjutant, passed away. He was buried under the trees in the small cemetery at Fort Walsh. This year also saw the end of James F. Macleod's tenure

223

- A Double Duty -

as Commissioner of the North West Mounted Police. While the official reason was that Commissioner Macleod had too great a work load as both Commissioner and Stipendiary Magistrate, there is ample evidence that he had displeased Sir John A. Macdonald who was annoyed at police expenditures and was looking for a sacrificial lamb.

When word got out that Commissioner Macleod was leaving, there was a flurry of correspondence to Sir John A. Macdonald by potential candidates who thought they could replace him. One of these was Lieutenant Colonel W. Osborne Smith, the original temporary Commissioner who was of the opinion that he would, "be of more use than a stranger in 'levelling up' the efficiency of the Force."[10] To the undoubted relief of Inspectors Neale and McIllree, Smith did not receive the appointment which went, instead, to Assistant Commissioner Irvine. Commenting on the change, Sir John A. Macdonald expressed the opionion that compared to Macleod, Irvine was "considerably more of a martinet."[11] This is in marked contrast to the possibly more accurate assessment of Major General Selby-Smith about five years previously who described Irvine as "almost too good natured to command obedience."[12]

Not satisfied with pay cuts, the parsimonious clerical minds in Ottawa also decreed that as of June 1, 1881 no married member could draw free rations, fuel or light for his wife and children.[13] This may not seem unfair but many of these wives, who were unpaid, assisted the force doing laundry, tailoring and looking after small detachments in the absence of their husbands. In an early attempt at cost recovery which was later to come into fashion with governments, it was decided that men who were hospitalized or on the sick list would have 25¢ a day deducted from their pay unless the illness or injury was directly attributable to duty. Not surprisingly, men began to desert and after nine left from Fort Walsh one day in November, Commissioner Irvine advised the Minister of the Interior that "in the spring, however, I fear that further attempts at desertion may be made."[14]

In addition to desertions, there was a certain amount of resistance to autocratic treatment and unnecessary disciplinary measures. At Fort Walsh it was customary at

- Tension Rising -

Saturday night roll call for the orderly sergeant to read out the orders assigning men to various duties. These orders always ended with "there will be a divine service held in the mess room at ten-thirty tomorrow. All those not on duty will attend." This announcement always elicited groans from the men.

One Sunday six men decided to play poker and shortly after breakfast they snuck off to the hay corral outside the barracks, found a sheltered spot, spread out a waterproof sheet and started to play "stud horse" poker. When they were dealing the last hand, the sergeant of the guard found them and marched them off to the guardroom. Commissioner Irvine asked one of them what the idea was and the man told him he objected to being forced to attend divine services. The men were released and after that the order stipulated that attendance was voluntary.[15] They were lucky they had not tried this in the time of Commissioner French.

By 1881 there were many changes taking place in the west. The Canadian Pacific Railway was advancing steadily across the plains and would soon bring in thousands of settlers. At the same time, the buffalo continued to disappear while the government tried to persuade or coerce the Indians to settle on reserves to the north.

Sitting Bull and the Sioux were still in Canada and Superintendent Crozier was much less sympathetic to their plight than Superintendent Walsh had been. Crozier invited Sitting Bull to a feast where he pressured him to return to the United States. Sitting Bull intimated that he would be encouraged by a letter from the officer commanding at Fort Buford stating that he would be well received. Crozier immediately despatched Inspector A.R. Macdonell to obtain the necessary document but when he returned with the letter Sitting Bull said he did not believe a word of it. After all the trouble he had gone to, Crozier was furious. Sitting Bull kept procrastinating, always hoping that his friend, Superintendent Walsh, might have gained some concessions in Ottawa and Washington. This delay in getting Sitting Bull to return to the United States was an irritant to Sir John A. Macdonald. He placed the blame squarely on Walsh, who was still in Ontario on sick leave, since he did not believe that he was being honest about his dealing with Sitting Bull.

- *A Double Duty* -

As time passed, more and more Sioux left for the United States but Sitting Bull stayed on, the eternal optimist, hoping for good news from Walsh. The Sioux at Wood Mountain were in sad condition, with no food and nothing to trade. Tensions increased and even an insignificant incident could trigger violence. One such incident was the appearance of a starving Blood Indian at Wood Mountain Post. He was sighted and pursued by the Sioux but managed to get into the post. The next morning the Sioux demanded he be surrendered to them. They milled about and shouted outside the closed gates and threatened to burn the buildings and kill the occupants. When Superintendent Crozier opened the gate to talk to them about the folly of an attack on the police, Sitting Bull attempted to force his way into the fort. Crozier seized him and threw him back out the gate. Sitting Bull's followers issued a number of threats but eventually left. The Mounted Police managed to smuggle the Blood Indian out of the post and he eventually got to Fort Walsh safely.

Jean Louis Légaré, the trader at Willow Bunch who was providing food to the Sioux at his own expense rather than see them starving, now decided to become involved in persuading them to surrender. He also held a feast at which he told the starving Indians that they should come with him to see Major Brotherton at Fort Buford. He promised to represent them there and if the responses they received did not satisfy them, he undertook to personally bring them back. Thirty travellers set out with Légaré, much to the chagrin of Sitting Bull who considered them deserters. He called a Council and despatched his nephew and adopted son, One Bull, and four warriors to follow and harass them. About half the "deserters" turned around and came back but sixteen carried on and surrendered to the United States Army at Fort Buford.

Meanwhile, Sitting Bull and his band had left for Fort Qu'Appelle in the vain hope that they would find Superintendent Walsh there. They were disappointed to learn that he was still in the east. Sitting Bull told Inspector Steele that he did not wish to return to the United States and he hoped "the Major" would have obtained a reserve for the Sioux in Canada. Sustained by rations obtained from Father Hugonard at the Le

- Tension Rising -

Bret Mission, Sitting Bull and his destitute followers continued to camp at Fort Qu'Appelle, still hoping that Walsh would return.

Eventually they lost hope and Sitting Bull took his dejected band back to Wood Mountain. Here he went to see Inspector Macdonell and unsuccessfully demanded more food. When nothing was provided, Sitting Bull got tough and threatened to take the supplies by force. He had picked the wrong man. Macdonell told him that he would "ration him and his men with bullets."[16] Unable to carry out his threats, the once seemingly invincible Sitting Bull backed away.

The Sioux then went to their last friend and supporter, Jean Louis Légaré. The trader gave them a meal, following which Sitting Bull asked Légaré to take them to Fort Buford. Légaré immediately began preparations for the journey while Sitting Bull procrastinated and delayed. Eventually they got underway but their progress was very slow and Légaré realized that their food supply would not last for the trip so he sent a request to Fort Buford for additional rations. The United States Army provided 1500 pounds of provisions and the trip was completed. Sitting Bull surrendered to Major Brotherton at Fort Buford on July 20, 1881 in the presence of Inspector Macdonell, ending a remarkable chapter in Canadian (and American) history.

The Sioux may have gone but further east Sir John A. Macdonald was still on the warpath. With Sitting Bull safely out of Canada he could turn his attention to his nemesis, Superintendent Walsh, who was still in Ontario on sick leave. Obviously sensing that he was in trouble, Walsh, a popular figure at home in Prescott, enlisted the support of some staunch Conservatives in the area. John Dunhille wrote to Sir John A. Macdonald, "at the request of Major Walsh's friends in South Grenville," referring to Walsh as a "hardworking Conservative" who had "rendered good service to that party during election campaigns." He noted that Walsh's many friends in the Riding "would like to hear of his being permitted to rejoin the force in the North West," adding that as far as he could learn "the Major is 'more sinned against than sinning.'"[17]

J.J. French, a Prescott barrister, wrote that "the friends of Major Walsh are numerous and influential in South Grenville and they are most anxious the cloud under which he seems to be labouring may be removed." He added that "if there should be any occasion for his not being reinstated in the force, will you kindly let me know so that his friends, who are mine as well, may be given a reasonable excuse."[18] Political peace in South Grenville appears to have carried the day and Superintendent Walsh eventually took up his post at Fort Qu'Appelle, but he was a marked man and Sir John A. Macdonald, who appeared to neither forgive nor forget, would bide his time.

While the surrender of Sitting Bull was taking place at Fort Buford, the North West Mounted Police had another demanding task in the organization and conduct of the visit to western Canada by the Governor General, His Excellency the Marquis of Lorne. This was a major undertaking which involved one fifth of the strength of the force who, in addition to the actual escort, had to cache provisions, gather camping equipment and provide transportation and labour. The escort was under Superintendents W.M. Herchmer and L.N.F. Crozier, assisted by Inspector P.R. Neale.

In June, Neale went to Winnipeg to purchase horses, wagons and buckboards. Three army ambulances were bought in St. Paul, Minnesota and shipped to Portage La Prairie, then the furthest point west on the tracks of the Canadian Pacific Railway. Meanwhile, the main body of the escort, under Sergeant Major Thomas Lake, left Fort Walsh for Fort Qu'Appelle, 315 miles north-east. Superintendent Herchmer, with more men and horses, set out from Battleford, 280 miles from Fort Qu'Appelle. Problems arose almost immediately. A thunder storm at Portage La Prairie scattered tents, wagon covers, bedding and equipment. The party enroute from Fort Walsh lost 15 horses in a stampede. The oats that Superintendent Herchmer intended to pick up at Fort Carlton were sent to Fort Battleford in error and he had to give up four of his horses to constables carrying the Indian treaty money. This was not an auspicious start for the venture.

Superintendent Herchmer reached Fort Qu'Appelle on July 21 and the travel weary Fort Walsh party arrived on July 26. On July 31 Herchmer and the escort started again from Fort Qu'Appelle and travelled to Fort Ellice where they met the Governor General who had come as far as Portage La Prairie by train then travelled onward

- Tension Rising -

aboard the steamer *Manitoba*. Besides providing the escort, Mounted Police duties included packing and unpacking baggage and equipment, pitching and striking tents and fitting, repairing and adjusting just about everything.

Having picked up the vice-regal party, the escort travelled back to Fort Qu'Appelle where Inspector Steele provided a guard of honour. The party then moved on to Fort Carlton and since they had to pass Duck Lake enroute, His Excellency was met by Chief Beardy who welcomed him. From Fort Carlton, the party travelled by steamer to Prince Albert and then to Battleford where the escort waited to take the Governor General to Government House. The Governor General held a colourful grand powwow at Battleford, with a Mounted Police guard of honour under Inspector W.D. Antrobus. The noted chief and orator, Poundmaker, was one of the main speakers.

From Battleford, the party headed for Calgary some 300 miles away, but they lost time on the way and, when provisions ran low, changed their plans and headed directly for Blackfoot Crossing where there were supplies. On September 10, a spontaneous Great Council took place at Blackfoot Crossing, with the vice-regal party in full dress uniforms and the aboriginal chiefs in war bonnets. The column then travelled to Fort Calgary and Fort Macleod before the Governor General left via Fort Shaw in Montana.

At this point another of the '73 Originals fell into disfavour, possibly due to what was then euphemistically termed intemperate habits. Turner said that Superintendent Jarvis resigned and settled in Edmonton but a letter from Frederick White, who was travelling in the west, informed Macdonald that Jarvis was dismissed for gross insubordination. White noted that matters at Fort Macleod were going badly, "liquor was plentiful and discipline nowhere."[19]

In October 1881, a chapter in the history of the North West Mounted Police closed with the capture and trial of Star Child, charged with the murder of Constable Graburn near Fort Walsh in 1879. When Star Child was reported to be in an Indian camp, Jerry Potts and four policemen were sent to apprehend him. They moved in at dawn and captured Star Child but in the process a rifle discharged, rousing the camp.

- A Double Duty -

The police party was quickly surrounded by hundreds of Indians who would have attempted a rescue but for the intervention of Chief Red Crow. Star Child was tried at Fort Macleod on October 18, 1881 by Magistrate James Macleod and Inspector Crozier. The jury, which was made up of six ranchers, acquitted Star Child and he was set free. He was later arrested on an unrelated charge of horse stealing and sent to the penitentiary. In an interview many years later, the son of Louis Léveillé recalled that his father believed Graburn was killed by a white man.[20]

As 1881 drew to a close, there were a number of ominous signs which Ottawa ignored despite the warnings of the Mounted Police. At this time large numbers of nomadic Indians still wandered the plains in search of food but conditions in the west were changing rapidly with construction of the Canadian Pacific Railway moving steadily across the plains. These changes caused grave concern to the Métis, who saw the influx of settlers as a threat to those already settled in the country. At Fort Qu'Appelle, hundreds of Métis petitioned the Governor General, expressing the opinion that they had received unfair treatment compared to the Manitoba Métis. They cited promises made during negotiation of the Fort Qu'Appelle Treaty, that Métis rights would be recognized and respected.

The party goers who had seen in the New Year of 1882 had hardly recovered from the festivities when trouble started. At Blackfoot Crossing on January 2, 1882 there was a potentially serious confrontation between the Blackfoot and members of the Mounted Police. The initial problem involved a quarrel between Charles Daly, an employee of the Indian Department, and Bull Elk, a minor chief. Bull Elk said that a beef head was sold to him then given to someone else so he tried to take it back.

Shortly after the disagreement, shots were fired with one bullet passing close to Daly's head. There was a twelve-man Mounted Police detachment at Blackfoot Crossing, but unfortunately under Inspector Dickens who was possibly the worst officer to ever serve in the Mounted Police. Dickens went to Blackfoot Crossing with Sergeant Howe and two constables to arrest Bull Elk. There were several high spirited young warriors at Blackfoot Crossing who, on their recent lengthy buffalo hunt in the United

- Tensions Rising -

States, had formed a Soldier's Lodge. Now, for the first time, the Blackfoot resisted the Mounted Police. When Sergeant Howe and Constable Ashe arrested Bull Elk, the warriors surged forward and knocked down Inspector Dickens while firing their weapons into the air.

Surrounded by 700 aggressive Indians, Inspector Dickens got a message to Crowfoot, who came to the scene of the standoff. Crowfoot told Dickens that the prisoner should be released in his custody on the promise that he would appear before Magistrate Macleod at an appropriate time. Dickens, never noted for his ability in a crisis, surrendered Bull Elk to Crowfoot. Sergeant Howe reported the problem to Inspector Crozier at Fort Macleod. Crozier, who was much tougher than Dickens, took 20 men to the Blackfoot camp, apprehended Bull Elk and took him to the police quarters where a preliminary examination was conducted. Crowfoot again demanded that Bull Elk be turned over to him but Superintendent Crozier refused. When Crowfoot asked whether the Mounted Police intended to fight, Crozier replied "certainly not, unless you commence."[21] Bull Elk was taken to Fort Macleod, tried and sentenced.

By this time the government in Ottawa realized that there would have to be additional members in the Mounted Police and authorized an increase in strength to 500 men in the case of an emergency or impending trouble. The large number of destitute nomadic aboriginals wandering the plains was considered a sufficient emergency and the increase was implemented.

While the liquor trade had been largely suppressed after the arrival of the North West Mounted Police, there were still some remnants of the whiskey trade. In early February 1882 Red Crow, chief of the Bloods, reported to Superintendent Crozier at Fort Macleod that there had been two liquor traders from Montana on the Blood Reserve. The two had returned to the United States for additional liquor supplies but said they would be coming back so an operation was set in motion to apprehend them. On the evening of February 2, three constables, Wilson, Callaghan and Leader, set out with the omnipresent Jerry Potts. They rode all night, leaving Constable Leader at

- A Double Duty -

Standoff and by daylight were near Lees Creek. After crossing the St.Mary's River they met Corporal La Nauze, who was already in the area, and rode with him to the boundary line.

The small party took up positions where they could maintain observation on the gap where the Sun River Trail crossed the Milk River Ridge. That afternoon their patience was rewarded when approaching figures were seen in the distance. After about two hours, a man passed by on horseback and was promptly taken into custody. A few minutes later, a second man, driving a team and wagon, was apprehended. A search found 20 gallons of alcohol, stored in five gallon coal-oil cans, which must have added something to the flavour.

The owner of the alcohol was an ex-policeman, by the name of Cochrane, who had been smuggling for some time. Cochrane was one of the west's characters. During his police service he had been with Inspector Walsh at the Sun River and accompanied Assistant Commissioner Macleod on his trip to Helena in March of 1875. The trip back to Fort Macleod was done in bitterly cold weather with no blankets, other than those under the policemen's saddles. One of the constables, Robert Wilson, noted in his diary that some of the evidence sustained them. The men were tried at Fort Macleod by Superintendent Crozier, fined $100 each and lost 3 horses, a wagon, saddles and harness.[22]

Although the Northwest Territories were officially dry, the use of alcohol was widespread, including use by members of the force. The difficult living and working conditions, isolation and lack of alternate social activities made drinking a perpetual problem for many members at this time and for years to come. Simon Clark noted in his diary the frequent arrests of former policemen, such as Jim Murray and Bob Watson, for smuggling whisky from Fort Benton. On one occasion he noted "the Police boys are on a drunk again. Tony LaChapelle arrived from Benton with quite a load of Jamaica Ginger and whiskey."[23] LaChapelle's name appeared frequently on the list of criminal cases tried before officers of the force, as did Bob Watson's.

- Tension Rising -

After Sitting Bull and most of the Sioux returned to the United States, their benefactor, Jean Louis Légaré, continued to trade at Willow Bunch. On the way home from Fort Buford in April, 1882 a band of 32 Crees robbed him of the food stocks on his wagons. His life was spared only because several weapons misfired and he managed to escape while his captors bickered over the spoils in his carts. At Wood Mountain Post, Légaré reported the incident to Inspector Macdonell, a brave, resolute officer who had been a protégé of Superintendent Walsh. Macdonell passed the word to local Indians and Métis to be alert for Cree raiders and soon had word of horses being stolen from a Métis by a party such as the one that had robbed Légaré. Macdonell set out for the area, taking Légaré with him. They found the Cree party and identified eight of them as having been in the group that had accosted the trader. The Cree were sent to Fort Qu'Appelle where they were tried and sentenced to hard labour.

Big Bear went out on the plains with his followers, after assuring Commissioner Irvine he would not cross the international boundary, and promptly went to Montana. Irvine kept the Americans advised on Big Bear's movements and said "I hope if he crosses the line the Americans will catch him and give him a sound thrashing."[24] Shortly afterward the United States Army mounted the Milk River Expedition to expel Canadian Indians and Métis north across the border. The troops burned the Métis village on the Milk River and scattered the Indians from their camps. Big Bear and his band were warned in advance and disappeared from their camping place before the soldiers arrived. They decided to return to Canada and in April 1882 were back in the vicinity of Fort Walsh.

Big Bear, who had been labelled a "trouble maker" because he was not willing to give up his land and rights, arrived back at Fort Walsh with about 130 lodges. He was reported to have said that if his people were not given ample provisions they would help themselves. Preparations were made for an attack; supplies were moved into the fort, the local trader's stocks of ammunition were secured in the police magazine and two 7-pounder mountain guns were positioned in the bastions.

- A Double Duty -

A message from Big Bear demanding food was delivered by 150 of his warriors. When they were told there would be no food supplied to non-treaty Indians, they rode around the stockade at full gallop, giving war cries, firing into the air and generally trying to intimidate the occupants of the fort. After some discussion, Big Bear's men withdrew from the area of the fort but loitered in the vicinity and provided another demonstration at the time of the full moon. Some time later Big Bear, accompanied by 500 Crees in war paint, arrived at Fort Walsh. Big Bear demanded food, clothing, arms and ammunition but again was unsuccessful. Several months later, as hunger took its toll, Big Bear met with Commissioner Irvine to tell him he would sign Treaty No. 6, which he finally did on December 8, 1882.

Nomadic bands of Assiniboines and Crees continued to wander the plains on both sides of the international boundary in search of food. The United States Army would push Canadian Indians back across the border whenever they found them and the Mounted Police tried to persuade the wanderers to move farther north away from the boundary. Commissioner Irvine wanted one large band of Assiniboines, with a few Crees, moved to a reserve near Battleford but had insufficient men to provide an escort. He assigned the task to Constable Daniel (Peaches) Davis, whose nickname came from his liking for canned peaches.

Davis was confronted with the task of moving 1,100 reluctant Indians across the plains on a trip that would last at least three weeks. He obtained 25 Red River carts and a large stock of food and was, finally, prepared to move off. Nothing happened! Rumours had spread that the Indians were to be forced onto a reserve so their chiefs, Grizzly Bear's Head and Poor Man, refused to move. The young men were riding around, firing into the air and getting excited. Davis knew he would get nowhere trying to threaten 1,100 Indians, so he fell back on the only inducement at his disposal - food. He said if they were not going to move he would return the food supplies he had drawn. The chiefs then agreed to go but wanted to be fed before they started. Davis said he would give them food at the first stop on the trail. The column moved along slowly, covering around ten miles a day, with Davis being continuously threatened. They

- Tension Rising -

reached the South Saskatchewan River in ten days and the Indians refused to go on. Davis crossed the river, put the water on to boil and brewed tea. The others soon crossed to join him.

One night a band of Blackfoot raiders ran off the horse herd, leaving Davis with no horses to ride or pull carts and more than 100 miles to travel. Fortunately, there was ample food. While scouting the area, Davis encountered some Métis camped nearby who had horses. They would not willingly help him so Davis took one of their horses in the name of the Queen and sent an Indians off to Fort Walsh for help. The message got through but neither the Indian nor the horse were seen again.

After a time Sergeant John Ward arrived with the necessary horses and Davis was once more ready to move on. The Indians now refused to go to Battleford so Davis left on his own with the supply carts. He was soon overtaken by the angry Indians who insisted he stop, make camp and have a meal. Chief Bear's Head told Davis his men were in a fighting mood and might take matters into their own hands. Constable Davis replied that if they did there would be some dead Indians. In the face of Davis' apparent lack of fear, the chief backed down. Eventually Davis got his charges safely to Battleford and had a well earned rest.

Life on the plains continued to change. With the arrival of the railway, the crime rate jumped 300 percent in one year and almost 700 percent in the next three years.[25] To avoid clashes between the Indians and the four thousand labourers working on construction of the Canadian Pacific Railway, the government decided to restrict the Indians to their reserves. This was a clear breach of trust since they had been guaranteed freedom of movement in treaty negotiations.

From 1882 onward, relations between the police and the Indians became increasingly strained and there were "many cases of mass resistance and general hostility among the Indians, a situation which the government could well have heeded."[26] In the House of Commons a journalist was quoted as saying "though so far the police have been able to make arrests of Indian depredators in the face of overwhelming odds, the general impression . . . is that the game of bluff is about played

- A Double Duty -

out, and that day when three or four red-coated prairie troopers, through sheer pluck and coolness can overawe a large band of Bloods, Piegans or Blackfeet, is now nearly or quite passed by . . . ."[27]

A decision was made that Pile of Bones or Wascana, now Regina, Saskatchewan, was to be the new capital of the Northwest Territories and headquarters and depot of the North West Mounted Police. The headquarters, housed in temporary portable buildings shipped in from the east, was laid out by Inspector Sam Steele on the homestead of Mr. George Moffat. Steele noted that "none of the officers liked the site", a sentiment shared by many recruits in the years that followed.[28]

North West Mounted Police At Fort Calgary   GAI NA-659-16

- 16 -

Trouble In The Force

Winter had a firm grip on the west as 1883 started and there was less crime than usual. This undoubtedly came as a relief to the thinly spread and overworked Mounted Police. As the railway moved across the plains and settlers started to appear in greater numbers, the apprehension of the Indians increased. Providing advice and assistance to poorly prepared newcomers became a major task for the police. The increased number of settlers meant a greater number of cattle so there was an increase in cattle theft, as well as the usual horse theft and smuggling. To control the area, a number of small detachments were established throughout what is now Southern Alberta.

In January 1883 the Canadian Pacific Railway tracks had reached to within a few miles of Maple Creek and by September trains had reached Calgary. Not everyone was happy about this progress and as the railway moved westward, the Indians viewed it as a "gigantic intrusion upon their old hunting grounds."[1] The Mounted Police worked hard to keep liquor from construction crews, to avoid confrontations between the natives and railway workers and generally to keep the peace. Their success was commended in a letter to Commissioner Irvine from W.C. Van Horne who said, "without the assistance of the officers and men of the splendid force under your command, it would have been impossible to have accomplished as much as we did."[2]

The Cree chief, Piapot, and his band had been at Davis Lake east of Fort Walsh, the location where Superintendent Crozier had provided tackle and nets and taught the Indians to fish. His band was supposed to go to a reserve near Fort Qu'Appelle but he was in no hurry to move. He eventually agreed to go if his band was given provisions, horses, wagons and camping equipment. In June 1883, after protracted negotiations with the Mounted Police, Commissioner Irvine hired freighters to carry the band's possessions and, grumbling and complaining, they moved off to Fort Qu'Appelle.

Piapot was a restless soul, much disturbed by the changes in the west and their impact on his people's way of life. One of the symbols of this hated change was the

- A Double Duty -

Canadian Pacific Railway. After a few months brooding on his reserve at Fort Qu'Appelle, Piapot and many of his followers moved west to where the new track was being laid. Here they lifted the survey stakes, disrupting construction and making it necessary for the work to be done again. He was not very popular with Canadian Pacific. When these tactics did not work and the railway kept on advancing, he took his band back to Fort Walsh where he complained that the reserve given to them at Fort Qu'Appelle was unsatisfactory. Piapot and his followers wanted to remain in the Cypress Hills and they loitered near Fort Walsh and Maple Creek, constantly demanding food.

In a bold attempt to obtain food from the railway, Piapot pitched his camp on the right-of-way and stopped all work. Corporal Wilde and a constable from Maple Creek were sent to remove the camp. The policemen arrived to find themselves facing several hundred menacing Indians. When Wilde told them to move they laughed. Piapot turned his back on Wilde, and his followers milled around, slapping the police horses in an attempt to dismount the men. Wilde took out his watch and told Piapot he had fifteen minutes to remove his camp. Piapot responded by saying they would stay there and his followers yelled and fired into the air.

At the end of fifteen minutes, Wilde dismounted and went straight to Piapot's lodge where he kicked out a pole and started to dismantle the lodge. The angry Indians pressed forward. At this point Piapot had two choices, he could kill or capture Corporal Wilde and the constable or move his camp. He chose to move. His name is still remembered on the Canadian Pacific right-of-way by a place named "Piapot" near the Alberta-Saskatchewan boundary, not far from the scene of his confrontation with the Mounted Police.

Later, some 130 workers on the Canadian Pacific Railway line at Maple Creek went on strike. A large Indian camp in the area was in a disturbed state and the climate was fraught with danger, so twenty-seven members of the Mounted Police were transferred from Regina under Inspector Samuel B. Steele. When a construction worker assaulted a foreman, the police immediately arrested him and the strike ended.

- Trouble In The Force -

This role of protector of Canadian Pacific Railway property gave the force an early reputation as being anti-labour.

By May 1883, with the Sioux gone, Fort Walsh was no longer required. It served largely as a magnet for nomadic Indians and Métis who gathered there in search of food. The government wanted the Indians to move onto their reserves farther north, away from the international boundary. A crew razed the buildings at Fort Walsh and transported any usable material to Maple Creek or Medicine Hat to construct buildings for the new detachments at these points. The arrival of the railway and the allocation of reserves to the north had ended the strategic importance of Fort Walsh.

That summer Star Child, who had been acquitted of the murder of Constable Graburn in 1879 at Fort Walsh, came back to Canada from a horse stealing expedition to Montana. Word of his presence reached Superintendent Crozier at Fort Macleod and he despatched Sergeant Ashe and a constable to the Blood reserve near Standoff. They located Star Child's shack, found him asleep and apprehended him without difficulty. He was escorted to Fort Macleod where he was tried by Magistrate James Macleod on a charge of bringing stolen property (horses) into Canada. He was sentenced to four years in Stony Mountain Penitentiary.[3]

There was continuing unrest among the bands along the North Saskatchewan, especially those of Beardy and Big Bear. In response to the increased tension, the Mounted Police established a 25 man detachment at the Hudson's Bay Company post at Fort Pitt, under Inspector Francis J. Dickens. Dickens was an unfortunate choice whose dismal career was marred by laziness, ineptitude and excessive drinking.

While there might have been some improvements, life in the North West Mounted Police was still hard and the good leaders, with genuine concern for the men in the force, were offset by those, both in Ottawa and in the west, who allowed intolerable conditions to exist when it was unnecessary. The food was poor and limited in variety, quarters were substandard, conditions were harsh, the pay was low and discipline was often a product of ignorance and arrogance rather than necessity. In return for these conditions, the men were expected to work long hours, be exposed to

- *A Double Duty* -

frequent danger and accept any mistreatment their superiors wished to impose. When the men had endured enough and considered their leaders were doing nothing to alleviate or improve conditions, their last option was resistance, a disturbance or an outright mutiny. There was a series of these minor and nonviolent mutinies from the first winter in Fort Macleod and Swan River Barracks. Conditions in 1883 caused more protests.

On March 6, 1883 when the bugle blew for evening stables at Fort Walsh the non-commissioned officers and only one other man fell in while the rest of the men remained in barracks and asked to see Inspector Shurtliff.[4] They told him that Sergeant Major Abbott was so tyrannical and overbearing toward them that they could not stand it any longer. The main spokesmen, Constables Edmonds, Ince, Murray and Montgomery, explained that they did not wish to be mutinous but had made up their minds that they would no longer serve under Abbott.

Shurtliff told the men they had committed a serious offence by being absent from parade and if they had complaints to make they should do it in the proper way. He defended the sergeant major whom he said had done his duty under very difficult conditions and unless the men could show that he had ill treated them, they would have to serve under him. The men considered his words for a few minutes then fell in on parade but, when Sergeant Major Abbott called them to attention, nobody moved. The men then said they would let anyone but Abbott march them to stables. Shurtliff told them they had to go with Abbott or face charges of mutinous conduct. The men then decided to obey and were marched away. That evening they submitted written complaints.

Not to be outdone by their comrades in Fort Walsh, the men at Fort Macleod decided to have a little mutiny of their own when they too found that their complaints were being ignored. Their food was inedible so the men were forced to eat in town at their own expense, there were no replacement uniforms and they were required to act as grooms and servants for visitors to the fort.

- Trouble In The Force -

In September 1883, ten years after Inspector Walsh had taken the first recruits on the arduous trip to Fort Garry, the men presented a long list of complaints to Superintendent Crozier. When no action occurred by the next Sunday, the men refused to mount guard or fall in for Church Parade, although they all walked to church independently. When Crozier saw only non-commissioned officers on the parade square, he checked to see what was going on. He then tried to blame Sergeant Major Bradley, who had recently arrived with a mandate to tighten up discipline. Crozier said there had been no problem before the arrival of Bradley but the men did not agree with him.

Every constable in the garrison signed a document saying that the sergeant major had nothing to do with their insubordination and the grievances had existed for the last six months. Crozier then professed to know of nothing that would cause the men's actions. This is an incredible statement given the long-term and obvious nature of their grievances. Crozier was either making a pitiful attempt to dodge responsibility or he was unaware of what was happening within his command, both of which would reflect badly on his professional competence. The men then submitted another list of their complaints and, after some discussion, most of the grievances were resolved.

Some causes of the Fort Macleod mutiny are good examples of unfair disciplinary practices. Many men will submit to very strict discipline if it is fair, reasonable and consistent. At Fort Macleod there were no replacement uniforms and a situation arose where the men could no longer be properly dressed, as required by orders, so they were charged with disobedience of orders and punished. Given that the provision of uniforms was the responsibility of the force, this was not discipline - it was stupidity. Unfortunately, this type of nonsense, which was common in some Army units and introduced in the Mounted Police during the tenure of Commissioner French, continued for many years. Because of hard conditions and questionable disciplinary practices, there were many desertions and men used any available subterfuge, such as feigned illness, to obtain a discharge.

- *A Double Duty* -

While their comrades at Fort Macleod and Fort Walsh were busy mutinying, the small detachment at Fort Calgary was busy with the Sarcee band. A Sarcee by the name of Crow Collar damaged some property in the ration house on the reserve and the Indian Agent called for help from the police detachment at Fort Calgary. Sergeant Ward went to the reserve and attempted to arrest Crow Collar but the Sarcee chief, Bull's Head, would not surrender him.

Superintendent McIllree and ten men came from Fort Calgary. McIllree spoke to Bull's Head and the minor chiefs, warning them that if they did not hand over Crow Collar he would arrest Bull's Head and take him to the guardroom. When they refused to hand over Crow Collar, the police arrested Bull's Head. The situation was now very tense; the Sarcees were highly agitated and night was falling so the police returned to the Indian Agent's house, leaving Bull's Head with his band. When reinforcements came from Fort Calgary the next morning, the Indians gave up Crow Collar. Both Crow Collar and Bull's Head languished in a cell for a few days and were then released on their promise to cause no more trouble.

The Canadian Pacific Railway, which had drawn the ire of Piapot, passed Maple Creek and moved toward Blackfoot country where it crossed their reserve. The Blackfoot were unaware that the railway line would follow this route. Politicians and bureaucrats in Ottawa were slow learners and, just as they had in Manitoba, they carried out major changes without consulting or even advising the people concerned. To add insult to injury, they did not offer compensation for building a railway across the Blackfoot reserve.

From the time the Mounted Police first arrived and Crowfoot formed a friendship with James Macleod, he had been prepared to compromise and help the newcomers. Now, Crowfoot, "who had been extremely tolerant, was deeply perturbed at what he considered an unwarranted wrong and insult." Commissioner Irvine had told Ottawa he thought the Blackfoot would resist having the railway cross their reserve unless there was some kind of compensation. He was right, "the first rails laid upon the Blackfoot land were torn up the following night."[5]

- Trouble In The Force -

Crowfoot was caught between his respect for the Mounted Police on one hand and his highly agitated young warriors on the other. The ink on the 1877 treaty was hardly dry before Ottawa was starting to break it. As a result, Crowfoot's young warriors were planning to attack the railway construction crews. Father Doucet, a Roman Catholic missionary with the Blackfoot, sent for Father Lacombe who was a friend of Crowfoot and highly regarded by the tribes of the Blackfoot Nation. Father Lacombe came to their reserve and Crowfoot called a Council. After heated discussions, Father Lacombe made a generous offer of compensation from the government for what he described as a "small amount of land" required by the railway right-of-way. With the help of Crowfoot he won the warriors over and the railway construction continued.

On September 1, 1883 Superintendent Walsh retired. His retirement coincided with the end of the first decade in the history of the North West Mounted Police. A colourful and flambouyant character, he had been at the centre of the force's activities for ten years, at Lower Fort Garry, on the march west, establishing Fort Walsh and dealing with Sitting Bull at Wood Mountain Post. John Peter Turner wrote that "of all the officers in the North West Mounted Police none had given better service to Canada in the great western transition than had Major Walsh. In fact, between 1875 and 1883, no man wearing the red tunic had been called upon to exercise a greater degree of courage, tolerance and tact."[6]

Unfortunately he was in the bad books of Sir John A. Macdonald and had no support from Commissioner Irvine who unfairly described him as "both utterly incompetent and untrustworthy" and added that "he does not command respect from officers or men and is very officious. Unfit to hold a commission in the Force."[7] The official records and many personal reminiscences do not support Irvine's character assassination. It is notable that Walsh, unlike many of the other officers, never had a mutiny in the troops under his command and there are many men who have praised his courage and determination. Commissioner French, who was very critical and not easily fooled, reported positively on Walsh that he treated his men and horses well.[8] Inspector

- *A Double Duty* -

Macdonell, who served under Walsh as a constable, sergeant and inspector, was a staunch supporter. Superintendent Walsh may not have been perfect but given everything he had done for Canada and the North West Mounted Police, he deserved a better finish to his career.

By this time it would have been reasonable to consider commissioned officers in the North West Mounted Police an endangered species. In late 1883, only four of the twenty-five original commissioned officers who were serving in July 1874 were still in the force; Crozier, Shurtliff, McIllree and Gagnon. While many had resigned for their own reasons, several others, such as French, Macleod, Walsh, Jarvis, Brisebois, Richer, Nicolle and LeCain were persuaded to go, if not actually pushed out the door. The first two commissioners had trouble with their political masters, French with the Liberals of Alexander Mackenzie and Macleod with the Conservatives of Sir John A. Macdonald, who was also largely responsible for ending the Mounted Police career of Superintendent Walsh.

The retirement of Superintendent Walsh was closely followed by the end of a landmark in the short history of the force. By 1883 the village of Fort Macleod had largely been destroyed by the Old Man's River so the original fort was abandoned and a new one built. This would have pleased the visiting clergyman who, not liking the location of the fort on an island, could not understand why the large number of policemen there, who appeared to have little to do, had not built a bridge or rope ferry.[9] Doubtless some of those policemen harboured similar views on the productivity of the clergy.

In a retrograde step, the government now transferred the control and management of the force from the Department of the Interior to the Department of Indian Affairs. This move signalled a major turning point in relations between the Mounted Police and the aboriginals. It allied the force more closely with the coercive and punitive attitudes of the Indian Affairs Department and helped to erode the trust with the Indians built up by the force over a decade.

- 17 -

A Decisive Decade

The decade from 1873 to 1883 brought the greatest change to Western Canada of any similar period in our history. In 1873, the vast area which is now Alberta, Saskatchewan and Western Manitoba, had few white settlers, no roads or railways and no effective system of law and order. The plains Indians were nomadic, following the buffalo which provided them with food, shelter and clothing. By 1883, there were white settlers, cattle ranches and farms, the buffalo had disappeared, a railway crossed the plains, the aboriginal tribes had been confined to reserves and the North West Mounted Police had brought law and order.

The fact that this change had come about without a major confrontation between the newly arrived settlers and the aboriginal people in the area was due largely to the positive influence and work of the North West Mounted Police. The Mounted Police had monitored the influx of large numbers of Sioux following the battle with Custer at Little Big Horn. They had also borne the brunt of ameliorating the starvation of thousands of Indians following the demise of the buffalo herds, in the face of the government's inability to cope with the problem. Time after time, when the Indian Affairs Department abdicated its responsibilities the Mounted Police rendered humanitarian aid on a massive scale.

The original deployment of the force from Fort Dufferin to Fort Macleod and Fort Edmonton, the crown jewel in the mythology of the force, was essentially a military operation. As such, it had serious shortcomings in planning, intelligence and logistics. The ultimate success of this deployment is more of a tribute to the courage and determination of the participants than to its planners or the government.

Once deployed in the west, the force made a major contribution to establishing good relations with the aboriginal people in the area. In doing so they also performed many of the daring feats which, justifiably, gave the Mounted Police a reputation for decisiveness, fearlessness and fairness. Their accomplishments are even more creditable when viewed in the context of the indifference and interference of the parsimonious government and and the harsh conditions under which they performed their difficult duties.

The government in Ottawa repaid the sacrifices and devotion to duty of the Mounted Police by reducing their already low pay and skimping on equipment, horses and quarters. The men were often subjected to unfair and arbitrary discipline from their officers. To even things out, the commissioned officers frequently drew the wrath of incumbent politicians, especially Sir John A. Macdonald and had their careers truncated.

The police looked on themselves as protectors of the Indians and had a somewhat paternalistic attitude toward them. It is doubtful whether any members thought of themselves as there primarily to allow construction of the Canadian Pacific Railway and the opening of the west to settlers. Initially, most of the Indians placed their trust in the police as the only whites in whom they had any confidence. The good relations between the Indians and the Mounted Police, carefully nurtured from the first meetings at Fort Macleod, were placed under considerable pressure, both by the ineptness of government officials and unfair and regressive policies. As these regressive policies took effect and the aboriginals realized that many of the promises made to them would not be kept, disillusion set in. Their initial respect for the police and their faith and trust in them was lost as members were required to enforce unpopular measures.

By 1879, as starvation increased, relations became strained and they were never to be the same again. The police, too few to force the Indians to do anything, had always relied on persuasion and were regarded as fair, firm and consistent in applying the law. When the government proved incapable of dealing effectively with the problem of starvation after the buffalo disappeared the Lieutenant Governor, Edgar Dewdney, resorted to insensitive measures, usually involving control of food supplies. "As Big Bear laboured to unite Amerindians, Edgar Dewdney, . . . worked to divide them. He did this by differential distribution of rations, using food as an instrument to keep the people quiet whenever a situation threatened to get out of hand. Dewdney also obtained an amendment to the Indian Act that provided for the arrest of any Amerindian found on a reserve not his own without official approval; he was determined that never again would Big Bear or any other chief convoke a large assembly. That this violated the law, not to mention basic human rights, was overlooked in the fear of an Amerindian war."[1] Possibly the most apt comment on the career of Dewdney was that of Frank Oliver in the *Edmonton Bulletin* who said "his appointment was a calamity, his administration a crime, its results a disaster and his retirement his most acceptable act."[2]

The Mounted Police were caught in the middle. They had to enforce bad policy and back up officials who were often incompetent. As their role in enforcing coercive policies increased, the mutual trust and respect between the force and the Indians was sharply reduced and there was now open defiance. In this climate the seeds were sown for many of the problems which plague the relationships between the Canadian government and aboriginal peoples to this day.

Beneath the calm exterior there was trouble brewing. By 1883 there was increasing unrest among the aboriginal peoples in the west and three Cree chiefs, Ermineskin, Bobtail and Samson, wrote to Sir John A. Macdonald that "if attention is not paid to our case now we shall conclude that the treaty made with us six years ago was a meaningless matter of form and that the white man has doomed us to annihilation little by little."[3] The Mounted Police warned the government in Ottawa that a continuing failure to redress the problems of the Indians and Métis would lead to confrontation. The failure of the government to heed these warnings set the stage for the 1885 Rebellion.

Looking back at this decisive decade there is much in which Canadians can take great pride. Canadians are reluctant to create heroes. If the events described here had happened in the United States, names such as Macleod, Walsh and Denny would be household words and their exploits would be taught to every child in school. Rather than create individual heroes, we have conferred hero status on the collective - the force

- A Double Duty -

itself. Sadly, many of those who made the greatest sacrifices in the early years of the force did not do well afterward, while others met with greater success. All of them earned the thanks of Canadians who saw the west settled without widespread bloodshed, but in the words of Frederick Bagley many were unfortunately "allowed by a grateful (?) country to end their days in poverty and want."[4]

As the decade ended there were storm clouds on the horizon. Both the Indians and Métis had petitioned Ottawa for redress of genuine grievances over land and other unresolved problems. Ottawa ignored these pleas and continued to take actions which were often against the law and frequently in direct violation of the treaties negotiated with the Indians. More than ten years previously, Alexander Morris, the newly appointed Lieutenant Governor in Fort Garry, had warned Sir John A. Macdonald that "little as Canada may like it she has to stable her elephant."[5] In this decisive decade Canada had stabled her elephant but the huge beast was restless and threatened to destroy her new stable.

APPENDIX A

What Happened To Them

This book covers a relatively brief period in western Canadian history. There are a number of strong characters involved so the reader may be left wondering what happened to them. The following material provides some information on the lives of several of the characters in this book following the events described.

Commissioner George A. French, who was seconded from the British Army, returned to duty with the Royal Artillery in England. He later served in India and Australia and retired as Major General Sir George French.

Commissioner James F. Macleod, a victim of Sir John A. Macdonald's ire, retained his position as a judge and was prominent in Alberta legal and social circles. He was probably the most universally respected and popular officer in the force in the early years.

Commissioner Acheson G. Irvine, known as Old Sorrel Top, was not a good disciplinarian and had many problems. He was pushed aside after the Northwest Rebellion of 1885 and became an Indian Agent and the Warden of Stony Mountain Prison which may have given him the opportunity to meet again some people he had sent there. He did not stand up for his officers in the face of political criticism.

Superintendent James Morrow Walsh went into the coal business. He later came into prominence as Commissioner of the Yukon Territory during the gold rush. His treatment by Sir John A. Macdonald is one of the more shameful chapters in the political history of our land.

Superintendent William Dummer Jarvis ran into difficulties when he came to Fort Macleod from Fort Saskatchewan. He was dismissed from the force.

Superintendent Samuel B. Steele ran afoul of Commissioner Lawrence Herchmer, the former Commissary Officer of the Boundary Commissioner, who was parachuted into the appointment of Commissioner of the North West Mounted Police by Sir John A. Macdonald, an old family friend. Steele went to the military in the Boer

- A Double Duty -

War and had a highly successful career in South Africa and World War I. He retired as Major General Sir Samuel Steele.

Superintendent Jacob Carvell, the old Confederate cavalryman, disappeared on leave in the United States in 1876, mailed his resignation in from Boulder, Colorado, and there seems to have been no subsequent word of him.

Superintendent William Winder left the force and went into the cattle and mercantile business in Fort Macleod.

Inspector Ephrem A. Brisebois was unable to muster any political support for reinstatement in the force. After a few years in Quebec, including some active political work, he was appointed Dominion Land Registrar in Minnedosa, Manitoba. He was active in the Militia in 1885. His position was abolished on a change of government and he died shortly after that, still a young man. He is buried in St. Boniface cemetery.

Superintendent Lief N.F. Crozier became an Assistant Commissioner. His many positive exploits were largely overshadowed by criticism of his actions in the 1885 campaign.

Superintendent Albert Shurtliff served for many years in the Fort Macleod area.

Sub-Inspector John H. McIllree joined the force in 1873 and retired in 1911 as an Assistant Commissioner in Regina. He was a quiet, steady officer.

Inspector James Walker left the force to be manager of the Cochrane Ranch. He was a prominent local citizen in Calgary, well known in military and ranching circles.

Inspector John French, brother of the Commissioner, left the force to farm at Qu'Appelle. He was killed in the 1885 Rebellion.

Sub-Inspector H.J. LeCain was not considered satisfactory by Commissioner French and was dismissed. A few years later he wrote to Sir John A. Macdonald from the United States, using the spelling LeQuesne, and told him that his problems had all been due to Carvell at Swan River Barracks.

Inspector Cecil Denny was not a favourite of Commissioner Irvine. He inherited a title as Baronet of Tralee Castle and was Sir Cecil Denny Bt. He pursued several careers, including Indian Agent, and Provincial Archivist for Alberta.

- What Happened To Them -

Superintendent William Herchmer became second in command of the force during the time his unpopular brother was the Commissioner. He died while serving.

William Parker, the reluctant ox driver and a chronicler of the march, rose to the rank of Inspector and eventually retired at Medicine Hat in 1912.

Trumpeter Fred Bagley, the youngest man on the march, rose to the rank of Staff Sergeant. He was later involved with the Army, retiring with the rank of Major. He was well known in Calgary, particularly in musical circles.

Sergeant Major (later Colonel) J.B. Mitchell left the force after delivering the ammunition on the Missouri River and returned to Gananoque. He became an architect, settled in Winnipeg, and was responsible for the design of many schools in that city. A junior high school in Winnipeg, is named after him.

Major Donald Roderick Cameron erstwhile Commissioner of the Boundary Commission, returned to duty with the Royal Artillery in England. His father-in-law, Sir Charles Tupper, tried to obtain a promotion or some other recognition for him because of his work on the Boundary Commission, but this was opposed by Prime Minister Mackenzie. Cameron retired as a Major General in 1888 and was appointed Commandant of the Royal Military College by Sir John A. Macdonald.

The Three Entrepreneurial Recruits who set up shop on the board sidewalks of Fort Benton, did well in at least two cases. The fate of the barber is unknown; Dr. Shaw became a well known dentist and prominent citizen in Southern Alberta: DeVeber, the physician and surgeon, also became well known in medical and political circles in Alberta, becoming a member of the Territorial Council, Alberta Legislature and the Senate of Canada.

Dave Akers the caretaker of Fort Whoop-Up stayed on there after failing to sell it to the Mounted Police and grew prize winning cabbages. He was shot by his partner, Tom Purcell

D.W. Davis who had been the chief trader at Fort Whoop-Up remained in Alberta and continued trading. He later became a Member of Parliament in Ottawa from 1887-1896.

- NOTES -

Abbreviations

AHR	Alberta History/Historical Review
GAI	Glenbow-Alberta Institute Archives
HBCA	Hudson's Bay Company Archives
HCD	House of Commons Debates
MPQ	RCMP Quarterly
NAC	National Archives of Canada
NARA	National Archives and Records Administration (US)
PAM	Provincial Archives of Manitoba
S&G	Scarlet & Gold

CHAPTER 1 - CANADA EXPANDS WESTWARD

1. Denny, Cecil E., *The Law Marches West* (Toronto: J.M. Dent & Sons, 1939), p. 60.
2. "Prairie Fire" by Bob Beal and Rod Macleod, pp. 19-20. Used by permission of McClelland & Stewart Inc. *The Canadian Publishers.*
3. NAC, MG 26, A-1, Macdonald Papers, Vol. 516, pp. 767-768, Macdonald to Cameron, November 23, 1869.
4. Steele, Samuel B., *Forty Years in Canada* (Toronto: McGraw-Hill Ryerson, 1972), p. 54.
5. Sharp, Paul F., *Whoop-Up Country* (Norman: University of Oklahoma Press, 1955), p. 40.
6. HCD 1870, p. 1310.
7. Canadian Heritage. Goldring, Philip, *Whisky, Horses and Death: The Cypress Hills Massacre and its Sequel* (Ottawa: Parks Canada, 1979), p. 61. Reproduced with permission of the Minister of Public Works and Government Services Canada, 1997.
8. Butler, William, *The Great Lone Land* (Edmonton: Hurtig Publishers, 1968).
9. PAM, MG 12, Archibald Papers, A-1, Christie to Archibald, April 24, 1871.
10. NAC, MG 26, A-1, Macdonald Papers, Vol. 518, Pt. 4, pp. 929-931, Macdonald to Cartier, June 16, 1871.
11. *Ibid.,* Vol. 518, Pt. 3, p. 513, Macdonald to Cartier, March 31, 1871.
12. NAC, MG 26, A-1, Macdonald Papers, Vol. 521, Pt. 3, p. 750, Macdonald to Colonel I.A. McNeill, October 19, 1872.
13. *Ibid.,* Vol. 252, pp. 113998-114008, Morris to Macdonald, January 16, 1873.
14. Excerpt from *Riel and the Rebellion: 1885 Reconsidered* by Thomas Flanagan, pp. 78-79, ©Western Producer Prairie Books, 1983, reprinted with permission of Douglas & McIntyre Greystone Books.
15. Goldring, *Whisky, Horses and Death,* p. 51.

CHAPTER TWO - THE FORCE IS FORGED

1. Stanley, George F.G., *Toil & Trouble: Military Expedition to Red River* (Toronto: Dundurn Press, 1989), p. 73.
2. Steele, *Forty Years,* p. 60.

- Notes -

3. NAC, MG 26, A-1, Macdonald Papers, Vol. 194, pp. 81206-81207, Campbell to Macdonald, July 11, 1873.
4. PAM, MG 12, Morris Papers, B-2 41, Campbell to Morris, August 14, 1873.
5. *Ibid.*, B-2 43, Morris to Campbell, August 25, 1873.
6. NAC, MG 26, A-1, Macdonald Papers, Vol. 253, pp. 621-624, Macdonald to Morris, September 10, 1873.
7. *Ibid.*, Vol. 252a, p. 11204, Morris to Macdonald, September 20, 1873.
8. *Ibid.*, Vol. 253, Pt. 3, p. 711, Macdonald to Dufferin, September 24, 1873.
9. PAM, MG 6, A-1, Walsh Papers, *Journal of Advance Party of the Mounted Police Under J.M. Walsh Ottawa-Fort Garry.*
10. NAC, RG 18, RCMP Papers, A-1, Vol. 1, File 22-74.Walsh to Richardson, October 3, 1873.
11. *Ibid.*
12. *Ibid.*, Walsh to Richardson, October 4, 1873.
13. *Ibid.*, Walsh to Richardson, October 8, 1873.
14. *Ibid.* Statement by Dixon, December 10, 1873, in a report from Secretary, Department of Public Works to Minister of Justice.
15. Fullerton, J.T., "Toronto to Fort Garry," *S&G*, Vol. 3 (1935), p. 17.
16. Daw, Ruth M., "Sgt-Major J.H.G. Bray, the Forgotten Horseman," in *Men in Scarlet*, edited by Hugh A. Dempsey, 152-162 (Calgary: Historical Society of Alberta-McClelland & Stewart, 1974), pp. 153-154.
17. *Ibid.*, p. 154.
18. PAM, MG 12, Morris Papers B-1 526, Osborne Smith to Morris, October 19, 1873.
19. NAC, RG 18, RCMP Papers, G, Vol. 3436, File O-1 - George A. French.
20. *Ibid.*
21. PAM, MG 6, B-5, Military District No. 10 District Orders, November 10, 1873.
22. PAM, MG 12, Morris Papers, B-2 126, Mackenzie to Morris, August 10, 1874.
23. *Opening Up The West: Reports of the Commissioner 1874-1881* (hereafter cited as *Annual Report*). (Toronto: Coles Publishing Co. 1973), p. 5.
24. Steele, *Forty Years*, pp. 60-61.
25. *Ibid.*, p. 62
26. PAM, MG 12, Morris Papers, B-2 116, Morris to Dorion, May 29, 1874.
27. Excerpt from *Colonel James Walker: Man of the Western Frontier* by J.W. Grant MacEwan, p. 31, ©Western Producer Prairie Books, 1989, reprinted with permission of Douglas & McIntyre Greystone Books.
28. NAC, RG 18, RCMP Papers, A-1, Vol. 1, File 7-74, French to Minister of Justice, January 7, 1874.
29. *Ibid.*, B-3, Vol. 3545, Letterbook of Commissioner G.A. French, French to Deputy Minister of Justice, December 24, 1873.
30. *Ibid.*, French to Minister of Justice, January 8, 1874.
31. NAC, Dufferin Papers, Dufferin to Thornton, March 19, 1874.
32. Steele, *Forty Years*, p. 61.

CHAPTER 3 - PLANNING AND PREPARATION
1. PAM, MG 12, Morris Papers, B-2 82, Morris to Minister of the Interior, December 4, 1873.

2. NAC, RG 18, RCMP Papers, A-1, Vol. 1, File 63-74, Morris to Minister of the Interior, April 25, 1874.
3. NAC, RG 18, RCMP Papers, B-3, Vol. 3545, Letterbook of Commissioner G.A. French, contains a handwritten document - "Commissioner French's Proposals of '74 March to the West." This section is largely based on that document.
4. GAI, M 477, Hardisty Papers, Box 3, File 96, fo. 545, Grahame to Hardisty, August 8, 1874.
5. NAC, RG 18, RCMP Papers, A-1, Vol. 1, File 4-74.
6. *Ibid.*
7. *Ibid.*, Vol. 1, File 5-74.
8. NAC, RG 18, RCMP Papers, B-3, Vol. 3545, Letterbook of Commissioner G.A. French, Jarvis to French, March 27, 1874.
9. GAI, M 43, Bagley, Frederick A., *The '74 Mounties by One of Them*.
10. Dempsey, Hugh A. (ed.) *William Parker: Mounted Policeman* (Calgary: Glenbow-Alberta Institute, 1973) p. 4.
11. Bagley, *The '74 Mounties*, p. 2.
12. *Ibid.*, p. 4.
13. *Ibid.*, pp. 6-7.
14. D'Artigue, Jean, *Six Years in the Canadian North-West* (Belleville: Mika Publishing, 1971), p. 16.
15. *Annual Report 1874*, p. 6.
16. Porter, G.C., "Colonel J.B. Mitchell, North West Mounted Police Survivor," *The Winnipeg Tribune*, November 30, 1940, p. 4.
17. Bagley, *The '74 Mounties*, p. 9.
18. *Ibid.*, p. 8.
19. PAM, MG 12, Morris Papers, B-2, L/BG 107/113/114, Urquhart to Osborne Smith, December 8, 1873 and Urquhart to French, December 17 and December 24, 1873.
20. HBCA B302/a/1, Lower Fort Garry Post Journals, fols. 168-170, December 28, 1873.
21. Bagley, *The '74 Mounties*, p. viii.
22. PAM, MG 12, Morris Papers, B-2 215, Becher to French, November 10, 1874.
23. NAC, RG 18, RCMP Papers, B-3, Vol. 3545, Letterbook of Commissioner G.A. French, French to Private Sec. to the Lieutenant Governor, December 16, 1874.
24. *Ibid.*, A-1, Vol. 1, File 30-74 contains details.
25. NAC, MG 26, A-1, Macdonald Papers, Vol. 370, pp. 172136-39, Smith to Macdonald, October 12, 1880.
26. *Ibid.*, Vol. 346, pp. 158595-602, Clark to Macdonald, May 18, 1874.
27. NAC, RG 18, RCMP Papers, G, Vol. 3436, File O-4 - James F. Macleod.
28. NAC, RG 2, Privy Council Order 603 dated May 28, 1874.
29. Royal Canadian Mounted Police, Turner, John Peter, *The North West Mounted Police 1873-1893*, 2 vols (Ottawa: King's Printer, 1950), p. 120. Reproduced with the permission of the Minister of Public Works and Government Services Canada, 1997.
30. PAM, MG 12, B-1, L/BJ 184, Morris Papers, Morris to Grahame, June 19, 1874.
31. *Ibid.*, B-1, L/BJ 183, Morris to Grahame, June 15, 1874.
32. GAI, M 477, Hardisty Papers, Box 3, File 96, fo. 549, McKay to Hardisty, August 28, 1874.
33. PAM, MG 12, Morris Papers, Grahame to Morris, June 15, 1874.
34. *Ibid.*, Report of Rev. John McDougall.

- Notes -

35. *Ibid.*
36. Steele, *Forty Years*, p. 62.
37. Canadian Heritage. Ross, David (ed.) *Jottings on the March From Fort Garry to the Rocky Mountains 1874 by James Finlayson of "B" Troop North West Mounted Police* (Winnipeg: Parks Canada, 1990). Reproduced with permission of the Minister of Public Works and Government Services, 1997. (Hereafter cited as Finlayson, *Diary*).
38. Excerpt from *Colonel James Walker: Man of the Western Frontier*, by J.W. Grant MacEwan, pp. 36-37, ©Western Producer Prairie Books, 1989, reprinted with permission of Douglas & McIntyre Greystone Books.
39. D'Artigue, *Six Years*, p. 24.
40. Porter, "N.W.M.P. Survivor."
41. Excerpt from *Colonel James Walker: Man of the Western Frontier*, by J.W. Grant MacEwan, p. 40, ©Western Producer Prairie Books 1989, reprinted with permission of Douglas & McIntyre Greystone Books.
42. GAI, M 44, Bagley, Frederick A., *Diary of a North West Mounted Police Trumpeter 1874-1884*, pp. 3-4.
43. Excerpt from *Colonel James Walker: Man of the Western Frontier*, by J.W. Grant MacEwan, p. 39, ©Western Producer Prairie Books 1989, reprinted with permission of Douglas & McIntyre Greystone Books.
44. Excerpt from *Vet in the Saddle: John L. Poett: First Veterinary Surgeon of the North West Mounted Police*, by Franklin M. Lowe and Edward E.H. Wood, p. 12, © Western Producer Prairie Books, 1978, reprinted with permission of Douglas & McIntyre Greystone Books.
45. *Annual Report 1874*, p. 70.
46. Denny, *The Law Marches West*, p. 15.
47. D'Artigue, *Six Years*, p. 34.
48. *Ibid.*, p. 28.
49. *Annual Report 1874*, p. 9.
50. D'Artigue, *Six Years*, p. 34.
51. Bagley, *Diary*, p. 5.
52. Excerpt from *Colonel James Walker: Man of the Western Frontier* by J.W. Grant MacEwan, p. 41, ©Western Producer Prairie Books, 1989, reprinted with permission of Douglas & McIntyre Greystone Books.
53. Bagley, *Diary*, p. 7.
54. NAC, Colonial Office Records, Vol. 1730, p. 92.
55. *Annual Report 1874*, p. 9.
56. Phillips, Roger and S.J. Kirby, *Small Arms of the Mounted Police* (Ottawa: Museum Restoration Services, 1965), p. 7.
57. Griesbach, W.A., *I Remember* (Toronto: Ryerson Press, 1946), p. 16.
58. NAC, RG 2, Privy Council Order 383 dated April 14, 1876.
59. *Free Press*, Winnipeg: July 9, 1874.
60. NAC, RG 18, RCMP Papers, G. Vol. 3436, File O-15 - Charles F. Young.
61. GAI, M 776, Macleod Papers, James Macleod to Mary Drever, July 10, 1874.
62. GAI, M 4166, Shaw Papers, "Frontiers of Western Canada 1880-1900: A Biography of Frederick Davis Shaw 1856-1926."
63. PAM, MG 12, B-2 122, Morris Papers, Morris to Mackenzie, July 10, 1874.

- A Double Duty -

64. Horrall, S.W., "The March West," in *Men In Scarlet*, edited by Hugh A. Dempsey, 13-26, (Calgary: Historical Society of Alberta-McClelland & Stewart, 1973), p. 20.
65. PAM, MG 12, B-2 122, Morris Papers, Morris to Mackenzie, July 6, 1874.
66. NAC, RG 18, RCMP Papers, A-1, Vol. 2, File 130-74, Bernard to French, July 10, 1874.

CHAPTER 4 - FORT DUFFERIN TO ROCHE PERCÉE

1. *Annual Report 1874*, p. 10.
2. *Free Press*, Winnipeg: July 10, 1874.
3. Finlayson, *Diary*, Entry for July 8, 1874.
4. Bagley, *The '74 Mounties*, p. 24.
5. *Annual Report 1874*, p. 26.
6. D'Artigue, *Six Years*, p. 45.
7. *Annual Report 1874*, p. 25.
8. Dempsey, *William Parker*, p. 9.
9. Maunsell, E.H., "With the North West Mounted Police Force From 1874 to 1877," S&G, 2 (1920), p. 52.
10. GAI, M 165A, File 14.
11. GAI, M 776, Macleod Papers, James Macleod to Mary Drever, July 10, 1874.
12. Finlayson, *Diary*, Entry for July 10, 1874.
13. GAI, M 611, The Northwest Expedition - 1874 of the North West Mounted Police: Diary of Henri Julien, p. 10.
14. Finlayson, *Diary*, Entry for July 11, 1874.
15. *Annual Report 1874*, p. 10.
16. Finlayson, *Diary*, Entry for July 11, 1874.
17. Turner, *North West Mounted Police*, Vol. 1, p. 131.
18. D'Artigue, *Six Years*, p. 42.
19. Julien, *Diary*, p. 11.
20. D'Artigue, *Six Years*, p. 43.
21. Julien, *Diary*, p. 12.
22. Finlayson, *Diary*, Entry for July 14, 1874.
23. *Ibid.*, Entry for July 15, 1874.
24. *Ibid.*, Entry for July 16, 1874.
25. *Free Press*, Winnipeg: July 16, 1874.
26. Mitchell, Colonel J.B., "Sir Sam Steele," *S&G*, (1919), pp. 23-25.
27. Finlayson, *Diary*, Entry for July 17, 1874.
28. *Annual Report 1874*, p. 35.
29. D'Artigue, *Six Years*, p. 40.
30. Bagley, *The '74 Mounties*, p. 26.
31. D'Artigue, *Six Years*, p. 45.
32. Maunsell, "With the North West Mounted," p. 52.
33. GAI, M 473, McIllree, J.H., *Diary of John H. McIllree*, Entry for July 19, 1874.
34. D'Artigue, *Six Years*, p. 13.
35. Bagley, *The '74 Mounties*, p. 34.
36. Finlayson, *Diary*, Entry for July 24, 1874.
37. D'Artigue, *Six Years*, p. 50.
38. *Free Press*, Winnipeg: August 24, 1874.

- Notes -

39. *Annual Report 1874*, p. 37.

CHAPTER 5 - ROCHE PERCÉE TO FORT MACLEOD
1. McIllree, *Diary*, Entry for July 30, 1874.
2. *Annual Report 1874*, pp. 38-39.
3. Horrall, "The March West," p. 21.
4. Sharp, *Whoop-Up Country*, p. 84.
5. McIllree, *Diary*, Entry for August 2, 1874.
6. Pearce, William, "Notes on the History and Settlement of the Canadian Northwest," p. 149.
7. McIllree, *Diary*, Entry for August 3, 1874.
8. *Annual Report 1874*, p. 39.
9. Denny, *The Law Marches West*, p. 27.
10. Julien, *Diary*, pp. 12-13.
11. Bagley, *The '74 Mounties*, p. 45.
12. *Ibid.*, p. 43.
13. Finlayson, *Diary*, Entry for August 11, 1874.
14. McIllree, *Diary*, Entry for August 13, 1874.
15. *Annual Report 1874*, p. 41.
16. *Ibid.*, p. 16.
17. *Ibid.*, p. 47.
18. Haig, Kenneth M., *Col. J.B. Mitchell* (Winnipeg, The Garry Press, 1957), p. 12.
19. GAI, M 6608, Carscadden, Joseph, *Journal of the North West Mounted Police Trek 1874*, p. 25.
20. "They Opened the Way for Peaceful Development of Canada's Broad Plains," MPQ, Vol. 11, Nos. 2-3 (Oct 45-Jan 46).
21. Finlayson, *Diary*, Entry for September 5, 1874.
22. *Annual Report 1874*, p. 46.
23. Carscadden, *Journal*, p. 37.
24. *Ibid.*, p. 38.
25. *Annual Report 1874*, p. 72.
26. Finlayson, *Diary*, Entry for September 10, 1874.
27. *Annual Report 1874*, p. 46.
28. Carscadden, *Journal*, pp. 46-47.
29. MacLaren, Sherill Maxwell, *Braeside: Three Founding Families in Nineteenth Century Canada* (Toronto: McClelland & Stewart, 1986), p. 137.
30. Carscadden, *Journal*, p. 43.
31. *Annual Report 1874*, p. 47.
32. Cruise, David and Alison Griffiths, *The Great Adventure: How The Mounties Conquered the West* (Toronto: Penguin Books, 1996), p. 311.
33. Carscadden, *Journal*, pp. 312-313.
34. Finlayson, *Diary*, Entry for September 10, 1874.
35. Turner, *North West Mounted Police,* Vol. 1, p. 149.
36. *Ibid.*, Vol. 1, pp. 150-151.
37. *Annual Report 1874*, p. 75.
38. Bagley, *The '74 Mounties*, p. 57.
39. McIllree, *Diary*, Entry for September 19, 1874.

40. Carscadden, *Journal*, p. 47.
41. *Chronicle of the Canadian West: North West Mounted Police Report for 1875* (hereafter cited as *Chronicle* Calgary: Historical Society of Alberta, 1975), p. 23.
42. Excerpt from *Colonel James Walker: Man of the Western Frontier* by J.W. Grant MacEwan, p. 50, ©Western Producer Prairie Books, 1989, reprinted with permission of Douglas & McIntyre Greystone Booksp.
43. GAI, M 776, Macleod Papers, Macleod to Mary Drever, September 28, 1874.
44. NAC, RG 2, Privy Council Order 893 dated July 18, 1874.
45. *Free Press*, Winnipeg: August 13, 1874, p. 3.
46. Finlayson, *Diary*, Entry for September 27, 1874.
47. Denny, *The Law Marches West*, p. 38.
48. Finlayson, *Diary*, Entry for September 29, 1874.
49. Turner, *North West Mounted Police*, Vol. 1, p. 159.
50. Denny, *The Law Marches West*, p. 41.
51. Sharp, *Whoop-Up Country*, p. 35.
52. Dempsey, Hugh A., "A Letter From Fort Whoop-Up," *AHR*, No. 4, (Winter 52), p. 27.

CHAPTER 6 - SWEET GRASS HILLS TO FORT DUFFERIN
1. NAC, RG 18, RCMP Papers, A-1, Vol. 5, File 222-75.
2. *Free Press*, Winnipeg: November 10, 1874.

CHAPTER 7 - ROCHE PERCÉE TO FORT EDMONTON
1. Steele, *Forty Years*, p. 67.
2. Featherstonhaugh, R.C., "March of the Mounties," *The Beaver* (Jun 40), p. 24.
3. NAC, RG 18, RCMP Papers, A-1, Vol. 3, File 18-5.
4. Steele, *Forty Years*, p. 70.
5. *Ibid.*, pp. 69-70.
6. *Ibid.*, p. 72.
7. *Ibid.*, p. 71.
8. D'Artigue, *Six Years*, p. 77.

CHAPTER 8 - FLAWED PLANNING, INTELLIGENCE AND LOGISTICS
1. Sharp, *Whoop-Up Country*, p. 90.
2. McDougall, Rev. John, *On Western Trails in the Early Seventies*, (Toronto: William Briggs, 1911), pp. 65-66.
3. NAC, Colonial Office Despatch 42, Vol. 1730, p. 110.
4. PAM, MG 1, B23-5, Hewgill, L.F., "In the Days of Pioneering," (Winnipeg: 1894), p. 1.
5. *Annual Report 1874*, p. 23.
6. Bagley, *The '74 Mounties*, p. 40.
7. *Annual Report 1874*, p. 9.
8. Dempsey, *William Parker*, p. 7. Also Parsons, John E., *West On The 49th Parallel: Red River to the Rockies 1872-1876*, (New York: William Morrow & Co., 1963), a photograph between pp. 98-99 shows Sgt Kay's Survey Party with a proper water cart.
9. Forrester, Margaret, "The Northwest Angle," *The Beaver* (Autumn 60), p. 38.
10. *Annual Report 1874*, p. 74.

- Notes -

11. PAM, MG 1, A-7, Military District 10, *Provisional Battalion of Canadian Light Infantry and Artillery Journal, 1871-74.*
12. *Annual Report 1874*, p. 11.
13. Pearce, *Notes on the History*, p. 165.
14. GAI, M 1000, Elizabeth Bailey Price Papers, "Early Days in Alberta", ms of Mrs. David McDougall.

CHAPTER 9 - ESTABLISHING LAW AND ORDER IN THE WEST
1. Denny, *The Law Marches West*, pp. 118-119.
2. *Ibid.*, p. 119.
3. Dempsey, Hugh A. (ed.), "The Last Letters of Rev. George McDougall," *AHR, 15*, No. 2 (Spring 67), p. 21.
4. *Annual Report 1874*, pp. 58-59.
5. Denny, *The Law Marches West*, p. 59.
6. *Annual Report 1874*, pp. 60-61.
7. Turner, *North West Mounted Police*, Vol. 1, p. 192.
8. NAC, RG 18, RCMP Papers, B-3, Vol. 3545, Letterbook of Commissioner G.A. French, French to Macleod, January 5, 1875.
9. *Ibid.*, A-1, Vol. 8, File 480-75, Macleod to French, December 21, 1874.
10. NAC, RG 18, RCMP Papers, A-1, Vol. 4, File 150-75.
11. Turner, *North West Mounted Police*, Vol. 1, p. 204.
12. Denny, *The Law Marches West*, p. 74.
13. NAC, RG 18, RCMP Papers, A-1, Vol. 4, File 150-75, Macleod to Bernard, April 4, 1875..
14. PAM, MG 12, Morris Papers, B-2 LB/G 226, Becher to Griffiths, February 8, 1875.
15. McKay, W.H., "The Story of Edward McKay," *Canadian Cattleman*, Sep 47, p. 76.
16. Ream, Douglas, *The Fort on the Saskatchewan* (Edmonton: Douglas Publishing, 1974), p. 115.
17. PAM, MG 12, Morris Papers, B-1 966, *Petition From Settlers in the Neighbourhood of Fort Edmonton* dated March 22, 1875.
18. NAC, RG 18, RCMP Papers, A-1, Vol. 6, File 282-75, Jarvis to French, April, 1875.
19. *Ibid.*, French to Jarvis, May 13, 1875.
20. *Ibid.*, French to Bernard, May 25, 1875.
21. PAM, MG 12, Morris Papers, B-1 1265, Irvine to Morris, June 12, 1876.
22. *Ibid.*, B-1 1136, Morris Papers, McDougall to Morris, October 23, 1875.
23. *Ibid.*
24. NAC, RG 18, RCMP Papers, A-1, Vol. 10, File 108-76, Crozier to Bernard, February 29, 1876.

CHAPTER 10 - PROBLEMS OF COMMAND
1. NAC, RG 18, RCMP Papers, A-1, Vol. 8, File 488-75, Telegram, French to Minister of Justice.
2. *Ibid.*, G, Vol. 3436, File O-1 - George A. French.
3. *Ibid.*, A-1, Vol. 607, Indexes and Registers 1874, Entry for December 14, 1874.
4. *Ibid.*, G, Vol. 3436, File O-1.
5. *Ibid.*

6. *Ibid.*, A-1, Vol. 2, File 209-74, Statement of Hugh Sutherland.
7. HCD 1875, pp. 993-994.
8. PAM, MG 12, Morris Papers, B-2 139, Mackenzie to Morris, December 11, 1874.
9. NAC, RG 18, RCMP Papers, B-3, Vol. 3545, Letterbook of Commissioner G.A. French, French to Deputy Minister of Justice, December 10, 1874.
10. PAM, MG 12, Morris Papers, B-2 LB/G 211, Morris to Secretary of State, November 11, 1874.
11. *Ibid.*, B-2 LB/G 221, Becher to Griffiths, January 14, 1875.
12. NAC, RG 18, RCMP Papers, A-1, Vol. 2, File 168-74, Bernard to French.
13. *Ibid.*, French to Minister of Justice, January 15, 1876.
14. *Ibid.*, Vol. 2, File 100-74, Dept. of Militia & Defence to Deputy Minister of Justice, August 14, 1874.
15. *Ibid.*, Vol. 1, File 67-4, Clark to Bernard, August 8, 1874.
16. *Free Press*, Winnipeg: August 6, 1874.
17. PAM, MG 6, Military District 10, District Orders, November 22, 1873.
18. NAC, RG 18, RCMP Papers, A-1, Vol. 9, File 82-76, D&E Division Defaulter Sheet, January 1876.
19. Carscadden, *Journal*, p. 8.
20. *Ibid.*, p. 84.
21. *Ibid.*, p. 40.
22. NAC, RG 18, RCMP Papers, A-1, Vol. 3, File 162-75, French to Minister of Justice.
23. *Ibid.*, B-3, Vol. 2229, Letterbook of Commissioner G.A. French, French to Minister of Justice.
24. *Ibid.*
25. NAC, RG 18, RCMP Papers, B-3, Vol. 3545, Letterbook of Commissioner G.A. French, Telegram, Bernard to French.
26. *Ibid.*, French to Bernard, February 12, 1875.
27. Excerpt from *Senator Hardisty's Prairies 1849-1889*, by James G. MacGregor, pp. 108-109, ©Western Producer Prairie Books, 1978, reprinted with permission of Douglas & McIntyre Greystone Books.
28. NAC, RG 18, RCMP Papers, B-3, Vol. 3545, Letterbook of Commissioner G.A. French, French to Jarvis, January 8, 1875.
29. *Ibid.*, French to Bernard, January 15, 1875.
30. *Ibid.*, French to Minister of Justice, April 3, 1875.
31. *Ibid.*, Griffiths (for French) to Cameron, November 28, 1874.
32. *Ibid.*, French to Cameron, December 6, 1874.
33. NAC, RG 18, RCMP Papers, A-1, Vol. 3, File 1-75, Nixon to Bernard, February 3, 1875.
34. *Ibid.*, Vol. 6, File 241-75, Nixon to Bernard, April 15, 1875.
35. *Ibid.*, Vol. 2, File 141A-74, Bernard to Nixon, October 26, 1874.
36. *Ibid.*, French to Bernard
37. *Ibid.*, Vol. 3, File 48A-75.
38. Dempsey, *William Parker*, Note 11, p. 160.
39. NAC, RG 18, RCMP Papers, B-3, Vol. 3545, Letterbook of Commissioner G.A. French, French to Minister of Justice.
40. *Ibid.*, Letterbook of Commissioner G.A. French, French to Minister of Justice, February 8, 1875.

- Notes -

41. *Ibid.*, B-3, Vol. 2229, French to Minister of Justice, May 7, 1875.
42. *Ibid.*, A-1, Office of the Comptroller, Vol. 5, File 225-75, French to Minister of Justice, April 12, 1875.
43. *Ibid.*, B-3, Vol. 3545, Letterbook of Commissioner G.A. French, French to Macleod, April 10, 1875.
44. *Ibid.*, B-3, Vol. 2229, Letterbook of Commissioner G.A. French, French to Macleod, April 13, 1875.
45. *Ibid.*, A-1, Vol. 2, File 114-74, Clark to Bernard, September 18, 1874.
46. *Ibid.*, A-1, Vol. 5, File 225-75, French to Minister of Justice, April 12, 1875.

CHAPTER 11 - SWAN RIVER BARRACKS
1. NAC, RG 18, RCMP Papers, A-1, Vol. 2, File 126-74, Report of Sutherland, Contractor, on the Progress of Fort Pelly.
2. Carscadden, *Journal*, p. 76.
3. Bagley, *The '74 Mounties*, p. 85.
4. *Ibid.*
5. NAC, RG 18, RCMP Papers, A-1, Vol. 5, File 206-75.
6. Bagley, *Diary*, p. 50.
7. *Ibid.*, p. 58.
8. *Ibid.*
9. NAC, RG 18, RCMP Papers, B-3, Vol. 2229, Letterbook of Commissioner G.A. French, French to Minister of Justice, December 8, 1875.
10. *Free Press*, Winnipeg: November 13, 1875.
11. NAC, RG 18, RCMP Papers, B-3, Vol. 2229, Letterbook of Commissioner G.A. French, French to Minister of Justice, December 8, 1875.
12. *Chronicle*, p. 25.
13. Bagley, *The '74 Mounties*, Appx J.
14. Steele, *Forty Years*, p. 96.
15. *The Mail*, Toronto: September 8, 1874.
16. McLean, *1885: Rebellion or Conspiracy?*, p. 32.
17. PAM, MG 12, Morris Papers, B-1 1039, Clarke to Morris, July 10, 1875.
18. NAC, RG 18, RCMP Papers, B-3, Vol. 2229, Letterbook of Commissioner G.A. French, French to Minister of Justice, August 6, 1875.
19. *Ibid.*, A-1, Vol. 6, File 333-75, French to Sec. to Lieut Governor, August 17, 1875.
20. PAM, MG 12, Morris Papers, B-1 1139, Langevin to Morris, October 25, 1875.
21. NAC, RG 18, RCMP Papers, A-1, Vol. 6, File 333-75.
22. GAI, M 517, Higginbotham Papers, File 82.
23. *Chronicle*, p. 32.
24. *Ibid.*, p. 7.
25. PAM, MG 12, Morris Papers, B-2 L/B G 283, Morris to French, August 11, 1875.
26. GAI, M 477, Hardisty Papers, Box 4, File 114, fo. 681, Christie to Hardisty, August 9, 1875.
27. *Chronicle*, p. 8.
28. NAC, RG 18, RCMP Papers, A-1, Vol. 8, File 454-75, Scott to Buckingham.
29. PAM, MG 6, A-7, Unpublished ms of Mrs. Beatrice Rickards, nd.
30. Turner, *North West Mounted Police*, Vol. 1, p. 247.
31. PAM, Rickards ms, pp. 17 and 21.

32. Young, Rev. George, *Manitoba Memories: Leaves From My Life in the Prairie Province 1868-1884* (Toronto: William Briggs, 1897), p. 284.
33. NAC, RG 18, RCMP Papers, A-1, Vol. 9, File 82-76, French to Minister of Justice.
34. *Ibid.*, Vol. 6, File 319-75, French to Minister of Justice, February 26, 1876.
35. PAM, MG 6, A-1, Letter of Henry Galt Carruthers, July 26, 1875.
36. *Chronicle*, p. 10.
37. Dempsey, *William Parker*, p. 18.
38. PAM, MG 12, Morris Papers, B-2 L/B G 272, Morris to French, July 21, 1875.
39. NAC, RG 18, RCMP Papers, B-3, Vol. 2229, Letterbook of Commissioner G.A. French, French to Minister of Justice, November 1, 1875.
40. *Ibid.*, French to Minister of Justice, November 30, 1875.
41. *Ibid.*, A-1, Vol. 9, File 30-76, French to Bernard, November 29, 1875.
42. *Ibid.*, Macleod to Bernard, December 10, 1875.
43. *Ibid.*, Vol. 8, File 488-75, French to Bernard, December 10, 1875.
44. *Ibid.*, Vol. 3, File 48A-75 - Character Sketches, January 14, 1875.
45. *Ibid.*, G, Vol.. 3436, File O-1, Minister of Justice to French, January 18, 1876.
46. *Ibid.*, Vol. 8, File 464-75, French to Minister of Justice, November 30, 1875.
47. *Ibid.*, B-3, File 2229, Letterbook of Commissioner G.A. French, French to Irvine, December 10, 1875.
48. *Ibid.*, A-1, Vol. 8, File 19-76, French to Bernard, December 17, 1875.
49. *Ibid.*, Vol. 10, File 118-76 - Suggested Visit.
50. *Ibid.*, Vol. 3437, File O-31, Griffiths to French, May 7, 1874.
51. GAI, M 4082, JEA Macleod Papers, Box 1, File 14, contains a list "From the file of Griffiths Wainwright Griffiths in the Office of the RCMP Ottawa." This list includes the quoted memo, French to Minister of Justice, January 14, 1875 which could not be found in the National Archives.
52. NAC, RG 18, RCMP Papers, A-1, Vol. 10, File 146-76, French to Bernard, March 30, 1876 quoting *Free Press*, Winnipeg: November 20, 1875.
53. *Ibid.*, French to Deputy Minister of Justice, March 30, 1876.
54. *Chronicle*, p. 6.
55. NAC, RG 18, RCMP Papers, Vol. 3437, File O-31 - Griffiths, Bernard to French, February 3, 1876.
56. *Ibid.*, French to Bernard, March 3, 1876.
57. *Ibid.*, Vol. 9, File 87-76, Report to Secretary of State, nd.
58. *Ibid.*, French to Bernard, March 3, 1876 and Nixon to Bernard, March 20, 1876.
59. *Ibid.*, Vol. 3437, File O-31 - Griffiths.
60. See 51 above. The list included a letter, French to Minister of Justice May 11, 1876. This letter could not be located in National Archives.
61. NAC, RG 18, RCMP Papers, Vol. 607, Indexes and Registers, 1874.
62. *Ibid.*, Vol. 11, File 184-76.
63. NAC, RG 2, Privy Council Order 718 dated July 22, 1876.
64. *Ibid.*, Privy Council Order 914 dated October 7, 1876.
65. Noble, Howat, "The Commissioner Who Almost Wasn't," *MPQ*, 30, No. 2 (Oct 64), p. 9.
66. French, George, "French Recalls Earlier Years," S&G, (1953), p. 37.
67. *Free Press* Winnipeg: August 30, 1876.

- Notes -

68. *Ibid.*, August 26, 1876.
69. NAC, MG 26, A-1, Macdonald Papers, Vol. 353, pp. 162678-81, French to Macdonald, November 27, 1878.

CHAPTER 12 - CHANGES ON THE PLAINS
1. Dempsey, *William Parker*, p. 16.
2. GAI, M 477, Hardisty Papers, Box 4, File 104, fo. 606, W. Leslie Wood to Hardisty, December 15, 1875.
3. GAI, M 517, Higginbotham Papers, Box 3, File 20, Notebook A, p. 62.
4. NAC, RG 18, RCMP Papers, A-1, Vol. 8, File 232-76.
5. Turner, *North West Mounted Police,* Vol. 1, p. 255.
6. PAM, MG 12, Morris Papers, B-2 181, Morris to Secretary of State, July 11, 1876.
7. *Annual Report 1876*, p. 22.
8. *Ibid.*, p. 23.
9. *Free Press*, Winnipeg: July 11, 1874.
10. PAM, MG 12, Morris Papers, B-2 177, Morris to Secretary of State, May 15, 1876.
11. Utley, Robert M., *Frontier Regulars: The United States Army and the Indians 1866-1880* (New York: Macmillan Publishing Co., 1973), p. 261.
12. Excerpt from *Colonel James Walker: Man of the Western Frontier*, by J.W. Grant MacEwan, p. 84, ©Western Producer Prairie Books, 1989, reprinted with permission of Douglas & McIntyre Greystone Books.
13. *Free Press*, Winnipeg: August 24, 1876.
14. PAM, MG 6, A-1, Letter of Francis Galt Carruthers, November 10, 1876.
15. Excerpt from *Senator Hardisty's Prairies 1849-1889*, by James G. MacGregor, p. 114, ©Western Producer Prairie Books, 1978, reprinted with permission of Douglas & McIntyre Greystone Books.
16. Turner, *North West Mounted Police,* Vol. 1, p. 195.
17. Excerpt from *Senator Hardisty's Prairies 1849-1889*, by James G. MacGregor, p. 120, ©Western Producer Prairie Books, 1978, reprinted with permission of Douglas & McIntyre Greystone Books.
18. PAM, MG 6, A-1, Letter of Francis Galt Carruthers, November 10, 1876.
19. *Ibid.*
20. GAI, M 1093, Sanderson Papers, p. 2.
21. *Free Press*, Winnipeg: October 3, 1876.
22. PAM, MG 6, Walsh Papers, A-1, *Letter to Cora Mowat Walsh*, May 28, 1890.
23. *Ibid.*, p. 4.

CHAPTER 13 - SITTING BULL AND THE SIOUX
1. PAM, Walsh Papers, *Letter to Cora Walsh*, The information in the early part of this chapter is based on this document.
2. *Annual Report 1876*, p. 28.
3. Johnson, Virginia Weisel, *The Unregimented General: A Biography of Nelson A. Miles* (Boston: Houghton Mifflin Co., 1962), p. 181.
4. Manzione, Joseph, *I Am Looking North For My Life* (Salt Lake City: University of Utah Press, 1991), p. 51.
5. *Ibid.*, pp. 42-43.
6. *Annual Report 1877*, p. 21.

7. *Free Press*, Winnipeg: May 26, 1877.
8. GAI, M 229, Simon Clark Diary.
9. *Annual Report 1877*, pp. 53-54.
10. Turner, *North West Mounted Police*, Vol. 1, p. 328.
11. *Ibid.*
12. *Ibid.*, p. 93.
13. *Annual Report 1877*, p. 36.
14. Utley, *Frontier Regulars*, p. 315.
15. Turner, *North West Mounted Police*, Vol. 1, p. 341.
16. PAM, MG 6, Walsh Papers, A-1, *Letter to Cora Walsh*, p. 1.
17. Utley, *Frontier Regulars*, p. 286.
18. Johnson, *The Unregimented General*, p. 181.
19. PAM, MG 12, Morris Papers, Father Scollen to Morris, September 8, 1876.
20. Hanks, Lucien M. and Jane Richardson Hanks, *Tribe Under Trust: A Study of the Blackfoot Reserve in Alberta* (Toronto: University of Toronto Press, 1950), p. 10.
21. Turner, *North West Mounted Police*, Vol. 1, pp. 345-346.
22. Denny, *The Law Marches West*, p. 119.
23. Manzione, *I Am Looking North*, p. 54.
24. Turner, C. Frank, *Across the Medicine Line: The Epic Confrontation Between Sitting Bull and the North West Mounted Police* (Toronto: McClelland & Stewart, 1973), p. 121.
25. *Annual Report 1877*, p. 42.
26. Turner, *North West Mounted Police*, Vol. 1, p. 361.
27. *Ibid/.* Vol. 1, pp. 365-367.
28. *Ibid.*, Vol. 1, p. 369.
29. *Ibid.*, Vol. 1, p. 370.

CHAPTER 14 - PROBLEMS ON THE PLAINS
1. NAC, RG 18, RCMP Papers, B-3, Vol. 2230, Letterbook of Commissioner James F. Macleod, Macleod to Irvine, March 5, 1878.
2. NARA, RG 393, Entry 1897, Department of the Yellowstone, Macleod to Miles, June 23, 1878.
3. Turner, *North West Mounted Police*, Vol. 1, p. 389.
4. Dickason, Olive Patricia, *Canada's First Nations* (Toronto: McClelland & Stewart, 1992), p. 300.
5. *Ibid.*
6. Turner, *North West Mounted Police*, Vol. 1, pp. 405-406.
7. Flanagan, Thomas, *Louis "David" Riel* (Toronto: University of Toronto Press, 1979), p. 105.
8. *Ibid.*, p. 107.
9. *Ibid.*, p. 106.
10. PAM, MG 3, D-1 565, Riel Papers, Handwritten ms. "About the Titons." [sic].
11. Johnson, *The Unregimented General*, pp. 219-220, Miles to Mary Miles, August 12, 1879.
12. Finerty, John R., *War-Path and Bivouac: or the Conquest of the Sioux* (Lincoln: University of Nebraska Press, 1955), p. 264.
13. *Ibid.*, p. 268.

- Notes -

14. Turner, *North West Mounted Police,* Vol. 1, p. 431.
15. Fitzpatrick, Frank J.E., *Sergeant 331,* (New York: 1921), p. 23.
16. Dickason, *Canada's First Nations,* p. 292.
17. Denny, *The Law Marches West,* p. 146.
18. NAC, MG 26, A-1, Macdonald Papers, Vol. 524, Pt. 2, p. 291, Macdonald to Macleod, June 23, 1879.
19. *Ibid.,* Vol. 361, pp. 167099-167111, Macleod to Macdonald, October 23, 1879.
20. Turner, *North West Mounted Police,* Vol. 1, p. 475.
21. *Ibid.*
22. *Ibid.,* Vol. 1, p. 447.
23. *Ibid.,* Vol. 1, p. 498.
24. NAC, RG 27, Lorne Papers, B-4, Vol. 1, p. 175, Macdonald to Lorne, November 5, 1880.
25. *Ibid.,* Vol. 1, p. 195-196, Macdonald to Lorne, January 25, 1881.
26. *Ibid.,* Vol. 1, p. 196, Macdonald to Lorne, January 25, 1881.
27. NAC, MG 26, A-1, Macdonald Papers, Vol. 210, pp. 242-243, Dewdney to MacPherson, August 4, 1881.
28. Dempsey, Hugh A., *Crowfoot: Chief of the Blackfeet* (Halifax: Formac Publishing Co., 1988), p. 119.

CHAPTER 15 - TENSION RISING
1. Sharp, *Whoop-Up Country,* p. 218.
2. Jennings, John Nelson, "The Plains Indians and the Law," in *Men in Scarlet* edited by Hugh A. Dempsey, 50-65 (Calgary: Historical Society of Alberta-McClelland & Stewart, 1973), p. 61.
3. *Annual Report 1880,* p. 28.
4. PAM, MG 6, A-1, Walsh Papers.
5. GAI, M 320, Edgar Dewdney Papers, Box 2, File 33, pp. 382-385, Macdonald to Dewdney, November 1, 1880.
6. NAC, RG 18, RCMP Papers, B-3, Vol. 2185, Letterbook of Commissioner A.G. Irvine, Irvine to Minister of the Interior, December 19, 1880.
7. NAC, RG 2, Privy Council Order 607 dated April 5, 1880.
8. Steele, *Forty Years,* pp. 143-144.
9. GAI, M 4166, Shaw Family Papers.
10. NAC, MG 26, A-1, Macdonald Papers, Vol. 370, pp. 172136-172139, Osborne Smith to Macdonald, October 12, 1880.
11. HCD 1881, p. 1327.
12. NAC, RG 18, RCMP Papers, Vol. 3437, File O-30 - Irvine.
13. NAC, RG 2, Privy Council Order 604 dated April 5, 1880.
14. NAC, RG 18, RCMP Papers, B-3, Vol. 2185, Letterbook of Commissioner A.G. Irvine, Irvine to Minister of the Interior, November 8, 1880.
15. "Remembrances of a Tenderfoot," *S&G* (XXXII), p. 409.
16. Steele, *Forty Years,* p. 160.
17. NAC, MG 26, A-1, Macdonald Papers, Vol. 376, pp. 175690-175692, Dunhille to Macdonald, September 28, 1881.
18. *Ibid.,* Vol. 379, pp. 117049-117050, J.J. French to Macdonald, December 7, 1881

19. See Turner, *North West Mounted Police,* Vol. 1, p. 626 and NAC, MG 26, A-1, Macdonald Papers, Vol. 295, pp. 134829-134848.
20. GAI, M 4561, Interview with Gabrielle Léveillé.
21. Turner, *North West Mounted Police,* Vol. 1, p. 631.
22. NAC, MG 29, E-47, *Diary - Robert N. Wilson.*
23. GAI, M 229, Simon Clark Diary, Entry for April 22, 1877.
24. GAI, M 320, Edgar Dewdney Papers, Box 4, File 57, p. 1194, Irvine to Dewdney, June 24, 1882.
25. Jennings, "Plains Indians and the Law, p. 62.
26. *Ibid.,* pp. 64-65.
27. HCD 1882, p. 542.
28. Steele, *Forty Years,* p. 166.

CHAPTER 16 - TROUBLE IN THE FORCE
1. Turner, *North West Mounted Police,* Vol. 2, p. 5.
2. *Ibid.,* Vol. 2, p. 2.
3. *Ibid.,* Vol. 2, p. 10.
4. NAC, RG 18, RCMP Papers, A-1, File 316-83.
5. Turner, *North West Mounted Police,* Vol. 2, p. 19.
6. *Ibid.,* Vol. 2, p. 25.
7. NAC, RG 18, RCMP Papers, A-1, Vol. 12, File 147-83.
8. *Ibid.,* Vol. 3, File 48A-75.
9. Sutherland, Alexander, *A Summer in Prairieland* (Toronto: Methodist Book & Publishing House, 1883), p. 43.

CHAPTER 17 - A DECISIVE DECADE
1. Dickason, *Canada's First Nations,* p. 304.
2. *Edmonton Bulletin* quoted in "Prairie Fire" by Bob Beal and Rod Macleod, p. 30. Used by permission of McClelland & Stewart Inc. *The Canadian Publishers.*
3. "Prairie Fire" by Bob Beal and Rod Macleod, p. 74. Used by permission of McClelland & Stewart Inc. *The Canadian Publishers,*
4. Bagley, *The '74 Mounties,* p. 58.
5. NAC, MG 26, A-1, Macdonald Papers, Vol. 252, pp. 113998-114008, Morris to Macdonald, January 16, 1873.

BIBLIOGRAPHY

Atkin, Ronald. *Maintain the Right: The Early History of the North West Mounted Police 1873-1900*. London: Macmillan, 1973.
Bagley, Frederick A. *Diary of a North West Mounted Police Trumpeter 1874-84*. Calgary: Glenbow-Alberta Institute Archives, M44.
_____ *The '74 Mounties by One of Them*. Calgary: Glenbow-Alberta Institute Archives, M45.
Beale, Bob and Rod Macleod. *Prairie Fire: The 1885 North-West Rebellion*. Toronto: McClelland & Stewart Inc., 1994.
Begg, Alexander. *History of the North-West (3 vols)*. Toronto: Hunter, Rose & Co., 1895.
Butler, William Francis. *The Great Lone Land*. Edmonton: Hurtig, 1968.
Canada, Royal Canadian Mounted Police. *Reports of the Commissioner 1874-1881. Opening Up the West.*, Toronto: Coles Publishing Co., 1973.
Carscadden, Joseph. *Journal of the North West Mounted Police Trek 1874*. Calgary: Glenbow-Alberta Institute Archives, M6608.
Clark, Simon. *Diary of a North West Mounted Police Experience in the NorthWest Territories 1876-1886*. Calgary: Glenbow-Alberta Institute Archives, M229.
Cruise, David and Alison Griffiths. *The Great Adventure: How the Mounties Conquered the West*. Toronto: Penguin Books, 1996.
D'Artigue, Jean. *Six Years in the Canadian North-West*. Toronto: Hunter, Rose & Co. 1882. Facsimile Edition, Belleville ON: Mika Publishers, 1973.
Daw, Ruth M. "Sgt-Major J.H.G. Bray, the Forgotten Horseman" in *Men in Scarlet*, edited by Hugh A. Dempsey, 152-161. Calgary: Historical Society of Alberta-McClelland & Stewart, 1974.
Dempsey, Hugh A. *Jerry Potts Plainsman*. Calgary: Glenbow Alberta Institute, 1966.
_____ *Big Bear: The End of Freedom*. Vancouver: Douglas & McIntyre Ltd., 1984.
_____ *Red Crow: Warrior Chief.* Saskatoon: Fifth House Ltd., 1985.
_____ *Crowfoot: Chief of the Blackfeet*. Halifax: Formac Publishing Co., 1988.
_____ ed. *Men in Scarlet*. Calgary: Historical Society of Alberta-McClelland & Stewart, 1974.
_____ "A Letter From Fort Whoop-Up." *Alberta Historical Review,* Vol. 4, No. 4 (Winter 1956): 27-28.
_____ "Robertson-Ross' Diary: Fort Edmonton to Wildhorse, B.C. 1872." *Alberta Historical Review*, Vol. 9, No. 3 (Autumn 1960): 5-22.
_____ "Brisebois: Calgary's Forgotten Founder" in *Frontier Calgary* edited by Anthony W. Rasporich. Calgary: McClelland & Stewart West, 1975.
_____ ed. "The Last Letters of George McDougall." *Alberta Historical view,* Vol. 15, No. 2 (Spring 1967): 22-30.

Denny, Cecil E., W.B. Cameron, ed. *The Law Marches West.* Toronto: J.M. Dent & Sons, 1939.

Dickason, Olive Patricia. *Canada's First Nations.* Toronto: McClelland & Stewart, 1992.

Eastman, Charles. *Indian Heroes and Great Chieftains.* Boston: Little, Brown & Co., 1919.

Edwards, John. *Extracts From the Notebook of John Edwards RE.* Winnipeg: Public Archives of Manitoba.

Fardy, B.D. *Jerry Potts: Paladin of the Plains.* Langley, B.C.: Mr. Paperback, 1984.

Featherstonhaugh, R.C. "March of the Mounties." *The Beaver* (June 1940).

Finerty, John F. *War Path and Bivouac: or the Conquest of the Sioux.* Lincoln: University of Nebraska Press, 1955.

Fitzpatrick, Frank J.E. *Sergeant 331: Personal Recollection of a Member of the Canadian Northwest Mounted Police 1879-1885.* New York: Published by Author, 1921.

Flanagan, Thomas. *Diaries of Louis Riel.* Edmonton: Hurtig Publishers, 1976.

_____*Louis "David" Riel: Prophet of the New World.* Toronto: University of Toronto Press, 1979.

_____*Riel and the Rebellion: 1885 Reconsidered.* Saskatoon: Western Producer Prairie Books, 1983.

Fooks, Georgia Green. *Fort Whoop-Up.* Lethbridge: Whoop-Up Country Chapter, Historical Society of Alberta, May 1983.

Forrester, Marjorie. "The Northwest Angle." *The Beaver* (Autumn 1960): 32-38.

Fort Macleod: The Story of the North West Mounted Police 1874-1904. Fort Macleod: Fort Macleod Historical Association, 1958.

Fullerton, J.T. "Toronto to Fort Garry." *Scarlet & Gold*, 17th ed., Vol. 3 (Jul 35): 17-18.

Goldring, Philip. *The First Contingent North-West Mounted Police 1873-74.* Ottawa: Parks Canada, 1979.

_____*Whisky, Horses and Death: The Cypress Hills Massacre and its Sequel.* Ottawa: Parks Canada, 1979.

_____ "The Cypress Hills Massacre - A Century's Retrospect." *Saskatchewan History*, Vol. 26, No. 3 (Autumn 1973): 81-102.

Grain, Carell, "Pioneers of a Glorious Future." *Scarlet & Gold*, XXIX (1947): 61.

Griesbach, W.A. *I Remember.* Toronto: Ryerson Press, 1946.

Haig, Kenneth M. *Colonel J.B. Mitchell.* Winnipeg: The Garry Press, 1957.

Hanks, Lucien M. and Jane Richardson Hanks. *Tribe Under Trust: A Study of the Blackfoot Reserve of Alberta.* Toronto: University of Toronto Press, 1950.

Hewgill, L.F. *In The Days of Pioneering.* Winnipeg: nd. pamphlet, Public Archives of Manitoba.

- Bibliography -

Historical Society of Alberta, *A Chronicle of the Canadian West: North-West Mounted Police Report for 1875.* Calgary: 1975.

Horrall, S.W. "Sir John A. Macdonald and the Mounted Police Force for the Northwest Territories." *Canadian Historical Review*, Vol. 53, No. 2 (Jun 72): 179-200.

Jennings, John Nelson. "The Plains Indians and the Law" in *Men in Scarlet*, edited by Hugh A. Dempsey. Calgary: Historical Society of Alberta, McClelland & Stewart, 1973.

———. "The North West Mounted Police and Canadian Indian Policy 1873-1896." Toronto: Ed D Dissertation, University of Toronto, 1979.

Johnson, Virginia Weisel. *The Unregimented General: A Biography of Nelson A. Miles.* Boston: Houghton, Mifflin Co., 1962.

Julien, Henri. *The North West Expedition - 1874 of the North West Mounted Police: Diary of Henri Julien.* Calgary: Glenbow Alberta Institute Archives, M611.

Kemp, Vernon. *Scarlet and Stetson: The Royal North-West Mounted Police on the Prairies.* Toronto: Ryerson, 1964.

Klancher, Donald J. and Roger E. Phillips. *Arms and Accoutrements of the Mounted Police.* Bloomfield, ON: Museum Restoration Services, 1965.

Klaus, J.F. "Early Trails to Carlton House." *The Beaver* (Autumn 66): 32-39.

———. "Fort Livingstone." *Saskatchewan History*, 15, 3 (Autumn 1962): 93-110.

Loew, Franklin M. and Edward H. Wood. *Vet in the Saddle: John L. Poett: First Veterinary Surgeon of the North West Mounted Police.* Saskatoon: Western Producer Prairie Books, 1978.

MacEwan, J. W. Grant. *Colonel James Walker: Man of the Western Frontier.* Saskatoon: Western Producer Prairie Books, 1989.

———. *Sitting Bull: The Years in Canada.* Edmonton: Hurtig Publishers, 1973.

MacGregor, James G. *Senator Hardisty's Prairies 1849-1889.* Saskatoon: Western Producer Prairie Books, 1978.

MacLaren, Sherril Maxwell. *Braehead: Three Founding Families in Nineteenth Century Canada.* Toronto: McClelland & Stewart, 1986.

Macleod, R.C. *The North-West Mounted Police and Law Enforcement 1873-1905.* Toronto: University of Toronto Press, 1976.

———. "Canadianizing the West: The North West Mounted Police as Agents of the National Policy 1873-1905" in *The Prairie West*, edited by R. Douglas Francis and Howard Palmer, 225-238. Edmonton: University of Alberta, 1992.

McDougall, Rev. John. *On Western Trails in the Early Seventies.* Toronto: William Briggs, 1911.

_____*Pathfinding on Plains and Prairie*. Toronto: William Briggs, 1898.

McIllree, John Henry. *Diary of John Henry McIllree*. Calgary: Glenbow Alberta Institute Archives, M473.

McKernan, James. "Expeditions Made in 1873." *Scarlet & Gold*, 2 (1920): 84-86.

McLean, Don. *1885: Métis Rebellion or Government Conspiracy?* Winnipeg: Pemmican Publications, 1985.

"Major General Sir George Arthur French." *RCMP Quarterly*, Vol. 1, No. 3 (January 1934): 99-101.

Manzione, Joseph. *I Am Looking North for My Life*. Salt Lake City: University of Utah Press, 1991.

Maunsell, E.H. "With the North West Mounted Police Force From 1874 to 1877." *Scarlet & Gold*, 2 (1920): 50-59.

Morgan, Charles E., "The North West Mounted Police: Internal Problems and Public Criticism 1873." *Saskatchewan History*, Vol. 26, No. 2 (Spring 1973).

Morris, The Hon. Alexander. *The Treaties of Canada With the Indians of Manitoba and the Northwest Territories*. Toronto: Belfords, Clarke & Co., 1880. Facsimile Edition: Saskatoon: Fifth House Publishers, 1991.

Morton, Desmond. "Cavalry or Police: Keeping the Peace on Two Adjacent Frontiers 1870-1900." *Journal of Canadian Studies*, 12 (Spring 1977): 27-37.

Morton, W.L. *Manitoba: The Birth of a Province*. Winnipeg: Manitoba Record Society Publications, 1965.

_____*Begg's Red River Journal and Other Papers*. Toronto: The Champlain Society, 1956.

Nevitt, R.B. *A Winter at Fort Macleod*. Calgary: Glenbow Alberta Institute-McClelland & Stewart West, 1974.

Noble, Howart. "The Commissioner Who Almost Wasn't." *RCMP Quarterly*, Vol. 30, No. 2 (Oct 64): 9.

Nute, Grace Lee. "On The Dawson Road." *The Beaver* (Winter 1954): 16-18.

Outlaws and Lawmen of Western Canada. Surrey, B.C.: Heritage House Publishing Co. Ltd., 1983.

Parsons, John E. *West On the 49th Parallel: Red River to the Rockies 1872-1876*. New York: William Morrow & Co., 1963.

Pearce, William. "Notes on the History and Settlement of the Canadian Northwest." Photocopy of ms prepared in 1925.

Phillips, Roger F. and Donald J. Klancher. *Arms & Accoutrements of the Mounted Police 1873-1973*. Bloomfield ON: Museum Restoration Services, 1982.

Phillips, Roger F. and S.J. Kirby. *Small Arms of the Mounted Police*. Bloomfield ON: Museum Restoration Services, 1965.

- Bibliography -

Ream, Douglas. *The Fort on the Saskatchewan.* Edmonton: Douglas Printing, 1974.

"Reminiscences of One of the Originals." *RCMP Quarterly,* Vol. 1, No. 1 (July 1933): 35-36.

Ross, David (ed). *Jottings on the March From Fort Garry to the Rocky Mountains 1874 by James Finlayson of "B" Troop North West Mounted Police.* Winnipeg: Parks Canada, 1990.

Sharp, Paul F. *Whoop-Up Country.* Norman: University of Oklahoma Press, 1955.

Spry, Irene M. *The Palliser Expedition.* Saskatoon: Fifth House Publishers, 1963.

Stanley, George F.G. *Toil & Trouble: Military Expedition to Red River.* Toronto: Dundurn Press, 1989.

_____ *The Birth of Western Canada: A History of the Riel Rebellion.* Toronto: University of Toronto Press, 1960.

Steele, Samuel B. *Forty Years in Canada.* Toronto: 1914. Toronto: McGraw-Hill Ryerson, 1972.

Sutherland, Alexander. *A Summer in Prairieland.* Toronto: Methodist Book & Publishing House, 1882.

"They Opened the Way for the Peaceful Development of Canada's Broad Plains." *RCMP Quarterly,* Vol. 11, Nos. 2-3 (Oct 45 and Jan 46): 141-154.

Treaty 7 Elders and Tribal Council. *The True Spirit and Original Intent of Treaty 7.* Montreal & Kingston: McGill-Queen's University Press, 1996.

Turner, C. Frank. *Across the Medicine Line: The Epic Confrontation Between Sitting Bull and the North West Mounted Police.* Toronto: McClelland & Stewart, 1973.

Turner, John Peter. *The North-West Mounted Police 1873-1893 (2 vols).* Ottawa: King's Printer, 1950.

Utley, Robert M. *Frontier Regulars: The United States Army and the Indians 1866-1890.* New York: Macmillan Publishing Co., 1973.

_____ *The Lance and the Shield.* New York: Henry Holt & Co., 1993.

- INDEX -

Adams revolvers, 52-54
Akers, Dave, 89-90, 116
Allen, 118, 181
Allen, Trader, 217
Antrobus, W. 189, 201
Archibald, Alexander,
Artigue, Jean D', 39, 158
Assiniboines, 123, 182, 196-97, 201
Assiniboine River, 97

Bagley, Frederick A., 38, 222
Baird, Lt G.W., USA, 198
Baker, I.G. & Co., 82, 112, 119 120, 180, 216
Battleford, 165, 229
Battle River, 165
Beardy, Chief, 166, 168, 200, 220
Bear Paw Mountains, 183, 214
Bernard, Hewitt, 118, 135
Big Bear, 124, 199, 200, 202, 208, 212, 234, 239
Black Bull, 253
Blackfoot, 2, 114, 122, 123, 165, 173, 178, 185, 188, 196, 221, 214, 235
Blackfoot Crossing, 186-87, 221, 229
Black Hills, 163
Black Horn, 176, 203
Black Moon, 171,
Bloods, 114,
Bray, Sgt Maj J.H.G., 119
Brisebois, E., 22, 113, 120, 160-61

Broad Tail, 184, 203
Bond, William, 112, 114
Boundary Commission, 14, 45, 91, 106-07, 110, 123, 134-36
Bow River, 76, 120, 160-61, 187
Bull Elk, 230
Bull's Head, 242
Button Chief, 188
Butler, William, 12

Cameron, D.R., 7, 11-14, 91, 104, 135, 151
Canadian Pacific Railway, 230, 237-38, 242
Carvell, Jacob, 22, 86, 94, 126, 140, 143
Chipewayan, 165
Chrisitie, W.J., 147
Clark, E. Dalrymple, 22, 42, 95, 129, 223
Clarke, Lawrence, 134, 144-45
Conrad, Charles, 88, 112
Cotton, J., 145, 209
Cow Island, 180
Crazy Horse, 164
Cree, 19, 122, 124, 165, 178, 186, 196, 199, 201, 221
Cripple Camp, 77, 91, 105
Crooked Arm, 181
Crow Collar, 242

- Index -

Crowfoot, 45, 112, 114, 163, 186, 188, 203, 214, 231, 242
Crow's Dance, 180-81
Crozier, L.N.F, 41, 112, 123-24, 199, 209, 219, 225, 228, 231, 237
Custer, Lt. Col. G.A., 163-64
Cypress Hills, 16, 71, 118
Cypress Hills Massacre, 20

Daley, Charles, 141
Daly, C., 170
Davis, Daniel (Peaches), 234-35
Denny, Sir. Cecil Bt., 81, 83, 111, 162-63, 189, 210, 221
Department of the Interior, 204
Department of Justice, 128, 152
Department of Militia & Defence, 107, 129
Department of Public Works, 148
DeVeber, L.P., 223
Dewdney, Edgar, 211, 214
Dickens, Francis J., 150, 230, 239
Dirt Hills, 74-75
Dixon, George, 25
Duck Lake, 165-66, 200-201, 220
Dull Knife, 203
Dumont, Gabriel, 98, 144
Dumont's Crossing, 98, 166

East End, 172
Elbow River, 120

Fargo, ND., 48
Farwell, Abe, 17
Finerty, John, 205
First Crossing of the Souris, 66
Fort Benton, 3, 9, 76, 82, 86, 88, 112, 119, 125, 172
Fort Brisebois, 160
Fort Calgary, 161, 221, 229, 242
Fort Carlton, 98, 123, 144-45, 147, 165-66, 169, 201
Fort Dufferin, 14, 50, 95, 105, 108, 119, 125-26, 136-37
Fort Edmonton, 12, 70, 82, 96, 101, 116, 120-21
Fort Ellice, 43-44, 94, 109, 116, 125, 128, 134
Fort Garry, 96
Fort Kipp, 104, 113, 115-16
Fort Livingstone, 93, 167
Fort Macleod, 111, 121, 132, 160, 166, 172. 179. 229. 241
Fort Pelly, 87, 93, 125, 133
Fort Pembina, 54
Fort Pitt, 100, 124, 169, 199, 239
Fort Qu'Appelle, 92, 108, 123, 148, 160, 228, 237
Fort Saskatchewan, 137
Fort Shaw, 112
Fort Walsh, 120-21, 160, 171-72, 192, 198, 228, 237, 239
Fort Whoop-Up, 10, 21, 45, 82, 89-90, 103-04, 116,

273

Four Horns, 175
Francis, Sgt Maj., 38, 159, 206
Frechette, Sub-Insp., 165, 171
French, G.A., 28, 77, 79, 81, 86, 88, 105, 115, 120-21, 124, 126, 132, 137, 142-43, 147, 151-53, 157-59
French, J., 141

Gagnon, Sévère, 100-01, 222
Genin, Jean-Baptiste, 183, 199
Graburn, Marmaduke, 208
Griffiths, Wainwright, 149, 153-56
Grizzly Bear's Head, 234

Hamilton, Sgt. Henry, 217
Hammond, George, 17
Hardisty, R., 120
Herchmer, Lawrence, 14, 76, 82, 91, 105
Herchmer, Wm., 220, 228
Hotchkiss gun, 205
Hudson's Bay Company, 1, 3, 93, 120-21, 123, 128, 133-34, 144, 146

Ilges, Major Guido, 199
Irvine, A.G., 8, 152, 161, 182, 199, 201

Jarvis, W.D., 22, 70, 97, 120-21, 133, 136, 229
Jingling Bells, 214
Julien, Henri, 52, 74

Kennedy's Crossing, 120

Kittson, Dr., 142, 181
Kittson's Butte, 181

Lacombe, Fr., 243
Laird, David, 108, 128, 187
La Nauze, Cpl., 231
Legare, Jean Louis, 171, 217, 226
Lestanc, Pere, 99
Léveillé, Louis, 77, 92, 118, 181, 209
Léveillé, Pierre, 64, 82-83
L'Hereux, Jean, 122
Little Black Bear, 122
Little Big Horn, 165, 171
Little Child, 180
Little Soldier, 17
Long Dog, 203
Lorne, Marquis of, 213, 228
Low Dog, 219
Lower Fort Garry, 27, 93, 133
Lucas, Pierre, 67

Mackenzie, Alexander, 11. 127, 144, 191
Macdonald, Sir John A., 11, 13, 15, 19-20, 143, 204, 210, 213, 219
Macdonell, A.R., 172, 225, 227
Macleod, James F., 20, 22, 40-41, 76, 81, 115, 118, 122, 124, 136-37, 151-52, 157, 159, 161, 210, 224
Manifest Destiny, 4
Manitoba Act, 10
Maple Creek, SK, 239

- Index -

Marty, Rev. Martin, 182, 207
Maunsell, E.H., 48
McCutcheon, R., 177
McDougall, Rev. George, 112
McDougall, Rev. John, 45, 97, 104, 124, 136
McDougall, William, 6-7
McIllree, John H., 29, 41, 147, 242
Métis, 6, 122, 144, 186, 203, 206, 214, 230
Miles, Gen. Nelson A., 178, 183-84, 198, 205-06
Milk River, 89, 120, 203,
Mills, David, 191
Missouri Coteau, 71, 92
Mitchell, J.B., 33, 39, 65, 78, 140, 158, 170 180
Mooney, Thomas, 132
Morris, Lt Gov. Alexander, 15, 108, 118, 128, 162, 168
Morriseau, F., 76, 82

Nataya, 162
Neale, Percy, 41, 228
Nez Perce, 183, 196
Nixon, Thomas, 135, 156
North Saskatchewan River, 99, 165
North West Company, 6

Ojibwa, 123
Old Man's River, 11, 113, 221
Old Sun, 45, 188

Old Wives Creek, 76, 91
Old Wives Lake, 75
Omenakaw, 220
One Bull, 226

Palestine, 142, 157
Palliser's Map, 104
Pearce, William, 109
Peigans, 114
Pembina Mountain, 63
Pembina Mountain Depot, 62
Pembina River, 62
Piapot, 212, 237-38
Pine Coulee, 112
Pinto Horse Buttes, 174, 182
Poett, John L., 48, 85
Poitras, Pierre, 207
Poor Man, 234
Potts, Jerry, 88, 11, 114, 117, 209
Power, T.C., 119
Pox, 162
Provencher, W., 124

Qu'Appelle River, 97

Red Crow, 189, 231
Red Dog, 197, 203
Red Deer River 162, 201, 208
Red River cart, 59, 107
Red Stone, 203
Richer, T., 60, 126
Riel, Louis, 6-8, 202-03, 213-15

Robertson-Ross, P., 13, 104
Roche Percée, 69, 96
Rocky Creek, 205
Rocky Springs, 88, 117
Rupert's Land, 1, 4

St. Peter's Springs, 68
Saulteaux, 165, 196
Scollen, Father, 179, 185
St. Laurent, 144
Selby-Smyth, Maj. Gen., 143, 145, 147
Shaw, Frederick, 223
Shell River, 142
Shoal Lake, 142, 150, 160
Shurtliff, A., 43, 69
Sioux, 75, 119, 162, 171, 174, 178, 182, 191, 196, 217, 226, 233
Sitting Bull, 164, 177, 182, 192, 199, 203, 207, 212, 218, 233
Smith, W. Osborne, 22, 27, 41, 109
Snider-Enfield Carbine, 52
Solomon, Moses, 17
Sounding Lake, 199
Souris River, 96
South Saskatchewan River, 83, 98, 162, 166, 169, 201
Spotted Eagle, 203, 219
Star Child, 209
Steele, Samuel B., 8, 23, 96, 101, 208-09, 229, 236
Stobart, Eden & Co., 201
Stone Dog, 203

Sturgeon Creek, 101, 120
Sun River, 113, 118
Sutherland, Hugh, 126
Swan River Barracks, 93, 116, 121, 125, 137, 139, 144, 147-48, 158, 160, 165-67
Sweet Grass, 12
Sweet Grass Hills, 82, 85, 91, 104
Swift Runner, 222

Tail Creek Crossing, 146
Tanner's Crossing, 142
Taylor, "Kamoose", 113
Terry, Gen. Alfred, 165, 191, 193
The-One-Who-Speaks-Once, 193
Three Buttes, 85, 112
Tillson, Lt. USA, 205
Toronto, 37
Treaty No. 7, 189, 196
Turtle Mountain Depot, 65

United States Army, 119, 122, 162, 164, 171, 180, 205, 227
Van Horne, W.C., 237
Victoria Mission, 100

Walker, James, 47, 136, 165-66, 199, 201
Walsh, J.M., 22-25, 83, 113, 118, 151, 171, 174, 177, 181, 183-84, 197, 203, 218-19, 227, 243
Weatherwax, "Waxy", 113

- Index -

Welch, Vernon, 81, 83, 118, 162

White Bird, 184

White Dog, 177-78

White Eagle, 172

White Mud River, 77

Wild Horse Lake, 86, 91

Winder, Wm., 22

Winnipeg, MB., 125-26

Wood End Depot, 71

Wood Mountain, 71, 76, 104, 160, 164, 171, 173-74, 204, 212,

Wood Mountain Post, 91-92, 116

Young, Capt. Charles F., 22, 28, 54, 126

PHOTO CREDITS

1. Hudson's Bay Company Archives, Provincial Archives of Manitoba.
   p. 43 (HBCA Reference P-438 (N9206)

2. Glenbow Archives, Calgary, Alberta.
   Cover (NA-973-1); p. 31 (NA-23-1); p. 114 (NA-1407-1); p. 118 (NA-1771-1); p. 130 (NA-2826-1); P. 177 (NA-659-15); p. 190 (NA-40-1); p. 194 (NA-5091-1); p. 236 (NA-659-16).

3. National Library of Canada
   Bibliothèque nationale du Canada
   p. 47 (C-061344); p. 51 (C-061346); p. 53 (C-061462); p. 61 (C-062549); p. 64 (C-062571); p. 70 (C-061449); p. 73 (C-062572); p. 74 (C-062596); p. 78 (C-062665); p. 84 (C-062677); p. 215 (C-062639).

4. Maps on pages 5 and 58 courtesy of Royal Canadian Mounted Police. These maps and quotation of Frederick Bagley in Preface reproduced with the permission of the Minister of Public Works and Government Services Canada, 1997.